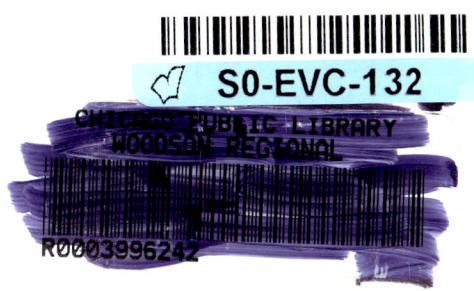

```
PN      Frank, Ellen Eve.
53
.F8     Literary
           architecture
```

Cop 1   18⁰⁰

	DATE	
~~REFERENCE~~		

WOODSON REGIONAL
LIBRARY CENTER
9525 SOUTH HALSTED STREET
CHICAGO, ILLINOIS 60628

© THE BAKER & TAYLOR CO.

Literary Architecture

Literary Architecture

Essays Toward a Tradition

WALTER PATER
GERARD MANLEY HOPKINS
MARCEL PROUST
HENRY JAMES

Ellen Eve Frank

UNIVERSITY OF CALIFORNIA PRESS
BERKELEY • LOS ANGELES • LONDON

University of California Press
Berkeley and Los Angeles, California

University of California Press, Ltd.
London, England

Copyright © 1979 by
The Regents of the University of California

ISBN 0-520-03352-3

Library of Congress
Catalog Card Number: 76-47970

Designed by Wolfgang Lederer

Printed in the United States of America

1   2   3   4   5   6   7   8   9

To my family

> The very place one is in, its stone-work,
> its empty spaces, invade you; invade all
> who belong to them . . . seem to question
> you masterfully as to your purpose
> in being here at all.
>
> WALTER PATER

1

The "Achieve and Mastery":
Literary Architecture Rent.
(Abbey Ruins, Jumièges)

AUTHOR'S NOTE

I began thinking about architecture as a possible analogue for literature in 1971. The core essays exploring this possibility were written in the years following, from 1972 to 1974. The enlargement upon the idea, the context into which I have placed these essays, came from my experiences after these essays were completed and was integrated into the manuscript in 1976.

Special care has been taken in the selection and arrangment of the photographs and in the printing of this book. I trust literary architecture can weather the time these processes have rightly taken.

ACKNOWLEDGMENTS

I should like to honor my teachers: Donald Davie, Herbert Lindenberger, Douglas Smith, Ian Watt, Wesley Trimpi, Professor Sir Ernst Gombrich. This book is a small gesture of my appreciation. I should also like to acknowledge the generous grants I received for this work: the Fulbright Foundation, Leverhulme Trust Fund, Ford Foundation; to thank the staffs of Stanford University, the Courtauld and Warburg Institutes for their help; William Petzel for his fine photographic skills; Catherine King for her typing. I also wish to acknowledge those who read the manuscript, either in its entirety or portions of it, and who gave me encouragement: Judith Allen, Rudolph Arnheim, Robin Bisio, R. Howard Bloch, Richard Bridgman, Carol Christ, Anne Mellor, Leonard Michaels, Alex Zwerdling; Lloyd Cross for his practical aid; and John Osman for his particular good will. I extend special gratitude to my sponsoring editor William McClung and to my designer Wolfgang Lederer for their commitment to this book and their care for its embodied form. Finally, I should like to thank my mother, Dorothy C. Frank, for her help in the preparation of the manuscript and for her kind support of my work.

E. E. F.

CONTENTS

Acknowledgments
page ix
List of Plates
page xiii
Introduction
page 1

I Literary Architecture: Walter Horatio Pater
page 15

II "The Poetry of Architecture":
Gerard Manley Hopkins
page 51

III "The Stored Consciousness": Marcel Proust
page 113

IV The Architecture of Fiction: Henry James
page 167

V The Analogical Tradition
of Literary Architecture
page 217

Notes
page 261
Index
page 309
Credits for Photographs
page 311

PLATES

1 Abbey Ruins, Jumièges. Editions Arthaud. . vii
2 South Chapel, Waltham Abbey. National Monuments Record, England. 16
3 Notre-Dame d'Amiens. Courtauld Institute. 27
4 La Madeleine, Vézelay. Photograph by Jean Roubier. 29
5 Notre-Dame d'Amiens. Courtauld Institute. 30
6 Notre-Dame d'Amiens. Photograph by A. F. Kersting. 35
7 La Madeleine, Vézelay. Courtauld Institute. 43
8. Notre-Dame d'Amiens. Courtauld Institute. 45
9 Notre-Dame d'Amiens. Courtauld Institute. 47
10 GERARD MANLEY HOPKINS: Tracery of a Gothic Window. Oxford University Press. . 52
11 GERARD MANLEY HOPKINS: Sketches from the early Diaries, 1863. Oxford University Press. 58
12 FREDERICK H. EVANS: Westminster Abbey, Apse from Choir. George Eastman House. 65

PLATES

13 GERARD MANLEY HOPKINS: Waves. Study from the Cliff Above, Freshwater Gate. July 23. 1863. Oxford University Press. . . . 67
14 GERARD MANLEY HOPKINS: Clouds. July 29 or 30 and July 31. 1863. Oxford University Press. 69
15 GERARD MANLEY HOPKINS: Sketch from the early Diaries, 1864. Oxford University Press. 71
16 GERARD MANLEY HOPKINS: Sketches from the early Diaries, 1864. Oxford University Press. 73
17 La Madeleine, Vézelay. Courtauld Institute. 79
18 Notre-Dame d'Amiens. Photograph by Jean Roubier. 85
19 WILLIAM BUTTERFIELD: All Saints, Margaret Street, London. *Building News* V, 1859. 93
20 FREDERICK H. EVANS: Lincoln Cathedral. Philadelphia Museum of Art. 99
21 FREDERICK H. EVANS: Wells Cathedral: Nave Looking West. Philadelphia Museum of Art. 105
22 Oxford Cathedral. National Monuments Record, England. 107
23 FREDERICK H. EVANS: Wells Cathedral. Stairs to Chapter House and Bridge to Vicar's Close. Philadelphia Museum of Art. . 111
24 Saint-Mathurin, Larchant. Photograph by Jacques Verroust. 115
25 Chartres Cathedral. Photograph by Theodor Seeger. 125
26 Notre-Dame d'Amiens. Courtauld Institute. 127

PLATES

27 FREDERICK H. EVANS: Church at Autun. Philadelphia Museum of Art. 129
28 Wells Cathedral. National Monuments Record, England. 131
29 Saint-Mathurin, Larchant. Photograph by Jacques Verroust. 140
30 Notre-Dame d'Amiens. Editions Arthaud. . 152
31 The Prince of Darkness and Foolish Virgins. West Portal, Strasbourg Cathedral. Photograph by Harald Busch. 163
32 ALVIN LANGDON COBURN: The Curiosity Shop. Frontispiece, Henry James, *The Golden Bowl* I (New York Edition, 1909). George Eastman House. 169
33 ALVIN LANGDON COBURN: An English House. Frontispiece, Henry James, *The Portrait of a Lady* I (New York Edition, 1907). George Eastman House. 180
34 ALVIN LANGDON COBURN: Some of the Spoils. Frontispiece, Henry James, *The Spoils of Poynton* (New York Edition, 1908). George Eastman House. 194
35 ALVIN LANGDON COBURN: The Doctor's Door. Frontispiece, Henry James, *The Wings of the Dove* I (New York Edition, 1907). George Eastman House. 199
36 ALVIN LANGDON COBURN: The Venetian Palace. Frontispiece, Henry James, *The Wings of the Dove* II (New York Edition, 1907). George Eastman House. 201
37 ALVIN LANGDON COBURN: Henry James, 1906. George Eastman House. 203

INTRODUCTION

Sit in a child's wagon. Someone pulls you through this house. You have entered white walls thick, prepared for the frescoing of your thoughts. Brown ground of earth is your floor, sky your ceiling. In the first room are Greek temples. You are pulled around them. In one corner you pass Roman ruins; in another, a plain English house with a flight of stairs to its roof. Then the second room. You do not know how you got there. Perhaps you were outside in passage, with Pegasus. In this room are cathedral façades, arches and spires, erect like sentries to Weather. Winged flight: the third room. You begin to smile. Here is a church entire, grey, light. But when you go inside you wish to be outside. So your guide pulls you faster until you no longer know whether you look up outside or are arched over inside. Winged flight: the fourth room. You walk, you have no guide. Here you find smaller rooms crowded with furniture or cleared in deference to window-views of churches, palaces, or people. Winged flight: the fifth is not a room at all but a hall. Every few feet issues a cord stretching out from under the wall. Windows mark the space above each cord. When you look through the windows, you see trails of houses and cathedrals, this cord stretching straight to Greece, that one shorter going to nineteenth-century France, another marked with speech-makers, still another with men writing on stone tablets. And then you are spun around, you cannot tell this way from that. You are outside. The white walls are gone. It is the world you are in. But ah, over there is the Parthenon, here a Gothic church, to the right your own house with a stairway to the attic and its own view. The world inside was no different, it was just bounded by white walls.

THE HOUSE I have described is the book before you, the open-air architecture of *Literary Architecture*. The five rooms are its five chapters, each filled with the furniture of its subject matter, each very specifically located, separated by halls of space. The tour is what I hope will be the experience of reading: a transitive activity connecting these separate rooms of vision and concluding in reflection on these connections. That we sit in a child's wagon to begin this tour is a gentle admonition that our activity of perceiving be undertaken with curiosity, the seeing and taking note of entrances and exits, peripheries and contents. For these are the tissue of this book: the architecture of literature as external configuration, as form and embodiment, of consciousness.

Literary Architecture is a building of connection. The particular subject, what may be thought of as the occasion, is the relationships between architecture and literature as announced in the writings of Walter Pater, Gerard Manley Hopkins, Marcel Proust, and Henry James; for each of these writers declares in one way or another that literature is like architecture. The larger subject is a proposition. There exists as a convention in literature the habit of comparison between architecture and literature extending from Plato to Samuel Beckett and discovering particular expression late in the nineteenth century and on into the twentieth. I propose that this convention constitutes a tradition which I should like to call literary architecture. I present the tradition of literary architecture by noting its occurrence and by asking this question: what may be accomplished when writers select architecture as art analogue for literature? The question is new to literary studies. It constitutes the motive for this book.

And yet this book as a building of connection is more than a structure with contents. For a building is not an object (product) only; it is, importantly, an activity. And it is the activity of building that constitutes my largest subject, that is, the nature of experience. Experience may be particularized in literary study to mean critical inquiry, methodology, reading; for our purposes, I should like it to be taken to mean our way of noticing or perceiving, our activity of being in the world. There is precedent for understanding experience and being as building: if we follow the word *building* to its etymological origins, we find it comes from an Indo-European word meaning "to be, to exist, to grow."[1] It is no surprise, then, that both building-as-object (product) and building-as-activity require and turn upon space constructs, the art of architecture. We may use the brief dream I have recorded as a literary example, for both building-as-object (product) of perception and building-as-activity of perceiving are present. The architectural structure (house) that we enter encloses its own kind of structure (architecture) as its contents (or, in literary language, its content): the Greek temples of Pater, the cathedral remains of Hopkins, the church of Proust, the writing-rooms of James. Our experience as an activity of being – entering and moving through interior space, see-

INTRODUCTION

ing wall-boundaries, looking through windows, feeling stress—is governed by and utilizes the architectural structures we perceive, as we perceive them. This is the constitutive experience. As we tour the rooms, we feel "point of view" as a position of place (where we stand when we view something), "circumspection" as moving around an object that we might see it from all sides, "introduction" as entering a new room-space, "conclusion" as the closing of a portion or lot of space. Similarly, "critical distance" becomes/is the physical space-relation between viewer and viewed (di-stance), "perception" is seeing through space, "perceptual construct" or "system" is architectural structure. Through literary architecture, the language of literary perception displays its enduring substantiality. Experience itself and the conditions of experience marry, may indeed be one with, the objects of experience.

My intention in this book, therefore, is not only to connect architecture and literature in particular writers and in literary history and theory; it is also to suggest the connection between architecture and literature in perceptual experience, as content and activity, subject and method. The tradition I propose, literary architecture, is also the one that I use as method; the one is a tradition or convention in art—literary, critical—the other a tradition or method in life—the activity of perception. The reading that I propose involves two steps: first, the noticing of internal architectural structures, those within the literary work, a James or a Proust novel, or even this book. These internal structures may be, for instance, cathedrals which symbolize character, temples which organize memory, or dwelling-houses which are settings for action. The second task of this sort of reading would be a looking-up from the book to notice the same or similar structures outside, in the physical, external world. (This approximates the exit from the house in the dream.) We may think of this second activity as the noticing of echoes or correspondences between internal and external structures; but "internal" structures are also structures of consciousness, conventions of perception, systems of belief, as well as the activities of thought and feeling. By "external," in addition to physical architecture and nature's architecture surrounding us, we must also understand all art-as-construct.[2]

Such a structure—one which discovers an internal, felt equivalent—makes *sense*, or means. We have here, in fact, one definition of meaning: that which has the same *nature* (the power of movement or correspondence between inner and outer) inside and outside which the occasion of place does not alter. Literature, then, may be described as *the giving of something* (place, form, or idea) *to meaning*, not the giving of meaning to something. That consciousness as structure (*human nature*) corresponds to or extends the world as structure is easy enough to understand: man and the world are composed of the same elements which either are or have the illusion of being spatial-temporal, the difference being combinations or proportions of elements. Man's main difference is that he imagines his consciousness or experience to be bounded or located in particular space, within white walls, bodies, time, while what is outside his personal realm he imagines to be boundless as he thinks the universe is boundless, timeless as it is timeless. Because of this structural correspondence, we may read all structures, not only those cited within this study, with a mental ruler and a table of equivalents: structures have

INTRODUCTION

either actual spatial extension (architecture) in the physical world or the language of spatial extension (literature) in the world of thought. They may be either as small as individual "cells," as in the prose of Walter Pater, or as large as the "womb-of-all, home-of-all, hearse-of-all night," as in the poetry of G. M. Hopkins.[3] To understand is to notice the internal or felt equivalent of the external structure; the activity of understanding is the activity of learning not what but how that external structure makes sense. Thus my book not only connects two separate arts, architecture and literature, but aspires also to connect subject with method. I should now like to add that it also aspires to connect method with meaning. A building of connection is also a building of meaning.

What I have called literary architecture in itself, and inevitably, proposes to make a connection of a very audacious sort. This is the larger connection of correspondence or equivalence between the two arts themselves, architecture and literature, the one whose characteristic form seizes actual space as territory, the other whose characteristic form spells time. Correspondence is actually active: it is a process of conversion obeying the laws of conservation in which there is no loss. Writers who select architecture as their art analogue dematerialize the more material art, architecture, that they may materialize the more immaterial art, literature. In this way, architecture and literature relinquish an analogical relationship to marry as literary architecture. The conversion, however, does not occur in the forward direction of construction or composition only. It requires a backward activity to precede it, the unbuilding or decomposing of existing structures, either actual architecture or present conventions of perception. The backward activity not only provides for the transformational process of building literary architecture; it actually makes possible that process by preparing ground or clearing the space necessary for the new—the artist's as yet unbuilt structure of seeing. (Ground clearing is especially important in the nineteenth and twentieth centuries when to build a view of the world is to *re*build an existing world view.) In literary terms, the process of building is "composing," the unbuilding is the "decomposing," or the activity of analysis.

Only in my last chapter do I relinquish particular focus on the literary architecture of my four principal figures. In this final chapter, I hope that, having experienced the activities of building, we may reflect back upon that experience and from it construe larger meaning. The delay is intentional: cognition—knowing—engages, while recognition—knowing that we know—disengages; recognition, in other words, requires the space-time construct *distance*. Only as conclusion may we understand fully the relation of correspondence, namely, the lucid coherence of literary architecture as practiced by these four writers: for relation requires experience to precede it. Therefore, while my theory of literary architecture emerges with the text, I present the formal tradition of literary architecture as a kind of Proustian retrospection, our reflection upon the buildings of literary architecture, something which occurs and can occur only after we have built the structures themselves.

It will be seen that my *Literary Architecture* thus cannot claim to be a traditional book, whether in its field, its subject, or its research. It attempts to take note of

INTRODUCTION

something which does not constitute an academic field but which, as its very subject is space—both ground and territory—does constitute a field of another sort, the field of literary and perceptual activity. This is a field which, though it is only just now beginning to be explored by critics, has been so explored by artists that it deserves to be named and recognized as a tradition proper, the tradition of literary architecture. Since this academically new field has been no field, there could be no traditional research within it; instead I have conducted a search, and my method has been one of following hunches, of asking how the architectural analogue serves literary art, and of looking for that "how" into our own activity of perceiving. Literature—our particular focus—is, of course, about itself and about life; that is, it is about our experience of being alive. I have tried not to turn to another system to explain literature and its meaning but to turn to the subject of literature, life, and to those self-consciously selected structures which these four writers use to help them organize their perceptions. My precedent is in the writers we are looking at: for Pater, Hopkins, Proust, and James teach us not only how to read but also how to see, not only the world of literature, not only the world of physical architecture, but also the structures of consciousness itself, most especially the structures of our felt and remembered experience of life.

I may be asked why there are few connective links between my chapters and why this study does not follow chronology so as to constitute a history. In answer, I must plead the nature of my subject matter. Writers who select architecture as their art analogue for literature choose to express time—what we may think of as the linearity, the storyness of history—in terms of space, that is, on location. They each place us within a particular spatial construct, a literary house, one with extension and peripheries which we are asked to observe. The chapters of *Literary Architecture* likewise are on location, respectful of the literary boundaries they observe. This positioning should allow us to survey a literary whole: we do not wander beyond our present (time) into another house; we do not wander beyond what is accessible. Each chapter should be read, then, as a taking-up only of the space its author-subject constructs upon, establishing us in relation to his spatial borders. So, too, this book is purposely not a history even though the information it presents may be read for and as history. For the minds it deals with are spacious minds. These writers see and express ideas as fields of extension rather than as lines of direction, much as they feel time, and therefore history, as connectedness, as spatial touching.

Thus while there is little forward (linear) direction in *Literary Architecture*, there is connectedness of another sort, of fields of vision and influence which radiate, each one obeying its nature. The order of presentation the book observes may be viewed as enlarging spheres. Pater fathers forth the aesthetic concept literary architecture, in fact coining the term; and while he did not achieve imaginative literary architecture with the largeness of Hopkins, Proust, or James, his ideas encompass all that their achievements realize. Hopkins (in history Pater's pupil) represents a use of the architectural analogue at its most economical, as a tool for poetry such that his dense, highly focused art gives us both his particular world and, in a sense, the whole world. Proust represents the analogue at its largest generically, in many-volumed fiction; the architectural analogue enables him to convert linear

INTRODUCTION

time, his private past and the historical past, into a literary art that does not fragment, does not go out of sight or out of reach despite its span. The architectural analogue permits time past to stay on view. James achieves a union of sorts as a writer of poetic fiction. Like Hopkins, James observes careful attention to each word as a tool for perception while using a genre of a much larger scale, his novels suggesting Proust's individual volumes. Thus we see three models of literary architecture following its articulation by Pater. And Pater's name raises another question which might be put to this study: where is John Ruskin, author of "The Poetry of Architecture," *The Seven Lamps of Architecture, The Stones of Venice*, in all this? I think I must answer that Ruskin is beyond, or at any rate, not within, the scope of this book. *Literary Architecture* is an inquiry into imaginative literature, not into art criticism or art history. And while Ruskin bequeathed to the nineteenth century a formalized means of "reading" architecture, it was Pater, not Ruskin, who applied architecture to literature by admonishing writers to use the architectural analogue in order to heal an exhausted literary art. This is not to suggest that Pater, Hopkins, Proust, and James are not each indebted to Ruskin; each is, and each pays him homage. Their relations to Ruskin are taken up as those relations seem to require, that is, when reference to Ruskin illuminates the imaginative literature we are studying.

I think of one question that remains: why these four writers and not others, such as Austen or Dickens? This is not just a period question, although it may be answered for period reasons as well as for literary reasons. The question brings us back to the primary meaning or function of the analogue, to architecture as it represents an embodied consciousness or form of consciousness, as it represents an awareness (idea) of consciousness. The four writers I have chosen select architecture in order to give to language and thought spatial extension, to present the where-ness of ideas and thoughts. By means of the analogue, they may give, or seem to give, substance to that which is no-thing, to that which does not occupy what we call substantial space. That they do this by giving spirit-thought a dwelling place or abode[4] is appropriate: *dwelling*, if traced to its Indo-European root, comes from a word which means "to rise in a cloud," the "dust," "vapor," or "smoke" which makes seeable, that is, gives substantial form to, the soul or spirit, our breath-being. (The Greek *thumos* also comes from this root.) A dwelling—body, architecture, literature—is spirit-thought bodied, seeable, given form. Constructing a building is *bringing into being*;[5] constructing a dwelling is bringing of being *into seeable form*. Dwellings or abodes are temporary: *abode* means, in fact, "the action of waiting," "a temporary remaining" before the spirit returns, with the death of the body, to its disembodied or extended state, the open field.

Pater, Hopkins, Proust, and James choose architecture as their art analogue for literature in part because it is the art form most capable of embodying thought-spirit, or essences, most capable of the conversion act. These four writers call the conversion activity translation; we may think of it also as *trans*-formation, of one art *form* into another, of being into embodied being. Austen and Dickens, on the other hand, work in a world of material or constructed equivalents—architecture and politics, architecture and character, and so forth—with-

INTRODUCTION

out converting either the material into the immaterial or the immaterial into the material and thus without doing or describing the trans-form act. Their fiction, as a consequence, does not show the fullest use or reach of the architectural analogue, nor does it offer to us a methodology for understanding the profound beauty and significance of literary architecture. Pater, Hopkins, Proust, and James, to the contrary, push the analogue to its perceptual limits. I choose them, therefore, for the particular largeness of their visions as they achieve form in great literature. That they write within a fifty-year spread is no coincidence: to writers more and more fearful of disappearance not only of the temporal past but of familiar concepts of identity (and such are those writing toward the close of the nineteenth century and on into the first decades of the twentieth), architecture provides a means of preserving or memorializing the past, and identity, even as it provides for the transformation of that past and of being into literary art. Literary architecture celebrates the perceiving mind of the self; but it does so never at the expense of the universe or whole, never to the exclusion of the world.

I
LITERARY ARCHITECTURE: WALTER HORATIO PATER

2

The literary architecture of association:
Waltham Abbey leads Pater to conjure
history and rule. Stone, for Pater,
was composed of "minute dead bodies."
Pater writes, "In architecture, close
as it is to men's lives and their history,
the visible result of time is a large
factor in the realised aesthetic value,
and what a true architect will always
trust to." Here, in Waltham Abbey
we can see the visible result of time
transform architecture into organic nature.
(South Chapel, Waltham Abbey)

ONE

Pater's Rooms: Concepts of Literary Architecture

SEVERAL YEARS after Walter Pater's death, the anonymous "F," presumably a student of Pater's at Oxford, wrote a modest and suitably quiet memoir of his don, not a tribute properly, but more a brief sketch appropriately drawn just before the twentieth century foreclosed the Victorian era. The short reflection, called "In Pater's Rooms," includes only four paragraphs, each topically discrete and without connective links. The first describes the room itself, the second Pater's literary attitudes, the third his taste in architecture; the last is a single sentence conclusion remarking that although "that Oxford room" is tenanted by another, it will remain Pater's as long "as English literature lasts."[1] The opening paragraph describing Pater's lodgings begins:

> The room was small, but the Gothic window with its bow enlarged it, and seemed to bring something of the outside Oxford into the chamber so small itself. The Radcliffe just a few hand-breadths away from the pane, the towers and the crockets of All Souls' beyond, and to the right the fair dream of St. Mary's spire, filling up the prospect with great suggestions—through the window one took in all these, and they seemed for a moment to become almost the furniture of the student's chamber.[2]

"F" then recalls his conversations with Pater, but in a tone so reminiscent of his master's that it almost betrays the motive for anonymity:

LITERARY ARCHITECTURE

We talked of literary success, and literary prospects for a beginner of good talents, who is willing to work and wait. Dare it be said aloud? most of the modern minor poets might be using their endowments better in writing prose in this "prose age"; the same qualities that minister to a tardy mediocrity in poetry and the world of imagination, would develop grace and artistic finish in prose, the world of fact, which sorely needs to be *more* than fact, if it is not to be less than truth.[3]

With what seems a careless innocence and ease, "F" has described and synthesized complexities of thought Pater himself was at pains to express and document throughout his literary career. Our concerns now are those transitions "F" omits or, rather, presumes: what relationship might something so seemingly peripheral as Pater's rooms have to his literary and aesthetic values, and what, in turn, do those values have to do with architectural style?

"F," obviously familiar with Pater's fiction, permits of the suggestion that to Pater rooms were the externalized configurations of internal consciousness, descriptive not only of the quality and structure of minds but filled with a metaphoric furniture of thought derived from particular sensuous experience of an outside world as it intruded through windows and doors, making its impress felt. Pater himself had written:

Into the mind sensitive to "form," a flood of random sounds, colours, incidents, is ever penetrating from the world without, to become, by sympathetic selection, a part of its very structure, and, in turn, the visible vesture and expression of that other world it sees so steadily within.[4]

It is difficult for any reader of Pater not to conjure up the rooms which open up in his fictional writings, the sequestered attic of Sebastian van Storck, the Rococo-frescoed halls of Antony Watteau, even the spare cell of the Prior Saint-Jean. But more elusive is the relevance of a *mind-room* equation to Pater's larger literary aesthetic. It is no secret that the aging Pater, in his essay "Style," made explicit the requirements for good and great literature:

> Given the conditions I have tried to explain as constituting good art;—then, if it be devoted further to the increase of men's happiness, to the redemption of the oppressed, or the enlargement of our sympathies with each other, or to such presentment of new or old truth about ourselves and our relation to the world as may ennoble and fortify us in our sojourn here, or immediately, as with Dante, to the glory of God, it will be also great art; if, over and above those qualities I summed up as mind and soul—that colour and mystic perfume, and that reasonable structure, it has something of the soul of humanity in it, and finds its logical, architectural place, in the great structure of human life.[5]

The passage announces Pater's controversial break from stylistic considerations to substantive ones, those concerning the subject matter of literature and its scope; but what is important for us here are Pater's requirements and the terms in which he couches them. "F" suggests at least one reason for Pater's notorious volte-face in the "Style" essay: presumably, Pater saw what "F" calls a "tardy mediocrity" in modern imaginative literature. While "tardy" sounds like Pater, his own terms are rather different, in slight ways and yet momentously. After noting a quality of mind which, characteristically nineteenth century, is "little susceptible to restraint" and yields "lawless verse," Pater condemns what he terms removable decoration in all literature for having a "narcotic force . . . upon the negligent intelligence to which

LITERARY ARCHITECTURE

any *diversion*, literally, is welcome, any vagrant intruder, because one can go wandering away with it from the immediate subject."[6] As remedy, Pater makes his request that literary style have two properties, "mind" and "soul."

By mind, the literary artist reaches us, through static and objective indications of design in his work, legible to all. By soul, he reaches us, somewhat capriciously perhaps, one and not another, through vagrant sympathy and a kind of immediate contact.[7]

Mind, however, Pater also calls architectural conception, and its literary effect is curative:

The otiose, the facile, surplusage: why are these abhorrent to the true literary artist, except because in literary as in all other art, structure is all-important, felt, or painfully missed, everywhere?—that architectural conception of a work, which foresees the end in the beginning and never loses sight of it, and in every part is conscious of all the rest, till the last sentence does but, with undiminished vigour, unfold and justify the first—a condition of literary art, which ... I shall call the necessity of *mind* in style.[8]

Mind and soul fused Pater calls literary architecture. In literary architecture, the soul of style, while important, affords only secondary colorations, picturesque ones at that, the light and shade, a literary *genius loci* of atmosphere, playing on and around literature's overriding architectural structure:

For the literary architecture, if it is to be rich and expressive, involves not only foresight of the end in the beginning, but also development or growth of design, in the process of execution, with many irregularities, surprises, and afterthoughts; the contingent as well as the necessary being subsumed under the unity of the whole. As truly, to the lack of such architectural design . . . informing an entire, perhaps very intricate, composition, which shall be . . . true from first to last to that vision within, may be attributed those weaknesses of conscious or unconscious repetition of word, phrase, motive, or member of the whole matter, indicating . . . an original structure in thought not organically complete.[9]

After describing the literary artist's task as one of "setting joint to joint," Pater concludes the passage with a double image, stating, "The house he [the writer] has built is rather a body he has informed."[10]

For Pater, the activity of great writing is the simultaneous activity of filling—informing—and of forming, the giving of full form/idea to that which is felt, sensed, or known but which has no embodied structure prior to the art act. Literary architecture is, consequently, an *alive* "reasonable structure": it is a body with a soul. In this context, the building of literary architecture is a composing of pregnant forms: it is pro-creative and full of care. The architectural analogue helps the reticent Pater to speak of such artistic making without embarrassment of exposure. But more significant for Pater, the analogue enables him to suggest that all structures mean regardless of scale, place, or occasion: Pater moves, in his passage of literary architecture, from art structure to human structure to life structure, from "colour" and "structure" (architecture) to "soul" and "mind" (man) to "soul of humanity" and "structure of human life."

There are more suggestive links between the materials and the structures of literary art. The mind-structure analogue—either Pater's room as "F" describes it or Pater's literary architecture—offers a distinct notion of inside and outside: the room "seemed to bring something of the outside Oxford into the chamber so small itself." Some correspondence, even if only in the most literal sense, exists between inside and outside, between a room and its "vagrant intruders." This correspondence has fruitful consequences; the trans-parent window enlarges the inner room-world, informing it by and with the external prospect, which itself is already *full* of "great suggestions": "through the window one took in all these, and they seemed for a moment to become almost the furniture of the student's chamber."[11] The activity "F" describes here is one of receiving, the artistic activity of influence or impression. For the activity of creating literary architecture, the direction changes to one of expression. One comes to expect Pater's announcement, made later, in his "Style" essay: "Well! all language involves translation from inward to outward."[12] Figuratively, literary architecture enables transmission, if not translation, from the inside out, and it also provides checks to lawlessness: intruders cannot enter wantonly, nor can what is inside grow wildly without structural checks.

As easy as this notion of inside and outside is, it is worthwhile to look at it for another moment, since the idea persists, and has persisted throughout Pater's fictional and critical writings as well as throughout the work of others who also select architecture as their art model. The imprisoned self in the one-time suppressed "Conclusion" of Pater's *The Renaissance*—suffering the intractability of a relativist aesthetic—also occupies a room of sorts. We cannot help but recall Tennyson's woeful "Soul" locked within "The Palace of Art"; but Pater has morbidly reduced palace to a chamber of Poe-like terror, just as elsewhere his rooms shrink still further to single cells, biologically and architecturally more minute and limiting:

WALTER HORATIO PATER

At first sight experience seems to bury us under a flood of external objects, pressing upon us with a sharp and importunate reality, calling us out of ourselves in a thousand forms of action. But when reflexion begins to play upon those objects they are dissipated under its influence . . . the whole scope of observation is dwarfed into the narrow chamber of the individual mind. Experience, already reduced to a group of impressions, is ringed round for each one of us by that thick wall of personality through which no real voice has ever pierced on its way to us, or from us to that which we can only conjecture to be without. Every one of those impressions is the impression of the individual in his isolation, each mind keeping as a solitary prisoner its own dream of a world.[13]

Pater's "Conclusion" makes the otherwise neutral word "translation" from the "Style" essay appear tinged with optimism and therefore, appropriately, encouraging. In suggesting the possibility of movement from the inward chamber to the outside, Pater, in "Style," is also suggesting the possibility of creating viable literary works of art. His summation—that great literature "finds its logical, architectural place, in the great structure of human life"[14]—so expands the cloistral chamber of *The Renaissance* as to offer a positive alternative to the philosophic and psychological confines of a relativistic and, by default, virtually solipsistic existence.

It is important, then, that Pater's anonymous elegist concludes his memoir with a recount of Pater's taste in architecture. Out of "F's" rendering Pater looms as no less a Victorian man of letters for participating in the charged architectural controversies persisting throughout his century. According to "F," Pater felt that

things of quite the first rank had been produced in the 'seventies and 'eighties: gross and flagrant mistakes had been made in modern Gothic and Renaissance; but churches and public buildings had lately been built as perfect in their way as the work of the twelfth or fourteenth century. He instanced St. Philips Church, which lies behind the London Hospital.[15]

"F" goes on to say that Pater's thinking about Whitechapel "led him to dwell with enthusiasm upon the perfect Norman of Waltham Abbey, that to the death of Harold, and that to the 'stirring, interesting writing of Professor Freeman, which I love to read.' "[16] [Plate 2] The attention paid here to Pater's stylistic sympathies throws into relief "F's" opening description of his don's rooms: no longer is it incidental that Pater's window was Gothic or that the metaphoric furniture of the room was towers and church-steeples of pre-Gothic (Norman), Gothic, and Gothic-Revival Oxford. The Gothic window qualifies Pater's vision: history and philosophy, political and aesthetic, cling to Gothic where they would not cling to buildings from another period or of a differing "mental style"; in turn, the towers and steeples cluttering Pater's room assume symbolic value, recalling to a reader religious and academic collisions of the past, perhaps the scarring Tractarian upheaval or the subsequent secularizing of an Oxford whose dons in the 1870s could relinquish celibacy vows. For Pater, too, as "F" well knew, architectural style triggers, intentionally, an associative remembering, buildings themselves sustaining qualities of expressive art-forms: one building beckons another, Whitechapel the Norman Waltham Abbey; Waltham Abbey then conjures history and rule, namely Harold, who finally solicits from Pater's memory affection for one man's writing, that of Professor Freeman.[17]

"F's" brief service to Pater's memory in 1899 managed to imply a great deal while saying little. In a few paragraphs the associative pattern comes clear, and reminiscence turns upon a coupling of architecture with literature. This, in fact, is one extraordinary service Pater's concept of literary architecture performs: in every kind of writing that Pater undertook, he celebrates the power for memory and association that architecture bestows. If a generic architecture (home, church, school), or architecture still more abstracted into sheer structure (rooms), has implications for Pater's conception of literature, so, too, do particular manifestations of architecture. On a formalistic level alone, qualities resplendent in architecture specifically Gothic find literary parallels in Pater's essays. Craftsmanship in Gothic construction, architectural or literary, is meant to suggest the imposition of an artist's individuality, his tastes and skill, onto the structure he builds as he translates outward his private vision. The "irregularities" and "surprises" of Gothic cornices and capitals, the "intricacies" of carved ornament or tracery inseparable in function from church structure – all these find reciprocal terms or characteristics in the literary architecture that Pater delicately evokes and qualifies in his essay "Style." [Plate 3] If we return, for a brief moment, to Pater's own prose, in this instance to the passage of advice regarding literary architecture, we see that Pater himself carries out what he admonishes others to do:

>   For the literary architecture, if it is to be rich and expressive, involves not only foresight of the end in the beginning, but also development or growth of design, in the process of execution, with many irregularities, surprises, and afterthoughts; the contingent as well as the necessary being subsumed under the unity of the whole. As truly, to the lack of such architectural design . . . informing an entire, perhaps very

intricate, composition, which shall be true . . . from first to last to that vision within, may be attributed those weaknesses . . . indicating . . . an original structure in thought not organically complete.[18]

"If it is to be rich and expressive" comes as an interruption or "surprise," "the contingent as well as the necessary" as an "afterthought" to the first part of the sentence, "forming an entire, perhaps very intricate, composition" carrying an intricacy or detail within it.

It is misleading, however, it is all too easy, to index Pater's writing by a metaphoric system in which preferences in architectural style denote equivalent preferences in history, philosophy, or aesthetics. This is to reduce Pater's oftentimes protean values to one scheme, implicitly and temporally consistent. It is much more profitable to recognize that the architectural door which swings wide on an historical past and on literary style also swings wide on private memory, and that it postulates something about its interiors: they are accessible, recoverable, describable. In one of his *Imaginary Portraits*, "Emerald Uthwart," for instance, a reader may "dive" with the Oxford student Emerald along a "passage," not, as we might expect, of old buildings, but of "old builders."[19] [Plate 4] In the same way, Pater may move, by induction or deduction, from literal or imaginary edifices, so as to reconstruct, often fictionally, a past made replete through creative rather than historical detailing. In such a context, Piranesian ruins (or empty spaces where buildings once stood) provide *materia* and creating room for a writer of historical fiction or philosophic fiction. Shifts of time—from a Rome in rubble to a whole Rome before its fall, and so to a nineteenth-century-recon-

WALTER HORATIO PATER

3

"Irregularities, surprises, afterthoughts":
"jut-jotting" rhythms of the Gothic. It is not
difficult to see how inspiring the Gothic was,
with its staccato intricacies and its pride of
territory. Such are the rhythms which attract
Hopkins as well as Pater. (Notre-Dame d'Amiens)

structed Rome (as in *Marius the Epicurean*)—show how effective architecture can be, as a provocation to synoptic fictions. Finally, a modern reader may look at "The Child in the House" or any other of the *Imaginary Portraits*, with an eye to architectural structure. In "Child," for instance, the "design"[20] which best describes "the process of brain building" is, by now predictably, the home of the story's central character, Florian Deleal: that structure then suggests mind-design, cognitive growth, nostalgia; and by implication, in accord with a terminology to be found in the aesthetic essays, it also suggests Pater's ideas about memory and fiction- or poetry-making. Such internal architecture does more than reveal the character's mind: through a perfect matching of thought to language or language to thought, the retreated writer himself goes public. Pater's careful literary monuments —his literary art entire—may be visited by all readers. Each may witness there the activity of growth itself of what would otherwise remain hidden, the private trains of thought (open sets) and of memory (closed sets) of the artist. Here we find another aspect of Pater's achievement: through his literary architecture readers may see the boundaries—the walls—of the artist's understanding and experience of the world at the same time that we see those limitations transformed into structures of meaning. Through creative expression Pater exposes the structural demarcations of his own collapsed life. These processes are tracked in detail, not only (subterraneanly) in his own fictions, but throughout his critical and historical writings. In the following section I shall concentrate on the interplay between fiction, architecture, and memory, especially as it was inherited by Pater out of a long tradition, and was then transformed by him.

4

The *mind* of literary architecture:
diving along a passage of *old builders*.
Here we see the world of time recorded
as architectural style. (Vézelay)

5

Notre-Dame d'Amiens: "L'église ogivale
par excellence," Pater claims in his
essay "Notre-Dame d'Amiens." Pater sees
in the "queen" of Gothic churches "certain
impressive metaphysical and moral ideas,
a sort of popular scholastic philosophy,
or as if it were the virtues and vices
Aristotle defines, or the characters of
Theophrastus, translated into stone."

TWO

The *Ars Memoria* Tradition: Architecture and Pater's Fiction

I come to the fields and spacious palaces of
memory (*campos et lata praetoria memoriae*)
where are the treasures of innumerable
images, brought into it from things of all sorts
perceived by the senses. There is stored up,
whatever besides we think, either by enlarging
or diminishing, or any other way varying
those things which the sense hath come to;
and whatever else ... which forgetfulness
hath not yet swallowed up and buried.
When I enter there, I require instantly
what I will to be brought forth,
and something instantly comes.

AUGUSTINE

*

Our susceptibilities, the discovery
of our powers, manifold experiences ...
belong to this or that other well-
remembered place in the material habitation ... and the early habitation thus
gradually becomes a sort of material shrine
or sanctuary of sentiment; a system of visible
symbolism interweaves itself through all
our thoughts and passions; and irresistibly,
little shapes, voices, accidents – the angle at which
the sun in the morning fell on the pillow –
become parts of the great chain
wherewith we are bound.

WALTER PATER

LITERARY ARCHITECTURE

> How indelibly [sensible things] affect
> us; with what capricious attractions and
> associations they figure themselves on the
> white paper, the smooth wax, of our
> ingenuous souls, as "with lead in the
> rock forever," giving form and feature,
> and as it were assigned house-room
> in our memory, to early experiences
> of feeling and thought, which abide
> with us ever afterwards, thus,
> and not otherwise.
>
> WALTER PATER

DESPITE THE LAPSE of time and the differences in tradition, it may be said that Pater and Augustine share assumptions about memory and place. For both, memory becomes a collection of mental images drawn from sense impressions and extended in time, linked associatively to place and figuring as edifices in the mind, or with Pater, edifices projected from the mental into material abodes. Pater, like Augustine, goes to places for their reconstructive value: "The quiet spaciousness of the place is itself like a meditation, an 'act of recollection,' and clears away the confusions of the heart."[21] But while Augustine summons up memories by an act of will, Pater and his fictional characters more often passively yield themselves to the influences of place and to the memories there associated. It is assumed that associations may be ordered in these memory store-houses, and that recollection of specific images or ideas, temporarily forgotten or buried, may be the aim of an associative ordering. Yet for Pater, order (or lack thereof) and association function, in addition, for a descriptive purpose, so as to portray what Pater calls the process of *brain-building*. If it is—and it is—unfair to say that Augustine is not concerned with cognitive processes, it would be as unfair to say that such was Pater's only concern. That "white paper" should figure as the recipient of sense impressions is far from incidental. It is here perhaps that Pater's purpose differs most widely from Augustine's: whereas Augustine reconstructs religious and meditative experience, Pater is concerned to suggest the active art of writing and creating. Sense images are recorded indelibly within the rooms of memory; but just as indelibly, and very much to the purpose for Pater, they may be recorded verbally as literary art. Quite simply, when Pater describes buildings—be they Vézelay or Notre Dame d'Amiens of his architectural histories, or else imaginative structures as in his fictions—he reciprocally talks not only about memory but about literature. Literature, by its analogous relationship to memory and architecture, comes to be defined as a process of recapituation, not only of a private past but of an historical one, what the nineteenth century might call racial, a past, as we have seen, recoverable through architectural renderings.

Pater, in his attitudes toward literature, architecture, and memory, holds assumptions and values which we shall find shared by others; and, in his own modest way, Pater attempts what flowers more fully elsewhere, especially in the subsequent literary creations of Gerard Manley Hopkins, Marcel Proust, and Henry James. Like these men after him, Pater inherits and brings together at the very least two seemingly separate and ancient traditions: the *ars memoria* tradition[22] which uses architecture as a quotidian structure for memory and a convenient metaphor for the mind; and what I call the *ut architectura poesis* tradition which suggests that writers respect and imitate in their literary style principles of architectural construction or structure. It is important to our concerns with Pater and with the larger implications of literary architecture, that what seem to be vestiges of the classical mnemonic system, the one to which Augustine in fact subscribed, do survive in nineteenth-century architecture manuals;[23] and, perhaps to our surprise, we find that these very manuals also borrow and use poetic or linguistic terms to describe the art of architecture. In this context, then, Pater's careful argument for literary architecture–rather than a newly formulated analogy between literature and architecture–represents for literary art what might be considered a repossession or borrowing back of terms and concepts which had once been literary commonplaces but which had been used more recently to dictate not literary but architectural practice in the nineteenth century.[24]

Although Pater himself rarely addresses the relationship between architecture and memory with the seeming explicitness that his architectural mentor, John Ruskin, does in the "Lamp of Memory" section in *The Seven Lamps of Architecture* (1849), for Pater as for Ruskin, architecture serves a memorial function: it recapitulates the historical past. Pater comments in "Prosper Mérimée":

> In that grandiose art of building, the most national, the most tenaciously rooted of all the arts in the stable conditions of life, there [are] historical documents hardly less clearly legible than the manuscript chronicle.[25]

Once again, the analogy between architecture and literature helps Pater to describe how he and others in the

6
Memorial architecture
with historical documents.
(Notre-Dame d'Amiens)

nineteenth century view buildings. While Pater and Ruskin cautiously avoid identifying the two art forms, Ruskin by remarking that one does not "read" certain building styles as one would read Milton, Pater by carefully hedging on his analogical formulation ("hardly less clearly"), the two overtly sanction the notion of shared qualities, even the belief that one art could, to use Ruskin's term, subsume the other.[26] Only with qualifications, then, does Pater agree with Ruskin that architecture, like poetry, is a "conqueror of forgetfulness."[27] If nature can no longer retain records of the past as it did for Romantic poets, architecture can. In "Emerald Uthwart," Pater, for instance, links architecture to consciousness when he conveys how King's School Canterbury records the past:

> Why! the Uthwarts had scarcely had more memories than their woods, noiselessly deciduous, or than their pre-historic entirely unprogressive, unrecording fore-fathers, in or before the days of the Druids. Centuries of almost "still" life—birth, death, and the rest, as merely natural processes—had made them and their home what we find them. Centuries of conscious endeavour, on the other hand, had built, shaped, and coloured the place, a small cell, which Emerald Uthwart was now to occupy; a place such as our most characteristic English education has rightly tended to "find itself a house" in—a place full, for those who came within its influence, of a will of its own.[28]

That there should exist a relationship between the individual and architecture as it embodies memory or the historical past, between Emerald and his school, means that there is an overlap between the aesthetic and the moral worlds. In part because architecture reveals the mind of its builders and of its period, it may impress its philosophical and ethical values upon those who dwell in it:

> The very place one is in, its stone-work, its empty spaces, invade you; invade all who belong to them ... seem to question you masterfully as to your purpose in being here at all, amid the great memories of the past, of this school; – challenge you, so to speak, to make moral philosophy one of your acquirements, if you can, and to systematise your vagrant self; which however, will in any case be here systematised for you.[29]

Pater is quite explicit that "impressibility" is a positive quality, especially for artists, and that architecture as physical edifice or literary structure, because it impresses aesthetically, determines or contributes to the moral quality of character impressed. If architecture assumes such power for Pater, we may begin to understand and anticipate how important architecture is for literature. We do know that Pater, throughout his own aesthetical, fictional, and philosopical writings, continually chooses to describe schools, churches, homes – structures in which a kind of learning is assumed to take place. In *Plato and Platonism* Pater comments:

> There exists some close connexion between what may be called the aesthetic qualities of the world about us and the formation of moral character, between aesthetics and ethics. Wherever people have been inclined to lay stress on the colouring, for instance, cheerful or otherwise, of the walls of the room where children learn to read, as though that had something to do with the colouring of their minds; on the possible moral effect of the beautiful ancient buildings of some of our own schools and colleges, on the building of character, in any way, through the eye and ear; there the spirit of Plato has been understood . . . [as has] the connexion between moral character and matters of poetry and art.[30]

LITERARY ARCHITECTURE

Memory housed architecturally becomes, thus, dynamic, to just the extent that its inhabitants become passively receptive.[31] The seesaw of static against kinetic, rest against motion, mind against soul, structure against inhabitant (not to mention structure against weather, territory against space) is endlessly in play; and just as in literary style, given optimum conditions, the passive and active coexist, so in the artistic personality the two work harmoniously if possible. In this way, an artist impressed may in turn construct or reconstruct, through memory, either the process of being impressed (his own growth), or else merely his particular, reflected, sense of an external world (his own decay).

It is possible to read Pater's fiction, then, in such a way as to take into account memory images and architectural structures as analogically suggestive, one of the other. As an example, we may look at a few passages from "The Child in the House," if only for the richness of interpretative possibilities. The story begins:

> As Florian Deleal walked, one hot afternoon, he overtook by the wayside a poor aged man, and, as he seemed weary with the road, helped him on with the burden which he carried, a certain distance. And as the man told his story, it chanced that he named the place, a little place in the neighbourhood of a great city, where Florian had passed his earliest years, but which he had never seen since, and, the story told, went forward on his journey comforted. And that night, like a reward for his pity, a dream of that place came to Florian, a dream which did for him the office of the finer sort of memory, bringing its object to mind with a great clearness, yet, as sometimes happens in dreams, raised a little above itself, and above ordinary retrospect.[32]

The initial relationship between dream and memory[33]

is based on place association. Pater sets up an associative chain in which there exists ostensible movement from parable, Bunyan-esque and general, to the particular or idiosyncratic, Florian Deleal. The house recalled is "raised" by dream rather than memory "above ordinary retrospect." After the passage just quoted, Florian, in the act of recalling (as distinct from the act of dreaming) places himself inside the house and thus identifies himself with soul and with the passive. He does this in order to describe an active process ("brain-building"):

> This accident of his dream was just the thing needed for the beginning of a certain design he then had in view, the noting, namely, of some things in the story of his spirit—in that process of brain-building by which we are, each one of us, what we are.[34]

Florian's verbal constructions betray, however, his assumptions about cognitive growth: they register passivity, that is, the refusal to take responsibility for growth of self. "With the image of the place so clear and favourable upon him, he fell to thinking of himself therein, and how his thoughts had grown up to him."[35] Florian then describes the old house:

> The old-fashioned, low wainscoting went round the rooms, and up the staircase with carved balusters and shadowy angles, landing half-way up at a broad window, with a swallow's nest below the sill, and the blossom on an old pear-tree showing across it in late April, against the blue, below which the perfumed juice of the rind of fallen fruit in autumn was so fresh. At the next turning came the closet which held on its deep shelves the best china. Little angel faces and reedy flutings stood out round the fireplace of the children's room. And on the top of the house, above the large attic, where the white mice ran in the twilight—an infinite, unexplored wonderland

of childish treasures, glass beads, empty scent-bottles still sweet, thrum of coloured silks, among its lumber—a flat space of roof, railed round, gave a view of the neighboring steeples; for the house, as I said, stood near a great city, which sent up heavenwards, over the twisting weather-vanes, not seldom, its bed of rolling cloud and smoke, touched with storm or sunshine.[36]

The ordering of association (which, incidentally, involves all the senses, not only sight) in this passage depends at first on the wainscoting which leads Florian around a spatially conceived house. Florian's tour ends, finally, above the attic, outside, on the roof-top. The physical movement as such is one of ascent, not descent, to bird's-nest, to pear tree, finally to attic and sky. Outside is something "wonderful, infinite and unexplored," while what is inside, by default, is relegated to the known and finite. The roof-top scene curiously repeats or imitates the aspiring or upward motion of Florian's physical progress through the house: "sent up heavenwards" are the cloud and smoke of the city mingled with natural atmosphere, storm and, alternatively, sunshine. The view reflects, rather oddly, Pater's conspicuously un-Ruskinian tolerance of the city with its effluvia, its fog, and smoke.

Architecture provides, then, not only a *design* establishing conditions of inside and out, but one making possible a *direction* of influences and soul growth. As home, it also suggests origins of feelings or moods as well as the beginnings of perceptual clarity: the distinctness between inner and outer yields to a fusion or blurring, which is how growth starts. "Inward and outward," so Florian says, are "woven through and through each other into one inextricable texture," half qualities from "the wood and the bricks," the other half "mere soul-stuff."[37] It is interesting that association patterns elsewhere in the story, those not linked to the architectural device "house," also stop or end at "church," and that the penultimate stop before that conclusion is invariably "home." We begin to think that there is only one way to church. When association connects itself with structure, in this instance the church in the city, its movement once again becomes pyramidal, as if it were graphing spiritualization in space:

> The coming and going of the travellers to the town along the way, the shadow of the streets, the sudden breath of the neighbouring gardens, the singular brightness of bright weather there, its singular darknesses which linked themselves in his mind to certain engraved illustrations in the old big Bible at home, the coolness of the dark, cavernous shops around the great church, with its giddy winding stair up to the pigeons and the bells. . . .[38]

Associative patterns based on buildings are not ordered temporally (there is no passage of time within Florian's home) but depend, rather, on spatial organization. Value judgments, too, link themselves to these spatial arrangements, the spiritual being above the attic, the soul within the house always escaping outward to spiritual light let in by windows or streaming onto the roof-top.

Pater's patterns of association, as we might fairly expect, do vary in important ways from those patterns used in classical memory systems.[39] Nonetheless, Pater's variations, while in some ways peculiar to him, may also suggest other services which the architectural analogy might provide for writers either familiar with Pater's work or inheriting a similar past. In classical theory, architecture as an artificial memory model is used most generally by a rhetor who places objects within a conceptualized and particularized structure in an order so that he may remember specific points or ideas. The associations proceed then from the arbitrarily placed objects. In Pater's fiction, however, individual objects placed in specific locations, though they trigger individual memories, more often function symbolically, so that a reader may gather from them, or adumbrate, meanings he wishes them to contain. Whereas we might say that the rhetor's placement of an object usually demands a coherence and order subservient to his argument, Pater's associations generally do not presuppose a direction logically based or logically maneuvered to persuasive ends. And whereas it seems that the order of steps in this artificial memory system is controlled by the carefully crafted model, in Pater the order, and what connects two things, is found in the thing itself as often as it is found in the structure. In other words, the object as symbol frequently contains that which generates recall of the next. It is true, however, that in Pater's fiction the architectural structures are in fact as arbitrary and idiosyncratic as associative ramblings would be without those structures. There seems to be a pretence in Pater—that architectural orderings involve a reduction of randomness, and a consequent diminishing, in importance of the specific things mentioned. When the motive in Pater's associative memory system is to emphasize the final step, as is generally the case with a rhetor, his structure is generally pyramidal; however, when the associative links themselves are each more important than any last step or conclusion, Pater refrains from using a

7
Rounding a
corner of the mind:
La Madeleine, Vézelay.

spatial structure having a top and a bottom. Indeed, it is not always clear that these structures have even an inside and an outside.

Pater insists that literary architecture should "foresee the end in the beginning," and this is a prescription which we shall encounter again and again as we read other writers who select an architectural analogue.[40] Foresight, in Pater's sense, is also characteristic of classical memory systems in which the end, or argumentative point, is preconceived and then broken down into a series of logical steps. In Pater's particular associative thought patterns, one similarly senses that he foresees the end of his associations in the beginning, that the enumeration of parts is a calculated elaboration of the points making up the whole. But for Pater, unlike classical rhetors, the component parts leading to the end never equal the end, and the last point is generally an added element that the constituent parts did not contain or do not produce. A holistic view of this sort allows Pater a retreat from an empirical position while in fact he has tempted the reader with a style seemingly empiricist, that is, the supposedly open-ended associative process. For Pater, the architectural device for associative memory has the advantage of avoiding the empiricist's bind of causality, seeming instead to establish fixed points and yet without becoming didactic and Cartesian. Whereas relativistic or impressionistic philosophy presumes to record impressions as they occur, without concern for the end, Pater's associations actually exist within a closed system in which the end is not only foreseen but prescribed.

From Pater's comments in "Style," if not indeed (and more compellingly) from his prose itself, one can see how he was attracted by stasis: a writer should "repeat"

8
"Cliffs of quarried
and carved stone . . .
radix de terra sitienti."
For Proust, this would be
an example of "church
epitomizing town,
representing it, speaking of it
and for it to the horizon."
(Notre-Dame d'Amiens)

his steps only that he may give the reader a sense of secure and restful progress, readjusting mere assonances even, that they may soothe the reader, or at least not interrupt him on his way.[41]

Pater, it seems, slows down the reader almost so as to distract attention from the end, and so to expand the spiritual qualities of the associative components. Superficially then, the soul of style dominates the mind, camouflaging the clear outline, the stated but meticulously disguised limits of Pater's epistemological system. One thinks that Pater takes a dynamic system and freezes it; and he does that, it is true, when he talks about holding onto the moment of flux and expanding it. But more often than not, the entire system is one of rest (that flux is within the "narrow chamber"), and the dynamic that exists does so within strict limits. Pater's alternation between motion and rest seems to direct us away from his thought peripheries, those severely limited and limiting epistemological assumptions, and force us back into the midst of his elaborations, of what seem now Pater's fetish, his self-consuming (and self-deceiving?) processes. That stasis, or rest, does in fact circumscribe the entire system is something Pater fears, just as he and his characters fear being closed in. Thus there exists always a break through to open windows, to skies, to that which is spiritually transcendent, anything which distracts from or invigorates a deterministic, generally pessimistic world view.[42] All processes of ordering, be they through architectural memory or literary architecture or both, support what cannot but appear as a conservative aesthetic, an aesthetic allowing for growth only in recapitulation.

The arrested beauty of Pater's literary architecture registers his inspired transformation of his own limita-

WALTER HORATIO PATER

9
"It is a spare, rather sad world
at most times that Notre-Dame
d'Amiens thus broods over."

LITERARY ARCHITECTURE

tions into art: sensuous experience for Pater never occurs in an external or natural world, but manages, nonetheless, to live within his careful language of interiors. In this way Pater's language itself is an accommodation to his fear of unbounded energy or natural weather. In passages where his characters are out of doors, there invariably occurs a retreat; and yet this is not surprising given Pater's view of the world and of the function of literature. To Pater, all fine art should be turned to "for a refuge, a sort of cloistral refuge, from a certain vulgarity in the actual world."[43] Pater's literary architecture—whether the structure of his sentences, the houses in his fictions, or the monuments in his histories—look out over his world of pain and protect him from it just as they magically let us see what he fears. Pater concludes his essay on Notre-Dame d'Amiens with just this marriage:

> It is a spare, rather sad world at most times that Notre-Dame d'Amiens thus broods over; a country with little else to be proud of; the sort of world, in fact, which makes the range of conceptions embodied in these cliffs of quarried and carved stone all the more welcome as a hopeful complement to the meagreness of most people's present existence, and its apparent ending in a sparely built coffin under the flinty soil, and grey, driving sea-winds. In Notre-Dame, therefore, and her sisters, there is not only a common method of construction, a single definable type, different from that of other French latitudes, but a correspondent sentiment also; something which speaks, amid an immense achievement just here of what is beautiful and great, of the necessity of an immense effort in the natural course of things, of what you may see quaintly designed in one of those hieroglyphic carvings—*radix de terra sitienti:* " a root out of a dry ground."[44]

Here the peculiar pain of Pater discovers expression in his

odd, transitive move from a situation open to his own pre-established and closed view of the world, from an overview to a coffin. And yet Pater's built literary world is informing and in forming; he offers to those after him an economical device for speaking of relation – between self and world, mind and other – in terms of space and place, that is, as we actually experience and recall our being, our life, our death: the spatial richness of architectural structure as it governs our physical experience of the world and our language-thought of spatial experience about that world.

II
"THE POETRY OF ARCHITECTURE": GERARD MANLEY HOPKINS

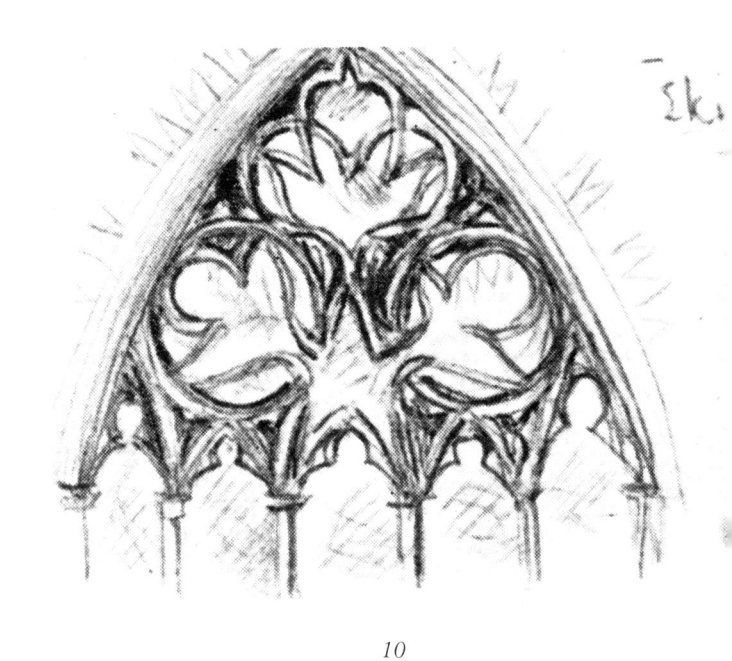

10
"The strong and noble inscape."
Gerard Manley Hopkins:
Tracery of a Gothic Window.

ONE

Architecture and Terminology

Stress, instress, scape, inscape, arch-inscape, sprung, pitch, centre-hung, end-hung, moulding, proportion, structure, construction, design – the literary terminology of Gerard Manley Hopkins is very familiar. While we know that Pater was one of Hopkins's teachers at Oxford, Hopkins's terms, at least at first glance, might seem to have little to do with the literary architecture of his don. That they are idiosyncratic and defy simple definition is well known; and that they have called for careful, oftentimes conflicting, interpretations by critics concedes both their potency and their enigmatic richness. I should like, nonetheless, to look at these terms again and to ask two simple questions: what do these terms have in common? and where do they come from?

Stress, sprung seem mechanical, *pitch* musical, *moulding* sculptural; *scape*, like *instress* and *inscape*, seems Hopkins's own, whereas *proportion, structure, construction, design* are so general as to be applicable to nearly any of the arts. Only *centre-hung* and *end-hung* remain. And these Hopkins defines explicitly:

> It strikes me that these two kinds of action and of drama thence arising are like two kinds of tracery, which have, I dare say, names; the one in which the tracery seems like so much of a pattern cut out bodily by the hood of the arch from an infinite pattern; the other in which it is sprung from the hood or arch itself and would fall to pieces without it. It is like tapestry and a

picture, like a pageant and a scene. And I call the one kind of composition *end-hung* and the other *centre-hung* and say that your play is not centre-hung enough. Now you see.[1]

Centre-hung and *end-hung* are architectural terms; and the art analogue Hopkins sets for literary drama is architecture. This ought to make us look at a book which Hopkins casually mentions in his early Diaries. Unfortunately Hopkins does not identify it, and we cannot identify it ourselves. But we know that it was a glossary of architectural terms and we may legitimately suppose that it was something like John Parker's *A Glossary of Terms used in Grecian, Roman, Italian and Gothic Architecture*,[2] if indeed it was not that very book. We come across it when Hopkins is discussing architectural motifs.

> Transoms in Decorated and Early English. In former not infrequently found for the purpose which they were intended to answer, before they became in Perpendicular only ornamental, viz. to give strength to mullions of tall windows. So also in Decorated where they are quite common in domestic architecture, but very rare in ecclesiastical. The Glossary mentions two examples. In long windows however as in towers (e.g. S. Mary's, Oxford) they are not uncommon. Their evidently deliberate rejection in ordinarily proportioned windows by the Decorated architects ought to be decisive against them.
> (JP, 14, 1863–64)

Do the remaining terms also derive from or refer to architecture? If we turn to Parker, perhaps the one Hopkins had cited, we find the following:

> stress: the result in a member of the action of external forces upon it. For example: tensile stress is the stress due to the action of two external forces tending to pull the

> constituents of a member apart: comprehensive stress is the stress due to the action of two external forces tending to push the constituents of a member together.
>
> scape: another term used for a column shaft, or for the apophyge, of a column.
>
> arch: an arrangement of wedge-shaped masonry, or bricks, built over an opening in a wall, in such a manner that the arch is self-supporting and will also take weight imposed on it.
>
> sprung, springer, springing, springing line, springing point: the point from which an arch springs, from the top of an abutment.
>
> pitch: the angle at which a roof slopes.
>
> moulding: a general term applied to all the varieties of outline or contour given to the angles of the various subordinate parts and features of buildings, whether projections of cavities, such as cornices, capitals, bases, door and window jambs and heads, etc.

As for *proportion*, Hopkins's use of the term rests explicitly on an analogy with architecture, as we see when he remarks on English and Italian sonnet form:

> Now in the form of any work of art the intrinsic measurements, the proportions, that is, of the parts to one another and to the whole, are no doubt the principal point, but still the extrinsic measurements, the absolute quantity or size goes for something. Thus supposing in the Doric Order the Parthenon to be the standard of perfection, then if the columns of the Parthenon have so many semidiameters or modules to their height, the architrave so many, and so on these will be the typical proportions. But if a building is raised on a notably greater scale it will be found that these proportions for the columns and the rest are no longer satisfactory, so that one of two things–either the proportions must be changed or the Order abandoned. Now if the Italian sonnet is one of the most

LITERARY ARCHITECTURE

successful forms of composition known, as it is reckoned to be, its proportions, inward and outward, must be pretty near perfection. (CD, 85–86, 1881)

Hopkins talks of *design* (which he elsewhere equates with pattern and inscape in poetry) when he discusses the use of dialect:

But its [dialect's] lawful charm and use I take to be this, that it sort of guarantees the spontaneousness of the thought and puts you in the position to appraise it on its merits as coming from nature and not books and education. It heightens one's admiration for a phrase just as in architecture it heightens one's admiration of a design to know that it is old work, not new: in itself the design is the same but as taken together with the designer and his merit this circumstance makes a world of difference. (LB, 87–88, 1879)

Thus we begin to see that while the terms Hopkins uses may have primary meanings in other arts, they all have architectural ones as well. Of the terms which remain, *structure* and *construction* are architectonic by definition. The only terms which do not occur in architectural glossaries of the time are Hopkins's own coinages *inscape* and *instress*. And in the context we have established, Hopkins's addition of the prefix *in* to *scape* and *stress* only serves to emphasize the architectural meanings, since it directs attention to notions of interior and exterior, inside and outside. For Hopkins, constructed and organic things both have insides and outsides, even man. The body may have, metaphorically at least, its structural ins and outs, its

> ... rack of ribs; the scooped flank; lank
> Rope-over thigh; knee-nave; and barrelled shank –
>   Head and foot, shoulder and shank – (Poem 71)

And its spiritual or emotional self must perforce respect the inhabited, structural boundaries: "Man's mounting spirit in his bone-house, mean house, dwells—" (Poem 39)

> Each mortal thing does one thing and the same:
> > Deals out that being indoors each one dwells;
> > Selves—goes itself; *myself* it speaks and spells,
>
> Crying *What I do is me: for that I came.* (Poem 57)

Instress and *inscape* require and depend upon architectural space concepts. Moreover, they suggest the possibility of access: what may be inner—either as skeletal or soul self—may speak, may be described, hence may be perceived. The act of perception, either as sight or cognition, becomes concretized into a kind of literal penetration to what we might call essence, the structural or soul "inscape" of person or thing. In his references to architecture, then, it appears that Hopkins has translated into his own literary terms and concepts some attitudes at least reminiscent of, if not inspired by, Pater.

11a
"*Flos, flower, blow,
bloom, blossom*":
architecture and etymology.
Gerard Manley Hopkins:
Sketches from the
early Diaries, 1863.

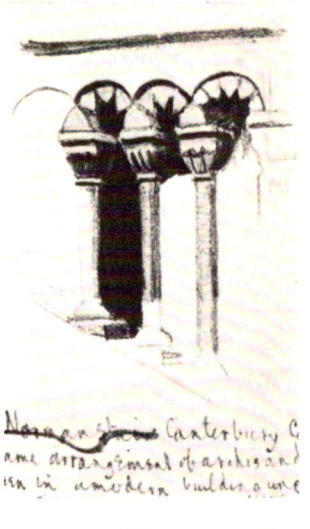

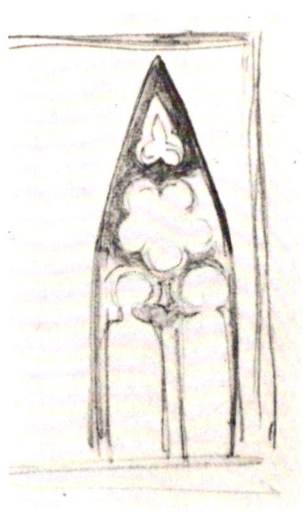

TWO

The *Note-books*: Architecture and Etymology

IF WE LEAF through Hopkins's notebooks, any surprise we may have at discovering that architecture has much to do with Hopkins's poetic, should subside: Hopkins's own sketches—of Norman and Gothic windows, stairs, tracery and transoms, arches and columns—lace the pages of his journals, either illustrating his often technical descriptions of buildings, or just oddly afloat between his discussions of word roots, thoughts, or weather observations. In the early Diaries alone there are at least two dozen verbal descriptions and more than a dozen drawings in one brief journal-year. While it is not at all extraordinary that Hopkins took an interest in architecture, especially since at Oxford he was in the midst of clamor and controversy over new college buildings, his interest is not to be explained so simply; and it seems fair to ask what relationship Hopkins's interest in architecture may have to his fascination with words and with nature.

At first it appears that Hopkins's two concerns, with architecture and with words, are discrete, and this seems to be confirmed by the apparent randomness of some journal entries. One such instance is a sequence of three recordings, the first concerning etymology, the second architecture, the third again etymology: [Plates 11a and 11b]

LITERARY ARCHITECTURE

Flos, flower, blow, bloom, blossom. Original meaning to be inflated, to swell as the bud does into the flower. Also φλέω (*abundo*) and *flaw* (storm), *flare* (English not Latin).

[Drawing of window given Fig. I.]³
Note. There is now going on what has no parallel that I know of in history of art. Byzantine or Romanesque Architecture started from ruins of Roman, became itself beautiful style, and died, as Ruskin says, only in giving birth to another more beautiful than itself, Gothic. The Renaissance appears now to be in the process of being succeeded by a spontaneous Byzantinesque style, retaining still some of bad features (such as pilasters, rustic-work etc.) of the Renaissance. These it will throw aside. Its capitals are already, as in Romanesque art, most beautiful. Whether then modern Gothic or this spontaneous style conquer does not so much matter, for it is only natural for latter to lead to a modern spontaneous Gothic, as in middle ages, only that the latter is putting off what we might be or rather are doing now. Or the two may coalesce.

τάλα (γαλακτος), γλαγος, *lac* (lactis), *leglin* (pail), *milk*, i.e., *mlik*.   (JP, 13, 1863)

Hopkins's comment, "There is now going on what has no parallel that I know of in history of art," teases us and distracts us. While Hopkins disclaims a parallel between the arts, he covertly structures one himself: his imagery darts out allusive sparks, the life-death-rebirth cycle of the Phoenix or some combative contest between forces, but the architectural event he nonetheless renders organic, natural, evolutionary; and the artist, for instance the unspecified architect, absents himself from this growth of style as if such growth were *sui generis*, an activity which he could only interfere with, never control. So, too, a paler Hopkins than the one we know unwinds the history of words, as if their growth were also evolutionary. Some word roots, perhaps the phonic *flo*, *blo*, *fla*, like certain architectural motifs, notably capitals and pilasters, persist while meaning, even usage, changes; other roots and motifs fade into retirement, outmoded. So Hopkins pursues one concern through twin modes: whether patterned in words or in architecture, what Hopkins looks for and describes is the retention, transition, revival of forms, calling for remarks on the capacity for development or change, or lamenting a regress from the structural to the ornamental.

Does not a Hopkins who documents the etymology of words as he does the history of architectural style also view words as building materials, concrete and visible, of structure-poems? From the ruins of language, does he not superintend the growth of a new style, a gardener-architect so tending vestigial remains that the audience may recover the origin of forms or words, even witness their rebirth or reinvigoration? In this Hopkins is like those writers of the earliest *ars memorativa* treatises who formed images for words from primitive etymological dissection of the word itself, hopeful that readers would remember a more vivid past. In his early Diaries Hopkins jotted down a poetic stanza in which the speaker threatens to topple a poem, to so dislodge the brickish building materials that poem and monument, one and the same, crumble in ruin.

> Let me now
> Jolt
> Shake and unset your morticed metaphors.
> The hand draws off the glove; the acorn-cup
> Drops the fruit out; the duct runs dry or breaks;
> The stranded keel and kelson warp apart; (JP, 40, 1864)

Concretized, his metaphors also cling to their etymological past: elsewhere in his journals Hopkins had remarked the origin of *keel*.[4]

> *Skill* etc.
> Primary meaning, to divide, cut apart. *Skill*, discernment. To *keel*, to skim. *Keel*, that part of a ship which cuts a way through the water. *Skull*, an oar which skims the water. (JP, 31, 1864)

A diacritical reading of the poem, demanded by the language itself, recovers primary word meanings so that reading becomes a kind of unbuilding, un-"morticing" of metaphors in order that they release a meaning submerged by time and usage. Hopkins's words and images, in their etymological origins, mime the idea they express: all mean and accomplish, in this journal fragment, an undoing, a dissection; reading becomes and requires analysis of the poem as a built structure. And that analysis is inseparable from remembering.

We might expect Hopkins's word accounts to fill his journals, but such is not the case. What had been incidental, the nature and weather observations, becomes normative; and Hopkins finally declares the journals his "weather record." The takeover does not, however, exhaust architecture. Instead themes, images, descriptions architectural begin to partner nature and weather descriptions. However, the partnership is curiously one-way. The architectural descriptions rarely, if ever, evoke, either mimetically or thematically, the natural. In fact, Hopkins's architectural discussions discover a scientific rigor, a demand for exactitude and precision of description such that technical terms are required so as to substantiate for us the kind of knowledge Hopkins possesses. Typical is Hopkins's record of the Cathedral at Exeter:

11b

Hopkins's one concern.
Above his drawing of Kirkham
Abbey, we can see that he
has written "*Nor* as 'better
nor that' is old English,
for *ne were* and is written
in old ballads etc.
sometimes *nar*."

Some notes to remember it by—two Norman towers; east of them choir, in 7 bays and a little one; nave, in 7, west; nave windows in basement story broad, geometrical . . .

(JP, 253, 1874)

or his account of William Butterfield's Babbacombe Church:

. . . the windows scattered; steeple rather detached . . . with an odd openwork diaper of freestone over marble pieces on the tower. . . . There is a hood of the same diaper at the east-end gable from the spring of the arch of the east window about upward. Tracery all simple. Inside chancel-arch much as at St. Alban's, Holborn.   (JP, 254–255, 1874)

Architectural terminology does not crop up only when Hopkins is recording throughout the notebooks his experiences of architecture. On the contrary, that terminology breeds and infiltrates, as if, in his desire for accurate, precise descriptions of the most minute natural forms or weather events, it is architectural terms that proffer themselves, irresistibly. Hopkins perceives nature as, or reconstructs her into, edifices: she has ribs, arches, traceries, transoms; she frets, copes, cusps, is fluted, moulded, vaulted; her elements—air, water—form into cloud, dew, then into chips of quarried building stone; she is seen in patterns of horizontal bands of colored stone as if on a polychromatic church wall. [Plate 12]

Perhaps the architectural vocabulary assumes the burden left over from abandoned etymological studies; perhaps, too, Hopkins's word curiosity expresses itself in his search for nature-descriptive terms and Hopkins turns to architectural language and images to facilitate these descriptions:

On this day the clouds were lovely. Opposite the sun be-

12

A grove of trees: organic
architecture outside-in.

Only the beak-leaved boughs dragonish 1
damask the tool-smooth bleak light.

Westminster Abbey: Apse from choir.

tween 10 and 11 was the disshevelled cloud [*sic*] on page opposite. The clouds were repeatedly formed in horizontal ribs. At a distance their straightness of line was wonderful. In passing overhead they were something as in the (now) opposite page, the ribs granulated delicately the splits fretted with lacy curves and honeycomb work, the laws of which were exquisitely traced.... (JP, 27, 1864)[5] [Plates 13-16]

Always Hopkins is suggesting an inhabitant/structure relationship: in his nature descriptions, it is nature which moves and shifts, as in the passage above; in his architectural descriptions, since architecture as completed structure is static, the inhabitant must shift in order to enjoy the optical varieties he does in a kinetic nature. In "To Oxford" optical illusion depends on the *inventio* of the speaker:

> Thus, I come underneath this chapel-side,
> So that the mason's levels, courses, all
> The vigorous horizontals, each way fall
> In bows above my head, as falsified
> By visual compulsion, till I hide
> The steep-up roof at last behind the small
> Eclipsing parapet; yet above the wall
> The sumptuous ridge-crest leave to poise and ride.
>   (Poem 12)

But what happens to nature imagery in this poem and others? May we not read it as description which, evoking the architectural, throws us back to the poet's perceiving mind, inhabitant of a world which he strangely rebuilds? Not quite. In "That Nature is a Heraclitean Fire and of the comfort of the Resurrection," for instance, a transposition of nature into architecture is indeed threatened, but nature does not relinquish her identity for an architectural one:

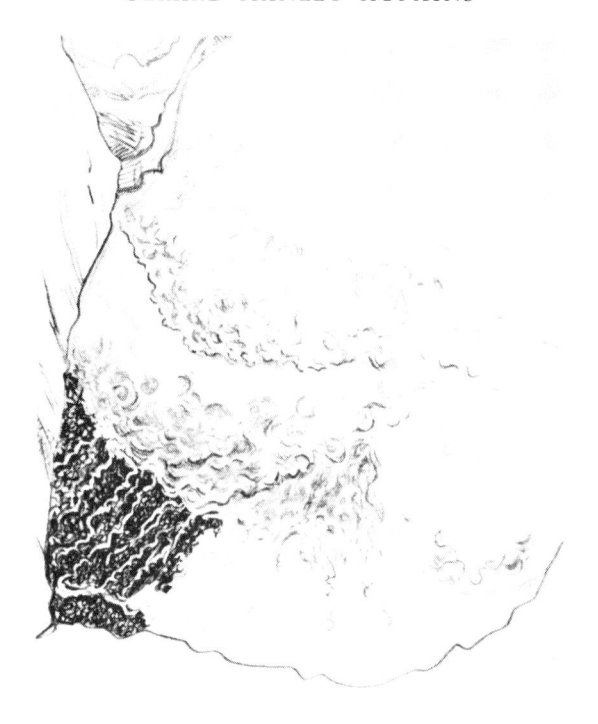

GERARD MANLEY HOPKINS

13
Gerard Manley Hopkins: Waves.
Study from the Cliff Above,
Freshwater Gate. July 23. 1863.
(This drawing is remarkably
suggestive of Leonardo da Vinci's
percussive water studies; in both
Leonardo's and Hopkins's drawings
the water twists are similar to
hair. Leonardo notes that
similarity in his notebooks.)

LITERARY ARCHITECTURE

> Down roughcast, down dazzling whitewash, ǀ wherever an elm arches,
> Shivelights and shadowtackle in long ǀ lashes lace,
> lance, and pair. (Poem 72)

The conversion of natural matter into architectural rarely, if ever, violates or abandons the one for the other, nature for architecture or architecture for nature. Instead the process of conversion discovers, releases, conveys energy, and that energy is expressed as poetic simile, whether in the poems themselves or in the descriptions which fill the notebooks. And while the notebook descriptions remind us of Constable's or Turner's, it is in the unrelenting search for simile that Hopkins becomes more than scientific naturalist.

While a completed architectural structure is static from the viewer's stance, as artifact it is dynamic, for its final form depends upon the disposition of stresses, themselves active. This stressful dynamism of architecture has much to do with its suitability as analogue for nature. In one passage in his journals, Hopkins rebuilds a rock-wall into a structure architectural and then not only remarks the internal stresses of that structure, but suggests as well the function of those stresses when the newly architectural and the natural collide:

> The seawall is picturesque and handsome from below—it is built of white and red and blue blocks and with a brim or lip or cornice or coping curved round to beetle over and throw back the spray without letting it break on the walk above: this shape and colour give it an Egyptian look.—The laps of running foam striking the sea-wall double on themselves and return in nearly the same order and shape in which they came. This is mechanical reflection and is the same as optical: indeed all nature is mechanical, but then it is not seen that mechanics contain that which is beyond mechanics. (JP, 251–252, 1874)

14
Gerard Manley Hopkins: Clouds.
July 29 or 30 and July 31. 1863.

LITERARY ARCHITECTURE

If we ignore for the moment the enigmatic, passive construction—"but then it is not seen that mechanics contain that which is beyond mechanics"—we discover what seems a seductively simple progression in Hopkins's thinking. Hopkins begins with an evaluation, the connotative spin-offs of the scene: the seawall is "picturesque and handsome." Yet his explanation is not evaluative but formalistic: the seawall is picturesque and handsome because of its construction. And curiously, its built form reveals and contains motive: its "brim or lip or cornice or coping" mechanically controls the spray, so that what is formalistic is not that alone but is also in some teleological way, mechanical. For Hopkins, nature and architecture are individually and interactively each mechanical; but by introducing the words *reflection* and *optical*, Hopkins games with us. While the interaction of wall and water may be a mechanical reflection, *reflection* picks up from *optical* another meaning, not thought rumination but reflection as sighting. Again Hopkins's description begs for an observer, someone to so sight the seawall: something cannot be optical, or by implication, mechanical, without being seen. And it is then that Hopkins, by innuendo, plays with the distinction between visual and religious perception. The seeing of structure, the recognition of mechanics—one's optical perception—is, potentially at least, a divine or religious act such that we suppose Hopkins to be indicting others, not himself, when he remarks "but then it is not seen that mechanics contain that which is beyond mechanics."

At times, as in the seawall passage above, Hopkins's verbs expose and establish for us the dynamic action he seeks to describe; *strike*, *double*, *return*, like Hopkins's

GERARD MANLEY HOPKINS

15

Gerard Manley Hopkins: Clouds and weather observations.
Hopkins, of the four writers I discuss,
is the only one who ventures out
into weather; he was not fearful of direct exposure
and did not use architecture as protection
from the energy of the elements. His keen weather
observations would seem to account in part for the equally
keen rhythm in his poetic literary architecture.

verbs elsewhere, define the mechanism as one of action and reaction. If the image Hopkins is attracted to is not in the midst of such action at the time of the description, Hopkins often speculatively remakes it or convinces himself, by some slowing down of time, that he can see in a moment the action of years; and in his reconstructions, mechanical action may explain growth and evaluation, and architectural simile may specify the structure and form of that growth. In recording an expedition to North Barrule, Hopkins notes holes in rocks, conceives of them as architectural shapes:

> Round holes are scooped in the rocks smooth and true like turning: they look like the hollow of a vault or a bowl. I saw and sketched as well as in the rain I could one of them that was in the making: a blade of water played on it and shaping to it spun off making a bold big white bow coiling its edge over and splaying into ribs. (JP, 235, 1873)

Part of Hopkins's expression of interaction depends upon an intricate structuring of analogies or images in which ethereal elements are rendered concrete, here water as "blade," then the entire water spray as a "bow" and finally "ribs." Hopkins's tools are like press moulds, themselves shaped in the same pattern as the final form of the object they in fact help make: the water makes and takes its form from the hole, the bow and ribs of a ribbed vault. Moreover, Hopkins often makes active what is inert. In recalling Denbigh Hill, Hopkins remembers the ruins which lay before him:

> Castle ruins, which crown the hill, were punched out in arches and half arches by bright breaks and eyelets of daylight. We went up to the castle but not in: standing before the gateway I had an instress which only the true old work gives from the strong and noble inscape of the pointedarch [*sic*].
> (JP, 263, 1875)

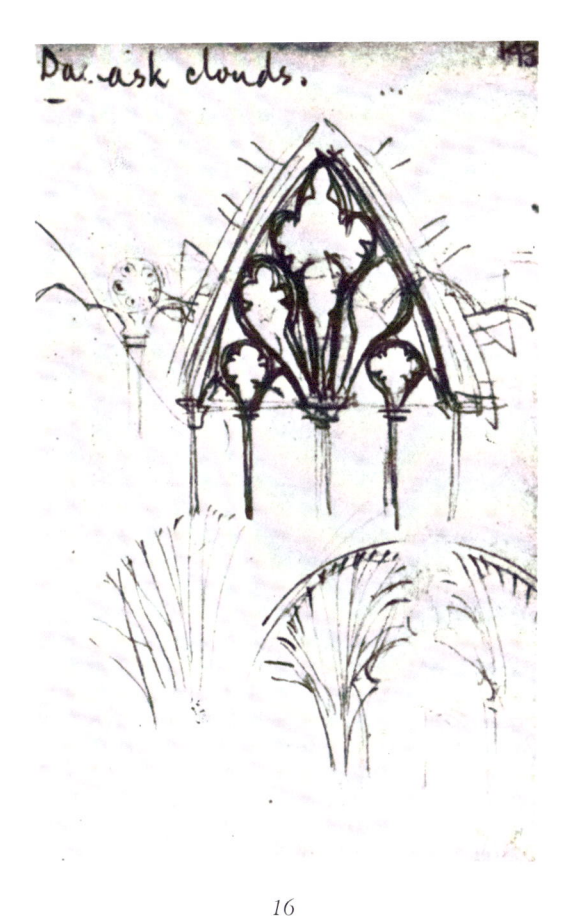

16
"Damask clouds" of architecture.
Gerard Manley Hopkins.
(Note in the bottom right the
springing-tree architecture and
compare with Plate 28, Wells Cathedral.)

Background sky becomes mechanically active: it "punches" out, not only silhouetting but shaping, moulding the ruins. Foreground and background vie with each other in what seems an optical equivocation, the background becoming a constructional member of the picture. The interaction of sky and ruin, then, makes a percussive impact upon Hopkins as viewer: "I had an instress," his statement of response, is attributed to the emotional or aesthetic richness of architectural form, the pointed arch. In this context, Hopkins's terms *instress* and *inscape*—involving as they do such obvious distinctions between inner and outer, the accessibility or interpenetrability of forms—are themselves not only mechanical, percussive action and reaction but, in the broadest sense, also architectural.

In order for things to strike, to hit, to punch, Hopkins continually converts the insubstantial into the substantial. Indeed, does not the notion of poetic stress suggest that words, like objects in nature, also *strike*? that they have a mechanical, hence optical, hence divine import? Hopkins is explicit that perception, even of words, is percussive: "The image (of sight or sound or *scapes* of the other senses), which is in fact physical and a refined energy accenting the nerves, a word to oneself, an inchoate word . . ." (JP, 125, 1868). It is no surprise, then, that a thing may word itself, that nouns, in taking on charges, become verbs, that things become their mechanical action or architectural shape. Images gain in density, in weight, in action; and oddly, in assuming purpose, as the seawall or water blade, they also assume a will and dynamism of their own. There is also a kind of medieval eye-ing of the object, and an eye-ing back, by the object, of the viewer. Hopkins remarks that "what you look hard at seems to look hard at you, hence the true and false instress of nature" (JP, 204, 1871).[6] Hopkins is careful to hedge: "seems to look hard at you." But if this seeming were simply a projection by Hopkins as observer, Hopkins would be the initiator of the dynamic interchange and that would be to doubt God's authority. Likewise, the kinds of percussive reverberations or mechanical interplay would then lose their physical stress; we must assume Hopkins to be literal even in his speculation. It seems that the stressful quality of interaction in fact depends upon its being physical; elements solidify into matter, action into assertion, making into moulding, and writing or speaking into physical striking. "Fineness, proportion of feature comes from a moulding force which succeeds in asserting itself over the resistance of cumbersome or restraining matter." Intensity of imagery, perhaps the life of Hopkins's poetry, depends upon the physical injunction of felt things, senses, nature artifacts. Just as artist may mould, so may soul shape; and just as rocks may be matter, so, too, it seems, may words and ideas assume density, duration, resistance, resilience; and the viewer-poet perceives tension, distortion, perspective, always in a stressed relationship with the things around him.

There is one final relationship Hopkins establishes between architecture and nature which I have yet to mention. It is the notion of complement: to construct nature churches, to structure–verbally–proximity between nature and architecture, to describe the impact architecture and nature each have on the other in any given scene–all suggest that something is gained in the way of beauty by the partnership between the man-made and the natural.

'Boughs being prunèd, birds preened, show more fair;
To grace them spires are shaped with corner squinches;
Enrichèd posts are chamfer'd; everywhere
    He heightens worth who guardedly diminishes;
Diamonds are better cut; who pare, repair;
    Is statuary rated by its inches?
Thus we shall profit, while gold coinage still
Is worth and current with a lessen'd mill.'

(Poem 96, vii)

While it seems that Hopkins creates a *pas de deux* relationship between architecture as support and nature as prima ballerina, he also argues for refinement, moderation, spareness. And for such an aesthetic value system, an architectural model is once again attractive. Poet-architect must complement, true; but more than that, he must "prune," "shape," "chamfer," "pare" and "repair." It is to Hopkins's poetic theory, then, and to the special richness and suggestiveness of the architectural analogue as he so conceived it, that we shall now turn.

THREE

Hopkins's Poetic Theory: Architecture's "Finer Edge"

HOPKINS'S REMARKS on poetic theory are sparse and scattered, confided in letters, preparatory lecture notes, or early Oxford essays. Nevertheless, even in these fugitive writings, we find that architecture is valuable to Hopkins as art analogue. Hopkins's architectural citings, in the context of his poetic theory, appear two ways, either as terminology or as clarifying illustration.

Hopkins's distinction between prose and poetry hinges on architectural concepts: "But what the character of poetry is will be found best by looking at the structure of verse" (JP, 84, 1865). It might help us, for the moment, to recall Hopkins's discussion of the seawall; just as the picturesque character of the wall of rock was explained in formalistic and functional terms, so Hopkins explains poetic character—poetry's moral/ethical nature as well as aesthetic distinctiveness—through a formalistic analysis. Structure determines character. That structure, what Hopkins subsequently refers to as construction, is controllable, man-made; more specifically, it consists of "continuous parallelism" of two sorts, the "marked" or abrupt, and the "gradual," "chromatic," a "chiaroscuro" parallelism. We cannot help but recall Walter Pater's important remarks on literary style:

The otiose, the facile, surplusage: why are these abhorrent to the true literary artist, except because in literary as in all other art, structure is all-important, felt, or painfully missed, everywhere?—that architectural conception of work, which foresees the end in the beginning and never loses sight of it.[7]

Pater, too, regarded words in a color sense, remarking that "the elementary particles of language will be realized as colour and light and shade through his [the writer's] scholarly living in the full sense of them."[8] What is significant about Hopkins's rendering is that the chiaroscuro of Pater, the soul rather than the mind of style, is also conceived of as structural. In this instance, Hopkins is consistent with contemporary architectural theorists who would also dismiss Paterian chiaroscuro in favor of what is called constructional color or constructional polychromy, color initiative of or contributing to structural organization of a building. [Plate 17]

As architectural style and language had shared, for Hopkins, organic life, both evolving in birth, death, rebirth patterns, so architecture in the context of Hopkins's poetic theory distinguishes itself from the organic, and is valued, in part, as structured or constructed artifice:

> The artificial part of poetry, perhaps we shall be right to say all artifice, reduces itself to the principle of parallelism. The structure of poetry is that of continuous parallelism.
>
> (JP, 84, 1865)

But something curious happens: architecture, although artificial structure, retains for Hopkins its generative capacities; and although architecture remains an art form structurally distinct from that of literature, what is architectural in literature begets wholly literary and expressive offspring. "The more marked parallelism in structure

17
Hopkins's soul of style:
constructional polychromy.
(La Madeleine, Vézelay)

whether of elaboration or emphasis begets more marked parallelism in the words and sense" (JP, 84, 1865). Similarly, "an emphasis of structure stronger than the common construction of sentences gives asks for an emphasis of expression stronger" (JP, 85, 1865). In this way, Hopkins makes causal and fathering what had only been analogous in his theory of language development. In fact, it is structure which draws the reader's attention to syllabic stress and emphasis.[9]

Although Hopkins was not to continue to use the word *structure* to describe the character of verse, he was nonetheless to use an expression also architectural, *construction*. And construction, like structure, assumes an aesthetic and ethical charge: rigorous construction in poetry is an antidote to what is licentious in English verse. While Hopkins means "licentious" literally as verbal excess, like the word *character*, *licentious* is rich with moral suggestiveness. Hopkins's pertinent remarks occur in a letter to Bridges in which Hopkins defends himself against the charge of lawlessness in verse: referring to "The Wreck of the Deutschland," Hopkins asks Bridges to have a second look.

> If you look again you will see. So that I may say my apparent licences are counterbalanced, and more, by my strictness. In fact all English verse, except Milton's, almost, offends me as "licentious." Remember this. (LB, 45, 1877)

Rigorous construction is prophylactic, in part because it calls attention to itself; and therefore what is libertine in verse is thrown into structural relief. We have the sense that Hopkins's verse structures react against the licentious as against a form of opulence and ease, poetic mellifluousness which is so smooth that it may act on a reader without the reader's awareness because it does not percussively jar him to contend with it. Licentious verse, then, is at once lawless and seductive, achieving a kind of surface perfection. Hopkins advocates correction; and verse, the sick patient, must recover in an unusual way.

> Perfection is dangerous because it is deceptive. Art slips back while bearing, in its distribution of tone, or harmony, the look of a high civilization towards barbarism. Recovery must be by a breaking up, a violence, such as was the Preraphaelite school. (JP, 79, 1864)

Mending itself is abrasive, jarring, sparring. We recall the Hopkins who "unmortices" metaphors, whose rhythm is abrupt, whose images strike the reader; and perhaps we begin to conceive a poet who values the imperfect artifact which testifies to being man-made because it does not tempt us as a false Una would. One's poetic building involves analytic unbuilding: it is little wonder that a Hopkins poem demands a diacritical reading. Dissection as poetic process forces the reader to look at and respect a poem's structure; it allows him not only to make demands—that the metaphors and images relinquish or yield up their primary and secondary meanings along with their past—but to judge a poem's worth on the basis of the result. It is in this context that Hopkins feared being misunderstood, that is, misread. For this reason also, it seems, Hopkins worried over prescriptive methods, how to go about informing the reader of the proper way to read his poems. Again Hopkins turns to the architectonic as correction, a poem's construction. In 1887 Hopkins wrote of the matter to Bridges,

> I do myself think, I may say, that it would be an immense advance in notation (so to call it) in writing as the record of

speech, to distinguish the subject, verb, object, and in general to express the construction to the eye; as is done already partly in punctuation by everybody, partly in capitals by the Germans, more fully in accentuation by the Hebrews. And I daresay it will come. But it would, I think, not do for me: it seems a confession of unintelligibility. And yet I don't know. At all events there is a difference. (LB, 265, 1887)

Despite his ambivalence, Hopkins presents the appropriate notation to Bridges. It seems that his request, too, for visible construction concedes the possibility of a non-percussive reader-poem relationship, undesirable as it is: words "are really matter open and indifferent," they may fall without striking the reader. In calling attention to construction, Hopkins assures himself of making a percussive impact. Oddly enough, the poem in question is one whose metaphors mime its theoretic concerns. The first stanza of "Harry Ploughman" is striking.

> HARD as hurdle arms, with a broth of goldish flue
> Breathed round; the rack of ribs; the scooped flank; lank
> Rope-over thigh; knee-nave; and barrelled shank—
>   Head and foot, shoulder and shank—
> By a grey eye's heed steered well, one crew, fall to;
> Stand at stress. Each limb's barrowy brawn, his thew
> That onewhere curded, onewhere sucked or sank—
>   Soared ór sánk—,
> Though as a beechbole firm, finds his, as at a rollcall, rank
> And features, in flesh, what deed he each must do—
>   His sinew-service where do.
>   (Poem 71)

Hopkins's poem which expresses "construction to the eye" in terms of poetic structure also expresses another kind of visible construction, the cathedral body, the "bone-house" of Harry Ploughman himself. In such an instance, architecture provides a reservoir of imagery capable of imitating the artistic intent of the poem. To cathedralize Harry further suggests what we might call stressed harmony: individual, faith, nature are each in service to the other, each revered. And in service to them all, what in fact structures their interrelationship, is the mechanical, either the literal motion of interaction "that onewhere curded, onewhere sucked or sank—Soared ór sánk" or the motion of poetic stress and syntax. Is it surprising, then, that a metaphor for a nature destructive, questioning harmony, physical and religious, among man, nature, and God, should also be architectural? While cathedralizing Harry in "sinew-service" to God, Hopkins decathedralizes a God destructive. He does so, however, only from a human perspective; from a divine one, God still sees harmony and that harmony expresses itself as a structural, architectural whole:

> Thy unchancelling poising palms were weighing the worth,
>   Thou martyr-master: in thy sight
> Storm flakes were scroll-leaved flowers, lily showers—sweet
>   heaven was astrew in them.   (Poem 28, stanza 21)

While the storm event is not neutral, it appears so because evaluation of it is relative: to God storm flakes are like Gothic ornamentation; to the nuns at sea on the *Deutschland* they were something very different. It seems, then, that to see construction, structural and ornamental, is to perceive harmony and beauty; not to see it, that is not to see the constructional order in Hopkins's poetry or in nature, is not to see divinity, harmony, beauty.

While we have been speaking of Hopkins's "visible" construction, we have yet to look at the elements of that construction, at least in any way other than a metaphorical one. The elements Hopkins wished to make visible, he in fact made concrete. In his notes on rhetoric, appropriately titled for our purpose "Rhythm and other structural parts,"[10] Hopkins gives to his building materials—syllables—architectural characteristics: their presence is physical, they have weight, strength, density; and they exist in an architecturally constructed universe which concedes only two spatial alternatives, interiors and exteriors, what Hopkins simply calls indoor and outdoor:

> [There are] two kinds [of accented syllables]: that of *pitch* (tonic) and that *of stress* (emphatic). We may think of words as heavy bodies, as indoor or out of door objects of nature or man's art. Now every visible palpable body has a centre of gravity round which it is in balance and a centre of illumination or *highspot* or *quickspot* up to which it is lighted and down to which it is shaded. The centre of gravity is like the accent of stress, the highspot like the accent of pitch, for pitch is like light and colour, stress like weight. (JP, 269)

Hopkins's poetic building blocks are substantial; language is not only structurally architectural, it partakes of the same physical characteristics as do the actual building materials of architecture, having weight, being subject to gravity, balance, stress, receiving light as accent. We may wonder whether the analogy is structural in other ways: are the stresses directional, constructional? To this point, Hopkins remarks that not the "length" but the "strength" of English syllables matters; and he adds:

> But besides the stress or emphasis and pitch or intonation of single syllables one against another, there is a stress or emphasis and a pitch or intonation running through the sentence and setting word against word as stronger or as higher pitched. (JP, 270)

GERARD MANLEY HOPKINS

18

"Stand at stress": the rhythms—and
other structural parts—of Hopkins's
poetry. Here we can see again those elements
of Gothic architecture that inspired Hopkins.
Are these springing lines suggestive
of Hopkins's sprung rhythm?
(Compare with Plate 23)
(Notre-Dame d'Amiens)

LITERARY ARCHITECTURE

We have, it seems, a poetic architecture which is mechanically engineered, a system of stresses, of words, syllables pitched, set one against another. The timing of Hopkins's description appropriately recalls the physical action of Harry Ploughman, "By a grey eye's heed steered well, one crew, fall to;/Stand at stress." We remember, too, the density, the direction, the stress and weight of Hopkins's nature descriptions. Throughout, the poetic clash of stresses and syllables one against another suggests the density and compression of architectural structures. [Plate 18; see also Plate 23] In a poem such as "Inversnaid," a poem we would think un-architectural, all these architectonic elements combine; and while the final poem is sonorous and compelling in rhythm, it is built of clashing stresses, of syllables striking against each other, piled on each other, each in a stressful relationship to what precedes and what follows. "Flutes," a word at once musical and architectural, stands at stress, receiving the weight and energy of the motion which builds to it, suspending us, holding us mid-air, before the softer falling home.

> This darksome burn, horseback brown,
> His rollrock highroad roaring down,
> In coop and in comb the fleece of his foam
> Flutes and low to the lake falls home.
>
> (Poem 56)

As syllables become transformed into matter, so they cease to exist in a neutral relationship to the poet; rather, weighted and occupying space, they seem cumbersome, to be contended with even by the skilled poet, as he tries to construct them into a poetic whole. Poet as architect must be stonemason as well: "Fineness, proportion of feature," Hopkins comments, "comes from a moulding force which succeeds in asserting itself over the resistance of cumbersome or restraining matter" (FL, 306, 1883). Hopkins recognizes the battle for poet and for architect; and in his sympathy and pathetic response to the latter, we begin to see another side of Hopkins's own relationship to his building materials.

FOUR

The Poet and the Architect

AMONG the William Butterfield papers now in the Starey collection rests a letter thanking the well-known architect for recommending buildings worthy of special study. The otherwise unremarkable letter closes, however, with a note somewhat unexpected in an admirer:

> I hope you will long continue to work out your beautiful and original style. I do not think this generation will ever much admire it. They do not understand how to look at a Pointed building as a whole having a single form governing it throughout, which they *would* perhaps see in a Greek temple: they like it to be a sort of farmyard and medley of ricks and roofs and dovecots.[11]

It is with an understandable feeling of irony that we learn the letter writer: Hopkins, whose own generation, but for a handful, never even knew his poetry, and the few who did oftentimes sadly failed to understand it. Three years before his letter to Butterfield, in 1874, Hopkins had visited Butterfield's All Saints "Babbicombe" Church,[12] recording the event in his journal:

> Then I went, with John Lynch, who had come to meet me, to Butterfield's Church at Babbicombe. It is odd and the oddness at first sight outweighed the beauty. (JP, 254, 1874)

Perhaps here, then, is some cause for the kind of affinity Hopkins may have felt for Butterfield. In a letter to his friend and mentor, Bridges, Hopkins had acknowledged that Butterfield's vice, "oddness," was his own:

GERARD MANLEY HOPKINS

No doubt my poetry errs on the side of oddness. I hope in time to have a more balanced and Miltonic style. But as air, melody, is what strikes me most of all in music and design in painting, so design, pattern, or what I am in the habit of calling "inscape" is what I above all aim at in poetry. This vice I cannot have escaped. Now it is the virtue of design, pattern, or inscape to be distinctive and it is the vice of distinctiveness to become queer. (LB, 66, 1879)

Hopkins's interest in Butterfield's architecture, like his careful admiration for Butterfield's "genius," persisted from the time Hopkins went up to Oxford through to his last poems. While Hopkins's poetry never attempts architectural description with the exactness or technical precision and specificity of his journal entries, a poem we looked at earlier, "To Oxford," refers in fact to Butterfield's Balliol chapel. It is worth noting again.

> Thus, I come underneath this chapel-side,
> So that the mason's levels, courses, all
> The vigorous horizontals, each way fall
> In bows above my head, as falsified
> By visual compulsion, till I hide
> The steep-up roof at last behind the small
> Eclipsing parapet; yet above the wall
> The sumptuous ridge-crest leave to poise and ride.
> None besides me this bye-ways beauty try.
> Or if they try it, I am happier then:
> The shapen flags and drillèd holes of sky,
> Just seen, may be to many unknown men
> The one peculiar of their pleasured eye,
> And I have only set the same to pen.
>
> (Poem 12)

What is as interesting as what Hopkins includes in this poem is what he omits: he does not mention color, easily the most controversial aspect of the building, but emphasizes instead direction or line. Perhaps there is reason: when he bows the horizontals he works with material resistant; and his reshaping then suggests the act of the artist, filtering, changing the objects of his perception just as he had similarly reshaped his nature descriptions into nature monumentalized. His attraction, then, is not to the individual "warp" but to something of far greater aesthetic import: to action which involves tension (to bow horizontals), strain, release, the action, in fact, of breathing. Perhaps we can understand why architectural structure and stress were particularly exciting to him.

If we pause, for a moment, to look again at Hopkins's letter to Butterfield, we see how we might have misread "To Oxford" by assigning weight to the particulars of the description rather than to the perceptual whole. When Hopkins suggests that Butterfield's audience could not see the whole of a building for the parts of it, we, too, might feel aptly embarrassed that, as Hopkins readers, we also tend to look at the "ricks and roofs and dovecots"–that is, at images singularly striking, jagged, discordant–rather than at the pattern and design of a whole poem. But part of our attention to details is surely intended: in his architectural city-scapes, Hopkins seems to distract attention, purposefully, from the whole scene by his attention to its parts, as in his description of Windsor castle.

As we approached Windsor the London smoke met us rolling up the valley of the Thames. Windsor stood out in the evening light: I think there can be no place like it–the eye-greeting burl of the Round Tower; all the crownlike medly [*sic*] of lower towers warping round; red and white houses of the town abutting on these, gabled and irregularly jut-jotted against them, making a third stage or storey.   (JP, 256, 1874)

GERARD MANLEY HOPKINS

What does this description hold for Hopkins? Why does he record it? At first it seems that he is misreading the scene just as Butterfield's viewers misread his architecture, noting the "crownlike medly" and the roofs and gables. Perhaps we might assume that his attractions are to the rhythms of the dotted hill; "jut-jotted" recalls some staccato rhythms of his poetry. But if we look more closely at the details Hopkins seems lost in, we might be surprised to find pattern. "Medly" is not defined but as a whole, "warping round"; and the irregular houses are patterned red and white, in fact comprising a stage or storey, a whole larger than its parts. There is no doubt but that the scene is intricate and may sustain detailing; nonetheless, we may image it as a detailed whole, rhythms working together to produce a pattern. Indeed, it would seem to be the particulars, the rhythms of Butterfield, that attract Hopkins to him; but these rhythms play within a larger whole, which Hopkins clearly sees. In the nave at Babbacombe, Hopkins, with what seems a twentieth-century sensibility, reads the ribbed diagonal web across the walls as playing against the continuous wall surface behind the web. He even goes to All Saints Margaret Street just to test his eye to see if his judgments remain correct and still stand:

> I wanted to see if my old enthusiasm was a mistake, I recognized certainly more than before Butterfield's want of rhetoric and telling, almost to dullness, and even of enthusiasm and zest in his work—thought the wall-mosaic rather tiresome for instance. Still the rich nobility of the tracery in the open arches of the sanctuary and the touching and passionate curves of the lilyings in the ironwork under the baptistery arch marked his genius to me as before. But my eye was fagged with looking at pictures.   (JP, 248, 1874) [Plate 19]

LITERARY ARCHITECTURE

19
William Butterfield's All Saints,
Margaret Street, London.
Hopkins comments on Butterfield's "oddness"
and on his own: "Now it is the virtue of
design, pattern, or inscape to be distinctive
and it is the vice of distinctiveness to
become queer." Butterfield's intricacies
of pattern here should remind us of Pater's
preferences in literary architecture.

While Hopkins's reading of buildings is formalistic, we have the sense that he makes literary demands of architecture just as he had made architectural demands of literature. "Rhetoric" and "telling" suggest his desire that architecture argue and story something; and "touching and passionate curves" suggests that he sought something at once sensuous and expressive in the angles and curves of architecture. We almost have the sense that Hopkins had an eye which could read abstract line and shape, which could find emotional satisfaction in what we have come to know as minimal art. We also have the feeling that Hopkins, like Pater, was attracted to forms which let light in, to spaces which structured or gave shape to light. But Hopkins is reluctant to make

GERARD MANLEY HOPKINS

value judgments, and we find only vague hints, not direct statements, which suggest what it is Hopkins seeks, and finds, in architecture. In describing Netley Abbey, for instance, Hopkins expresses his greatest praise: "a pair of plain three-light lancets in each clearstory of the S. transept, which dwell on the eye with a simple direct instress of trinity" (JP, 215, 1871). Hopkins's architectural values combine, it seems, the structural and the religious so that structure signifies devotion. We can see how nature reconstructed into architecture, through poems or descriptions in the journal, becomes a religious statement, especially since it is not a generic architecture but specifically cathedrals; and the act of so transposing nature into monuments becomes one of worship and may be "touching" or "passionate" by turn. Not surprisingly, it is Gothic architecture which best fulfills Hopkins's religious yearnings, his desire for the sensuous and sturdy combined as ornament and structure; yet his theories of proportion lead him to value, and to find harmonious with his religious preferences, Classical architecture also. We cannot help but be impressed by the catholicity of Hopkins's taste: his is neither the eclecticism of the undiscerning nor the rigid, dogmatic preference of the religious who regard style as an expression of divine truth; rather, Hopkins seeks capability in form and style, asking what each offers aesthetically and ethically, what each has come to mean historically.

FIVE

The "Achieve" and "Mastery": Hopkins's Poetry

Duns Scotus's Oxford

TOWERY city and branchy between towers;
Cuckoo-echoing, bell-swarmèd, lark-charmèd,
    rook-racked, river-rounded;
The dapple-eared lily below thee; that country and
    town did
Once encounter in, here coped and poisèd powers;

Thou hast a base and brickish skirt there, sours
That neighbour-nature thy grey beauty is grounded
Best in; graceless growth, thou hast confounded
Rural rural keeping – folk, flocks, and flowers.

Yet ah! this air I gather and I release
He lived on; these weeds and waters, these walls are
    what
He haunted who of all men most sways my spirits to
    peace;

Of realty the rarest-veinèd unraveller; a not
Rivalled insight, be rival Italy or Greece;
Who fired France for Mary without spot.

(Poem 44)

Neither the syntax nor the diction of "Duns Scotus's Oxford" is difficult, and the sense, therefore, of the poem is easily accessible. The poem suspends its mood between celebration and lament. The celebration is for Duns Scotus himself and an Oxford which retains and triggers memory of him, and the lament is for the gracefulness of the past, a past still at the heartfelt center of Oxford. But the lament, nostalgic as it may be, is oddly submerged in the celebration; and when it surfaces, it is transformed into something harsher, not a loss per se but more a criticism of a modern Oxford which defies the harmony between city and country, a harmony of old. The poem then venerates memory, memory whose power and energy render her more immediate than the actual baseness of nineteenth-century Oxford.

The value system is rendered through metaphor —predominantly architectural and natural—through rhyme and rhythm: when nature and architecture are integrated, Oxford is celebrated; when they are at odds, an Oxford of the past is longed for. The opening stanza describes the city, but—as one finds out only in the subsequent stanza—only the city center, what comes to be its essence.

> TOWERY city and branchy between towers;
> Cuckoo-echoing, bell-swarmèd, lark-charmèd,
>   rook-racked, river-rounded;
> The dapple-eared lily below thee; that country and
>   town did
> Once encounter in, here coped and poisèd powers;

The opening line establishes the condition of harmony, that architecture be natural and nature be architectural. Towers frame the view, opening and closing the verse line and receiving its stresses; "branchy" and "towery" so go together, by virtue of rhyme and placement, that trees and towers seem to share each other's qualities, together a woven or patterned interlacing network. While the first image, "towery city," seems to establish the foreground of our visual field, Hopkins throws the background—"branchy *between* towers"—also to the fore, as if harmony requires and depends on a frontality of

GERARD MANLEY HOPKINS

forms which are reciprocally architectural and natural ("towery" and "branchy"), equal in importance to each other. The exchangeability, even confusion, of forms is rendered complete in the next line, in which bells and birds occupy the other's roost, take on the other's sound; and we almost have the sense that the "dapple-eared lily" hears them. "Coped" may be architectural and ecclesiastical, "poised" an abstract quality and a mechanical one, too. The contrasting present-day Oxford is the brickish Victorian Oxford whose shapeless suburbs extend into nature and defy harmony: *base* and *brickish* appear the harsher juxtaposed with *towers, powers, flowers*, with *weeds, waters, walls*. The stress we feel, rhymed and constructive, is in the gathering and releasing, in breathing; and harmony almost seems linked to and like that natural process. Mental peace, like architectural harmony, also requires and results from an integration of weeds, waters, and walls; "insight," the special quality which Hopkins selects to distinguish Duns Scotus, constitutes a pun on visual perception, suggesting that the ability to integrate the natural with the man-made, the religious with the organic, Oxford as city with Oxford as country, is a quality rare and worthy. At once visual perception becomes a moral and religious act, one which the poem supports.

While "Duns Scotus's Oxford" seems to build from city to man, from image to action, "Spelt from Sibyl's Leaves" seems to unbuild.

Spelt from Sibyl's Leaves

EARNEST, earthless, equal, attuneable, | vaulty, voluminous, . . . stupendous
Evening strains to be tíme's vást, | womb-of-all, home-of-all, hearse-of-all night.

LITERARY ARCHITECTURE

Her fond yellow hornlight wound to the west, ǀ her wild hollow hoarlight hung to the height
Waste; her earliest stars, earlstars, ǀ stárs principal, overbend us,
Fíre-féaturing heaven. For earth ǀ her being has unbound; her dapple is at an end, as-
tray or aswarm, all throughther, in throngs; ǀ self ín self steepèd and páshed—qúite
Disremembering, dísmémbering ǀ áll now. Heart, you round me right
With: Óur évening is over us; óur night ǀ whélms, whélms, ánd will end us.

Only the beakleaved boughs dragonish ǀ damask the tool-smooth bleak light; black,
Ever so black on it. Óur tale, O óur oracle! ǀ Lét life, wáned, ah lét life wind
Off hér once skéined stained véined varíety ǀ upon, áll on twó spools; párt, pen, páck
Now her áll in twó flocks, twó folds—black, white; ǀ right, wrong; reckon but, reck but, mind
But thése two; wáre of a wórld where bút these ǀ twó tell, each off the óther; of a rack
Where, selfwrung, selfstrung, sheathe- and shelterless, ǀ thóughts agaínst thoughts ín groans grínd.   (Poem 61)

Unlike "Duns Scotus's Oxford," where evocation of Scotus himself is linked to city and to air preserved almost hermetically, in "Spelt from Sibyl's Leaves" there is no such evocation of the past but rather a "disremembering," appropriate, as we will see, to the unbuilding, the "dismembering" in the poem.

> For earth ǀ her being has unbound; her dapple is at an end, as-
> tray or aswarm, all throughther, in throngs; ǀ self ín self steepèd and páshed—qúite
> Disremembering, dísmémbering ǀ áll now.

GERARD MANLEY HOPKINS

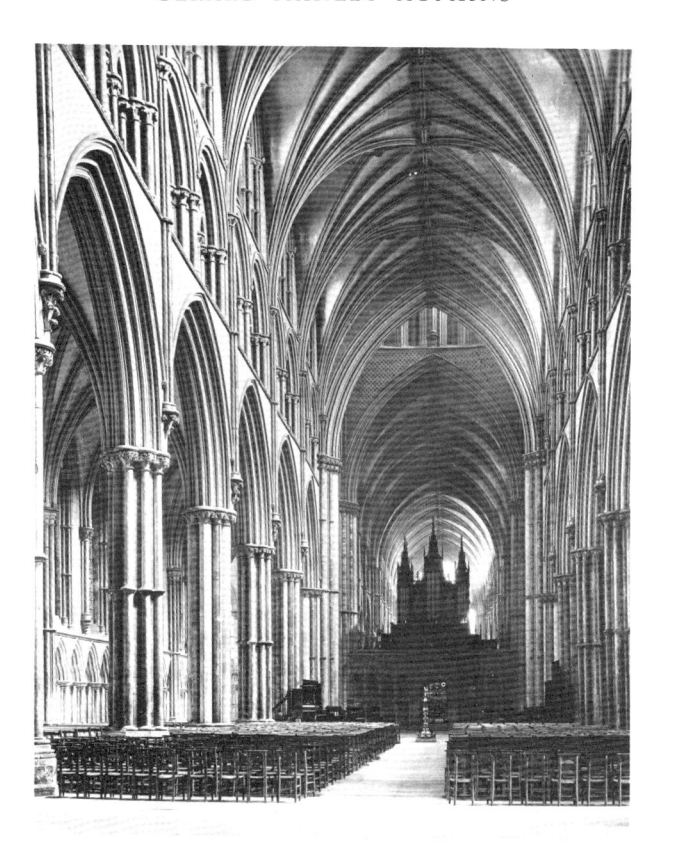

20

EARNEST, earthless, equal, attunable, ¹ vaulty,
voluminous, . . . stupendous
Spelt from Sibyl's Leaves

Here in the Lincoln Cathedral
we see the hollow center,
the building space of literary architecture
as an art of rhythmed enclosure.

LITERARY ARCHITECTURE

Nature does engender: Sibyl's leaves spell and spill, a proliferation verbal, cognition depending upon verbalization; and in a circular way, it is a cognition of that very proliferation. Does wording render idea concrete, accessible? Does nature, not man, spell—that is, word—and make concepts apprehensible?

The first long stanza of "Spelt from Sibyl's Leaves" opens with the struggle for description and definition of something not concrete: space. If Hopkins cannot define it by activating it or filling it—as in "branchy between towers," "branchy" giving substance to "between" in "Duns Scotus's Oxford"—he does so by enclosure: space may be defined as "content" if something else gives it peripheries and appropriate shape; something may be empty if it is enclosed:

EARNEST, earthless, equal, attuneable, | vaulty, voluminous,
   ... stupendous
Evening strains to be tíme's vást, | womb-of-all, home-of-all,
   hearse-of-all night.

The first adjectives seem beyond physical rendering; but "vaulty" gives extension, cathedral shape; "voluminous" gives mass, weight. Similarly, birth, life, and death are rendered in images also of enclosure, images again suggesting contents and outside limits; definition, verbally sought, of what is abstract and conceptual is in fact accomplished by physical delineation which is implicitly architectural, having spatial dimension, weight, and size. So, too, the movement of the poem seems to involve a locating or placing of ideas made substantial: light may be "wound," thread-like, or "hung"; it has dimensions, position, so that nature, tortured on Judgment Day, is some oddly cathedral-like structure, built, demolished and rebuilt again within the life-span of the poem. Images of roundness run through the first stanza: "wound," "overbend," "round"; and the emotion in response to the event is rendered, potentially at least, in the terms or shape of the event itself, "Óur évening is over us; óur night ǀ whélms, whélms / ánd will end us." "Whelming," as something partial, attracts its natural partner "over"; and our emotion, "overwhelming" takes on the literalness of enclosure. Evening seems to move literally, mechanically, into night. And structuring seems to be remembering, "spooling" in contrast to the unstructuring or architectural "dismembering" and "disremembering." Nature acts on what is man-made, on definition or "thinging," on light which is "toolsmooth":

> Only the beakleaved boughs dragonish ǀ damask the toolsmooth bleak light; black,
> Ever so black on it. Óur tale, O óur oracle!

If definition is a way of rendering and making accessible what is abstract, so, too, is winding a kind of organizing what is random and disordered. The poem's end seems enclosureless: the Last Judgment, what amounts to "undoing," is imaged by the absence of peripheries, night being no longer a "hearse" but now "sheatheless" and "shelterless." That final night cannot be enclosed or have perceptual limits suggests that it cannot therefore be grasped, worded, or defined. Instead, we have an image of sacrifice on a torture rack, but no saint, not even Christ, is being tortured: "self" is. And, crucially, "self" is defined, figured forth, "selved," as thought substantialized or concretized. Hopkins, though, goes still further: even torture is, in a sense, potentially generative. In the poem's end, thought retains its substance and, therefore, its mechanical capabilities: "thóughts agaínst thoughts ín groans grínd" as if thoughts have weight, direction, position. [Plate 18] And grinding, while a wearing down, also suggests a productive and generative friction: metaphor pruned, worn down, shaped, releases the intellectual and poetic energy of probing, defining, rendering or transposing. In this way, the end of the poem is almost affirmative: thoughts have taken on the architectural, physical characteristics that syllables had in Hopkins's "Rhythm and other structural parts," and we have the sense that although all else may be destroyed in the end, the artist, perhaps Hopkins as artist, can create poems so long as thoughts can generate other thoughts, syllables other syllables, poems other poems.

Some of Hopkins's poetic terms, such as *pitch* and *stress*, are both musical and architectural, and as much may be said of the images in "Spelt from Sibyl's Leaves" and in another poem, "On a Piece of Music."

(On a Piece of Music)

HOW all's to one thing wrought!
The members, how they sit!
O what a tune the thought
Must be that fancied it.

Nor angel insight can
Learn how the heart is hence:
Since all the make of man
Is law's indifference.

[Who shaped these walls has shewn
The music of his mind,
Made known, though thick through stone
What beauty beat behind.]

Not free in this because
His powers seemed free to play:
He swept what scope he was
To sweep and must obey.

Though down his being's bent
Like air he changed in choice,
That was an instrument
Which overvaulted voice.

What makes the man and what
The man within that makes:
Ask whom he serves or not
Serves and what side he takes.

For good grows wild and wide,
Has shades, is nowhere none;
But right must seek a side
And choose for chieftain one.

Therefore this masterhood,
This piece of perfect song,
This fault-not-found-with good
Is neither right nor wrong,

No more than red and blue,
No more than Re and Mi,
Or sweet the golden glue
That's built for by the bee.

[Who built these walls made known
The music of his mind,
Yet here he has but shewn
His ruder-rounded rind.
His brightest blooms lie there unblown,
His sweetest nectar hides behind.]

(Poem 148)

Here the same concretizing takes place that occurred in the other poems; and "mind" itself looms an architectural structure such that inside and out seem to define self and not-self:

LITERARY ARCHITECTURE

> Who shaped these walls has shewn
> The music of his mind,
> Made known, though thick through stone
> What beauty beat behind.

So, too, definitions of values, aesthetic and ethical, hinge on an architectural image. Harmony, or discord for that matter—the mind's character and the artist's—are revealed by an architectural analogue, the artifact or structure, either as mind or as product.

> What makes the man and what
> The man within that makes:
> Ask whom he serves or not
> Serves and what side he takes.

It is not surprising if, on reflection, the mind as structure, so imaged in "On a Piece of Music," makes us think that God's mind, gigantic yet structural or architectural, was also figured forth in "Spelt from Sibyl's Leaves," a mind extending into nature the way God's mind does in "The Wreck of the Deutschland." Just so, order in "On a Piece of Music" is imaged by architectural members, and that order testifies to divine or ethical control:

> How all's to one thing wrought!
> The members, how they sit!
> O what a tune the thought
> Must be that fancied it.

We may well recall Robert Browning's "Abt Vogler" where, in the same way, music takes the form of a piece of architecture; but for Hopkins, the artifact, not only as an extension of the artist, but as an emblem of him, is imaged by construction. We sense both an internal and an external pressure, man shaped and shaping; and "what

GERARD MANLEY HOPKINS

21
How all's to one thing wrought!
The members, how they sit!
O what a tune the thought
Must be that fancied it.
On a Piece of Music
(Wells Cathedral: Nave Looking West)

side he takes" assumes a literalness of actual position. By contrast, that over which the artist exerts no control is imaged as organic growth, defined not as the tree-steepled Oxford was but as was modern Oxford and her shapeless suburbs.

> For good grows wild and wide,
> Has shades, is nowhere none;
> But right must seek a side
> And choose for chieftain one.

Architecture may embody nature, but more important, it should offer structure to nature, not miming a structureless opulence and variety. [Plate 22] Here again Hopkins's value system reminds us of that in his schoolboy poem, "The Escorial," in which poet-architect rejects Gothic forms with their "engemming rays," their "foliag'd crownals" all "in a maze of finish'd diapers" (Poem 1) of a nature untended. We also have the sense that, for Hopkins, structure protects; while soul may be imaged organically, as flower, as nectar, the creating and created mind walls it in, over-bending the flower of soul or idea, that it be safe from destruction.

> Who built these walls made known
> The music of his mind,
> Yet here he has but shewn
> His ruder-rounded rind.
> His brightest blooms lie there unblown,
> His sweetest nectar hides behind.

Stress, grind, and density of syllables are notably absent from the neatly mellifluous stanzas of "On a Piece of Music," so that it is *more* obscure than the strenuously mannered "Sybil's Leaves."

22

Nature vaulted and traced:
Oxford Cathedral.
Here we can also see what Ruskin
called an elastic tension which communicates
"force from part to part."

LITERARY ARCHITECTURE

It should not surprise us, after looking at these three poems, to find that Hopkins, when doubting his own generative, creating capacity, images that capacity or lack thereof architecturally. In one of his most personally poignant poems, the structure, built from nature, the stuff of nests and twigs, is architecturally laced and fretted:

> Oh, the sots and thralls of lust
> Do in spare hours more thrive than I that spend,
> Sir, life upon thy cause. See, banks and brakes
> Now, leavèd how thick! lacèd they are again
> With fretty chervil, look, and fresh wind shakes
> Them; birds build—but not I build; no, but strain,
> Time's eunuch, and not breed one work that wakes.
> Mine, O thou lord of life, send my roots rain.
>
> (Poem 74)

While the imagery suggests the procreative, it seems more the fathering forth of an artifact-child that Hopkins so desires. The sought-for rain almost suggests a need for growth in order to build, the need for sustenance in order to create rather than sustenance of which the direct product is the artifact. For Hopkins the nest, the structural home for offspring, suggests that poems house ideas, that they are constructed nature monuments; and we have the sense that, for Hopkins, his recasting of nature constitutes a survival or preservation effort. For this purpose, as poetic metaphors, art, science and nature, music, architecture, mechanics and optics, are all potentially compatible. Throughout his oeuvre, Hopkins varies the theme, but for the most part, in all he images construction—whether of body, artifact, created world of human mind—as architectural structure. Man's body not only houses but grounds, substantiates, his spirit: in "The Caged Skylark," we find both ideas, momentarily perhaps, compatible: potentially, the bird's nest is no prison.

> As a dare-gale skylark scanted in a dull cage
> > Man's mounting spirit in his bone-house, mean house, dwells—
> . . . .
> Man's spirit will be flesh-bound when found at best,
> But uncumberèd: meadow-down is not distressed
> > For a rainbow footing it nor he for his bónes rísen.
>
> (Poem 39)

So, too, does Hopkins figure mind as structurally limited and delimiting: in "The Lantern out of Doors," he writes,

> Death or distance soon consumes them: wind
> > What most I may eye after, be in at the end
> I cannot, and out of sight is out of mind.
>
> Christ minds: Christ's interest, what to avow or amend
> > There, éyes them, heart wánts, care haúnts,
> > > foot fóllows kínd,
> Their ránsom, théir rescue, ánd first, fást, last friénd.
>
> (Poem 40)

Here again, mind is defined by the literal peripheries of perception, distance. We have, in a sense, a double idea, that projection is out of the mind, "out" meaning from out of, generated from inside and projecting out; that which is deduced, understood from sight is also "from" the mind, and sight itself is an act of the mind. To "eye after," to sight—we are prepared for what happens in the poem: the mind is defined by and becomes its own action, and appropriately is transformed from noun into verb.

LITERARY ARCHITECTURE

23
Architecture at its softest; it is not
for this that Hopkins turns to architecture.
(Compare with Plates 3 and 17, above.) Here the
architecture—its stone stairs—
registers transformation from accurate use.
The sea of stairs, while structurally
so different from Hopkins's preferred
architectural forms, does suggest Hopkins's
lines on vision—death and distance:

Death or distance soon consumes them: wind
What most I may eye after, be in at the end
I cannot, and out of sight is out of mind.
The Lantern out of Doors

(Wells Cathedral)

GERARD MANLEY HOPKINS

III
"THE STORED CONSCIOUSNESS": MARCEL PROUST

But a cathedral is not only a thing of
beauty to be felt. It may, for you,
no longer be a source of teaching
to be followed, but at least it is
a book to be read and understood.

MARCEL PROUST

24
The aspiration.
(Saint-Mathurin, Larchant)

ONE

Church Architecture: The Structure of *A la recherche du temps perdu*

When, in 1919, Marcel Proust wrote to the Comte Jean de Gaigneron, he commended, with almost excessive ingenuousness, the Comte's insight into his novel *A la recherche du temps perdu*. Proust also confided to the Comte what now seems but a gratuitous revelation, that the structure of *A la recherche* is like a cathedral.

> When you speak to me of cathedrals, I cannot but feel touched at the evidence of an intuition which has led you to guess [*deviner*] what I had never mentioned to anyone, and here set down in writing for the first time – that I once planned to give to each part of my book a succession of titles, such as *Porch*, *Windows in the Apse*, etc. . . . so as to defend myself in advance against the sort of stupid criticism which has been made to the effect that my books lack construction, whereas I hope to prove to you that their sole merit lies in the solidity of their tiniest parts. I gave up the idea of using these architectural titles because I found them too pretentious, but I am touched at finding that you have dug them up by a sort of intelligent divination.[1]

The Comte de Gaigneron had divined what became public and explicit only subsequently, in the posthumous publication of the last volumes of *A la recherche*. There, in now celebrated passages, Proust's narrator declares his structural purpose, taking care to avoid the pretension Proust expressly eschewed in selecting his

LITERARY ARCHITECTURE

titles. Architect and dressmaker, Marcel balances the enormity of his "architectural labours"–to "build" a book "like a church"–with the humility of a seamstress's craft. He plans to work in the manner of his nurse, Françoise:

> As all the unpretentious persons who live close beside us acquire a certain intuitive comprehension of our work . . . I would work near her [Françoise] and almost in her manner–at least as she used to, for she was now so old she could scarcely see any more–for, pinning on an extra sheet here and there, I would construct my book, I dare not say ambitiously "like a cathedral," but simply like a dress. (II, 1113)

But once he has thus qualified his ambitiousness, Marcel abandons the simile of artist-dressmaker, elaborating instead his task as church architect. Whatever discomfort he continues to feel (the result of choosing one simile in favor of another) is dealt with by uncertainty and hope, feelings which newly administer the salve of professional modesty. The image of his book as "church" is nonetheless striking; and we might do well to recall Hopkins's poetic churches and witness them transformed here into a monument of fiction no less awesome or grand:

> And yet, while all my useless duties to which I was ready to sacrifice the real one went out of my head in a few minutes, the idea of the thing I was to construct did not leave me for an instant. I knew not whether it would be a church in which the true believers would be able little by little to learn some truths and discover some harmonies, the great, comprehensive plan, or would stand, forever unvisited, on the summit of an island, like a druid monument. But I had decided to devote to it all my strength, which was leaving me slowly, as though reluctant and wishing to allow me time, having completed the outer

structure, to close the funereal door. Soon I was able to shew a few sketches. No one understood a word. Even those who were favourable to my conception of the truths which I intended later to carve within the temple congratulated me on having discovered them with a microscope when I had, on the contrary, used a telescope to perceive things which, it is true, were very small but situated afar off and each of them a world in itself. (II, 1118)

This chapter will concern itself with these images, Proust's and his narrator's, of fiction as architecture, as cathedral, temple, even rooms. What relationship does architecture, as art analogue of fictional literature, have to Proust's conceptions and methods of literary structure, subject, and style? And what, then, does architecture so conjoined with literary art have to do with Proust's evaluation and use of memory in *A la recherche du temps perdu*?

Perhaps the passage above constitutes the defense proper, the "proof" which Comte de Gaigneron perceptively did not need, that *A la recherche* does not "lack construction." If the defense is tardy, occurring after some two thousand pages of text, it is deliberately so: chronologically, it masks as a kind of retrospective insight into the structural order of *A la recherche*, thereby gaining force and value, like those after-pages in which a writer, reflecting upon his work, confers upon it what Proust praises as "retrospective illumination," an "ulterior" beauty surpassing the work itself (II, 491). But the defense does double duty, for it evidences and substantiates the writer's controlled "foresight of the end in the beginning," what Pater had specified as a prerequisite of great literary architecture: and in fact these last pages were written before the text itself.[2]

LITERARY ARCHITECTURE

Marcel's architectural simile clearly achieves more than strategical defense: not only does the image endow the book with "teachfulness" ("true believers" might "learn" there) and symbolic monumentality, legendary and mysterious (a "druid monument"); it also enables the narrator to describe "making" (is this like Hopkins's "process"?) and so release discussions of literary structure from the confines of descriptive formalism into vistas of interpretative possibility. The formal distinction between outer structure and inner detail, between exterior and interior, might, for instance, suggest those perceptual and conceptual antinomies between a generalized harmony (inaccuracy?) and a particularized truthfulness (accuracy?), between distance and size (the confusions of relative measurement, telescope versus microscope), between continuous and contiguous worlds ("each of them a world in itself"). Likewise, the evocation of literary artist as Gothic craftsman who carves images (or "truths"!) suggests something about the materials and functions of language, its permanence, solidity, and spatial potential.

These matters Marcel, for the moment, only suggests. Regarding the other riches bestowed by the architectural image, Proust's narrator is explicit. By evoking comparison with a Gothic cathedral, Marcel reserves for the literary artist the right to an incomplete work:

> And in those great books there are certain portions which there has been time only to sketch in and which no doubt will never be completed because of the very magnitude of the architect's plan. How many great cathedrals remain unfinished! (II, 1112)

But perhaps most important to the narrator, the image of the cathedral secures the book as an edifice constructed in

MARCEL PROUST

"Time." Marcel, fearing his own waning strength, comments:

> In any event, if I still had the strength to accomplish my work, I realized that the nature of the circumstances which today ... had given me at one and the same time the idea of my work and the fear of not being able to carry it out would assuredly before all else imprint upon it the form I had once dimly sensed in the church at Combray, during certain days which had deeply influenced me, a form which usually remains invisible to us, the form of Time. This dimension of Time which I had once vaguely felt in the church at Combray I would try to make continually perceptible in a transcription of human life necessarily very different from that conveyed to us by our deceptive senses. (II, 1121)

While the young Marcel might have only "dimly sensed" the significance of the church at Combray, the mature narrator had, even in the early pages of the book, enlarged the naive view to something more. Although nature herself was indifferent to the singularity of the church (Madame Loiseau's fuchsias leave her flower-pots to cool "their purple cheeks against the dark front of the church") (I, 47), the narrator's mind defied this visual evidence and exploded between church and town an abyss. Saint-Hilaire stood apart precisely because it occupied "four dimensions of space—the name of the fourth being Time" (I, 46). The special "geometry" of the church is likewise the geometry—and the innovativeness—of the novel: the varieties of temporal extension, with the capacity for contradictory, because instantaneous, contraction, are not only essential and necessary to both architecture and literature; they also reveal and constitute both the material and the "dematerialized" essence of both art forms and of literary architecture.

LITERARY ARCHITECTURE

Contemporary criticism, with its hawk-eyed attention to literary structure, has observed Marcel's remarks and from them construed the serviceability of his architectural references. One of the most outstanding Proust critics, Gilles Deleuze, in an otherwise revolutionary reading of Proust's art, alludes to the cathedral only as an image sanctioning "incompleteness."[3] Richard Macksey, in a more modest essay, finds in the steeple of Saint-Hilaire what Georges Poulet calls "temporal perspective," the unity of *A la recherche* and the signature of Proust's genius. In this symbol, fragments of time and space, character and narrative incident, are reconciled and united by a "vital simultaneity," a unifying point of view which newly combines what had been discrete and mutually exclusive, especially the Méséglise and Guermantes ways.[4] I should like to suggest that while the text corroborates Deleuze's observation, Deleuze nonetheless slights the church analogue, perhaps of necessity, in concession to the demands of his persuasive polemical stance. And although Poulet and Macksey concede architecture's temporal significance, their notion of a simultaneity and a whole (of recombined fragments and reconciled opposites) seriously undermines, if it does not violate, Proust's painstaking definition of a whole which preserves rather than annihilates difference, distance, extension, fragmentation, as narrative necessities and epistemological truths. Proust is careful to suggest that Time, hence the novel, "traverses" fragments which do not themselves constitute a whole or confirm a unity. And—almost ironically for Poulet and Macksey—it is the church of Combray which displays these "crossroad" links. The church

occupied, so to speak, four dimensions of space—the name of

the fourth being Time—which had sailed the centuries with that old nave, where bay after bay, chapel after chapel, seemed to stretch across and hold down and conquer not merely a few yards of soil, but each successive epoch from which the whole building had emerged triumphant. (I, 46) [Plate 25]

Proust's whole breaks with the Coleridgean model in which parts relinquish their identity by relation to other parts and to the whole.[5] Rather, the formal structure of the novel, its ability to "sail," to "stretch," to "span" and "cross," fashions, not a unity of identity or recombination of parts, but a unity which establishes exchange and communication between discrete and separate fragments ("each [truth] a world in itself") without destroying that dimension which causes and characterizes such fragmentation. In the closing passage of a book composed of multiple events, perspectives, attitudes, Marcel puts forward the image of a simultaneity which demands and maintains the discontinuous and disjunctive nature of Time.

> I would not fail to stamp it [my work] with the seal of Time . . . and I would therein describe men—even should that give them the semblance of monstrous creatures—as occupying in Time a place far more considerable than the so restricted one allotted them in space, a place, on the contrary, extending boundlessly since, giant-like, reaching far back into the years, they touch simultaneously epochs of their lives—with countless intervening days between—so widely separated from one another in Time. (II, 1123-1124)

With a kind of imitative pun, Marcel expresses the idea of disjunction by a syntactical displacement, an interruption; the parenthetical phrase about distance in fact distances: Marcel's giants "touch simultaneously

LITERARY ARCHITECTURE

epochs of their lives—with countless intervening days between—so widely separated from one another in Time." Even in the syntax, that which distances need not fragment; it can also "span" and "connect" sentence elements which nonetheless remain distinct and separate. Proust's words and syntax can span because he conceives of and uses them dimensionally, for their depth. *Simultaneity* is the name for such touching or connectedness in time; *transparency* or *superimposition* is its spatial name.

It is notable that Proust's literary concept of a unity of the discontinuous, structuring and allowing an inclusiveness and variety, finds its counterpart in the architectural theory Proust ardently explored in the works of Viollet-le-Duc and Emile Mâle. But still more striking, the notion of disconnectedness in the service of another unity, stands at the heart of the architectural essay Proust chose to study and translate, John Ruskin's *Bible of Amiens*. The cathedral, writes Proust, "is a book to be read and understood"; it is built of many rough stones which the architect must not "mutilate," for "there is history in them."[6] Proust quotes Ruskin:

> And in all their [the stone's] veins and bones and flame-like stainings, and broken and disconnected lines, they write various legends, never untrue, of the former political state of the mountain kingdom to which they belonged, of its infirmities and fortitudes, convulsions and consolidations, from the beginning of Time.[7]   [Plates 27 and 25]

From Ruskin Proust learns that the greatness of Gothic architecture is due, in large part, to its freedom from rules of order, symmetry, unity, rules which represent the enslavement of laboring and creating minds. Ruskin is explicit:

MARCEL PROUST

25
"Bay after bay, chapel after chapel, seemed
to stretch across and hold down and conquer
not merely a few yards of soil, but each
successive epoch from which the whole building
had emerged triumphant." (Chartres Cathedral)

LITERARY ARCHITECTURE

26
Here we see space-time, that is, time as
and inseparable from space. Distance measures,
therefore, both time and space intervals at once;
it clearly requires two (*di*) positions in
space-time—where we stand as viewers and where
we look to (*di* indicating subject and object
distinction). If we look down the center, we are
actually looking through—*per-ceiving*—
space-time which we can only see *in* the context
of the surrounding or enclosing structure.
Space-time throws into relief the human scale:
notice the chairs. (Notre-Dame d'Amiens)

And it is, perhaps, the principal admirableness of the Gothic schools of architecture, that . . . out of fragments full of imperfection, and betraying that imperfection in every touch [the architects] indulgently raise up a stately and unaccusable whole.[8] [Plates 6 and 7]

These "fragments"—like "surprises," "accidents," sudden "changes" and incomplete images, reminiscent of Pater's literary architecture as well as of Hopkins's Denbigh Hill—do not violate "unity," but rather assume an importance of their own such that Ruskin singles out for

MARCEL PROUST

description and analysis partial views and "pieces" of buildings. [Plate 3] In this, Ruskin, like Proust after him, breaks from traditional architectural concerns with the orders and unities, shifting his attention to qualities of craftsmanship and problems of truthfulness, of novelty, of accumulation of details. It seems a misreading of Proust to search for and describe a unity which reconciles opposites and neutralizes tension between discrete parts; for Proust's literary debt, in this instance, is to a man who does not value conventional wholes. Ruskin describes the changeful variety of Gothic architecture:

> Undefined in its slope of roof, height of shaft, breadth of arch, or disposition of ground plan, it can shrink into a turret, expand into a hall, coil into a staircase, or spring into a spire, with undegraded grace and unexhausted energy; and whenever it finds occasion for change in its form or purpose, it submits to it without the slightest sense of loss either to its unity or majesty,—subtle and flexible like a fiery serpent, but ever attentive to the voice of the charmer.[9] [Plate 27]

Daring interruptions of the formal plan would rather give additional interest to symmetry than injure it. Proust's cathedral Saint-Hilaire, partly in homage to Ruskin, likewise preserves what is broken and discontinuous. The "communication" which takes place between the separate naves and bays of Saint-Hilaire, like that communication between narrative incidents and characters in *A la recherche*, depends upon discontinuity, the gap or space between, which may receive or transport a charge, what Ruskin calls tension: that communication is again at the basis of Ruskin's concept of the Gothic.

In Gothic vaults and traceries there is a stiffness analogous to that of the bones of a limb, or fibres of a tree; an elastic

27
The splendor of Gothic architecture: the elasticity
of architectural form and structure
discovers an equivalence in style and structure
of literary architecture.
(Church at Autun)

tension and communication of force from part to part, and also a studious expression of this throughout every visible line of the building.[10]   [See Plates 22 and 28]

Proust's critics Poulet and Macksey seem to ignore the important shifts in late nineteenth-century architectural tastes and the possible relationship between these shifts and Proust's self-conscious architectural analogue for literature. Poulet and Macksey argue that the steeple of Saint-Hilaire symbolizes the unity and connectedness of *A la recherche* because the steeple offers a view which connects fragments of countryside. Macksey writes:

> This new law of *temporal* perspective was beautifully perceived by Georges Poulet in the emblem which crowns Combray, the spire of Saint-Hilaire. From the vantage of this point surmounting the work of centuries, the opposition of the mutually exclusive ways of Méséglise and Guermantes was resolved, the arch was closed.[11]

Poulet and Macksey furthermore overlook the explicit inadequacy of this view from the tower. While, it is true, the tower enables such an overview, it does so at the expense of a ground view – its enlargement or grounded extension – which is also necessary. The Curé of Saint-Hilaire points this out: from the steeple

> you can see at the same time places which you are in the habit of seeing one without the other . . . from the top of Saint-Hilaire . . . the whole countryside is spread out before you like a map. Only, you cannot make out the water; you would say that there were great rifts in the town, slicing it up so neatly that it looks like a loaf of bread which still holds together after it has been cut up. To get it all quite perfect you would have to be in both places at once; up here on the top of Saint-Hilaire and down there at Jouy-le-Vicomte.   (I, 81)

28
Gothic architecture organic:
"bones of a limb, fibres of a tree."
(Wells Cathedral)

Poulet's and Macksey's concept of unity, in other words, violates the *di-stance*, that is, the space, hence time, of the novel. More crucial yet, it is the distance and the discontinuity of a ground view – the Martinville towers – which stimulated Marcel's first attempt at art, at discovering truths behind the appearances of things. Marcel's Saint-Hilaire, as "Time incarnate," spans epochs and ways, traverses them, crosses space, much as the narrative I spans and links the episodes of *A la recherche*, connecting characters in space-time while surprising the reader with accidents and changes. Marcel's *A la recherche*, his book as cathedral, carefully presents his "conception of truths" carved within the temple, truths which, "it is true, were very small but situated afar off and each of them a world in itself" (II, 1118).

TWO

Rooms of Self: The Quest for Definition

> The Proustian equation is never simple.
> SAMUEL BECKETT

A LA RECHERCHE opens with a simple equation. The context for the equation is this: Marcel awakes, recollects that he has been asleep, that while he was asleep he thought he was still awake reading, but that in this sleep-reading he had misconstrued the subject matter of his book. Then comes the equation, in the form of appositives, but constituting a definition: "I myself seemed actually to have become the subject of my book: a church, a quartet, the rivalry between François I and Charles V" (I, 3). If paraphrase suggests the complexity of a context which Proust's narrative grace had made seem of dreamlike ease, then perhaps the simple equation likewise dissembles a complexity which, if unwound, in fact consumes twelve volumes of text. Of course, in one sense, the dream-book is *A la recherche*; and perhaps the subject of the book is all four—self, church, quartet, history. But is each individually *the* subject? Does the equation propose identification between each member (self equals church, but church also equals quartet, etc.)? And are self, church, quartet, history therefore interchangeable? Finally, if the structure of the book is that of a church, as Proust and his narrator claim, are subject and structure—church—the same? Is the subject of the book architectural/literary structure? I should like to suggest

LITERARY ARCHITECTURE

an alternative to Marcel's equation: if a church is, as Proust states, a work of art (in addition to being the literal structure housing works of art, a treasure-house of frescoes, etc.), then the subject matter of *A la recherche* is art (and history is art, and music is history is art . . .). But what does architecture have to do with self? And what do the two of them have to do with subject and structure? While these questions seem endless, the entire "Overture" plays them out in narrative and dream sequences so that the reader, before he begins Book I proper, learns to read in one subject the language of another. In other words, the reader learns to translate one art form into another,[12] much as Swann, in order to remember Vinteuil's sonata, had to transform music into architecture.

> He was able to picture to himself its [the music's] extent, its symmetrical arrangement, its notation, the strength of its expression; he had before him that definite object which was no longer pure music, but rather design, architecture, thought, and which allowed the actual music to be recalled. (I, 160)

For Swann, memory must "toil to lay down firm foundations," to make "facsimiles," albeit *in materia* of something "fleeting, fugitive," and insubstantial. Swann's translation is richly suggestive. But perhaps, for the moment, it is enough to point out that such translation enables preservation and recall; that "design, architecture, thought" become equivalent parts of a new equation, perhaps suggesting something about the matrix of memory and the patterning of impressions; and that "extent," "arrangement," "notation," and "strength" qualify the plastic, dimensional potential of thought as well as the structure of architecture. Translation here, then, involves not only a change from one art into another but also a corresponding change of sense from the audible to the visible and palpable.

In the "Overture," however, the narrator is less explicit; and description, even suggestion, do the service of analytic inquiry. The first and primary relationship that "self" establishes is with architecture, not yet the church at Combray, but the bedroom, its structure and the placement or displacement of furniture. The opening equation, at least between self and architecture, becomes manifest as a kind of exchange or metaphorical equivalence between self and room: both share the experience of sleep and unconsciousness; and Marcel himself figures as a piece of the furniture surrounding him. Marcel savors "in an instantaneous flash of perception, the sleep which lay heavy upon the furniture, the room, the whole surroundings of which I formed but an insignificant part and whose unconsciousness I should very soon return to share" (I, 4). Sleep and death are both unconsciousness, as if unconsciousness were the general condition whence Marcel came and to which he shall return, while consciousness–life–is but a brief interruption. Proust implies here that the perceiving and narrating self at this interval between sleep and waking resides nowhere, is neither in nor identical with the body (which is part of the room). Marcel's experience, itself narratively muted, is produced almost percussively, as if a shotgun should explode a soft, white magician's balloon: Marcel's sleepy, innocuous description is a "flash of perception." The experience asks to be registered and stored by the reader if he wishes to know, by the end of the "Overture," what the architecture of rooms and descriptions of self have to do with each other and with literature.

The first task of awakening–its connotations are intended—is, strangely enough, the task of locating oneself spatially or architecturally; for, contingent upon external physical context, is identity of self. Shelved into his narrative strata is Marcel's explanation: "And when I awoke at midnight, not knowing where I was, I could not be sure at first who I was" (I, 5). "Place," and place memory, provide definition; and expectedly, place comes to express what it had defined, self, ego, identity. Place comes to be room for self and condition of self; and knowledge of place is knowledge of extent, how much space is filled or occupied by the self, where in place-space the self ends and other begins. The reader learns that domestic architecture, like a new double-duty litmus paper, registers and characterizes individual consciousness and the parallel consciousness of civilization. No knowledge of self ("not being") is an "abyss"; rudimentary knowledge is a "cave dwelling"; Marcel's self-knowledge is a French bedroom; and visual recall of past bedrooms enables Marcel to "put together by degrees the component parts of my ego" (I, 5).

As Marcel revisits his memory-rooms, an organic body-memory comes to aid his struggling mind:

> And even before my brain . . . had collected sufficient impressions to enable it to identify the room, it, my body, would recall from each room in succession what the bed was like, where the doors were, how daylight came in at the windows, whether there was a passage outside, what I had had in my mind when I went to sleep, and had found there when I awoke. (I,5)

From these memory-rooms, Marcel discovers feelings of that particular self who slept there and the relationship he had established with the outside world. Body recalls in an order: what→where→how→where→what, from physical-room to mind-room; the final sequence moves from space to access to contents. This approximates the order to consciousness: space→contrast ("form" that is "in," "out," "center," "edge")→perception (seeing – the physical act requires contrast; *form* in fact comes from the Indo-European word meaning "to sparkle, gleam," while *idea* comes from a word meaning "to see")→conception (making of models, screening out or particularizing)→consciousness.[13] The self figures as the "heart" of these body-rooms, bed as a nest fashioned from those fragments of furniture and room appropriate to that time, that place, that age, season, and mood. One such nest, for instance, is built from "the corner of [his] pillow, the top of [his] blankets, a piece of shawl, the edge of [his] bed, and a copy of the evening paper" (I, 6). Marcel has concocted from fragments which remain discrete and identifiable a protective whole, just as Degas deliberately broke from traditions of pictorial composition, cutting-off and framing a partial scene which suggests that there is more outside, that the artist who grabs only a corner of the whole does so to show not only fragment and whole, but the selection itself as it reveals his private vision of himself in relationship to the outside world.[14] These remembered rooms, for Marcel and for the reader, come to signify, then, not only character but the shaping mind of the artist. The reader learns to read back from "structure" to "subject."[15]

Proust, however, does more than establish a deductive, contingent relationship (from room to mind): he posits an identity of sorts. The mind, like the liquid poured into a container, assumes the room's shape:[16] Marcel recalls a "room in which my mind, forcing itself for hours on end to leave its moorings, to elongate itself upwards so as to take on the exact shape of the room"; he succeeds in "filling [the room] with my own personality until I thought no more of my room than of myself" (I, 7, 8). In this way, perhaps, rooms as literary structures—even *A la recherche*'s Gothic cathedral—release as much information about the nature (the *shape*) of the artist's mind and his vision as do explicit statements or oblique references to the writer's craft. And, in the sense that "vision" or a particular subjective way of perceiving the world constitutes, for Proust, literary "style,"[17] then structure and style, form and language, also come together in an architectural image. At last Marcel makes it clear. The furniture Marcel's grandmother prefers, that "in which could still be discerned a flourish, a brave conceit of the past," was "as charming to her as one of those old forms of speech in which we still see traces of a metaphor whose fine point has been worn away by the rough usage of our modern tongue." The analogy is explicit: George Sand's pastoral novels are structured as rooms, and filled with the furniture of language:

In precisely the same way the pastoral novels of George Sand . . . were regular lumber-rooms of antique furniture, full of expressions that have fallen out of use and returned as imagery, such as one finds now only in country dialects. And my grandmother had bought them in preference to other books, just as she would have preferred to take a house that had a gothic dovecot, or some other such piece of antiquity as would have a pleasing effect on the mind, filling it with a nostalgic longing for impossible journeys through the realms of time.

(I, 31)

Thus for Proust concepts which seem primarily architectural, such as those of structure, space, shape, furniture, take on a literary suggestiveness as well. To know either "structure" or "subject," "room" or "self," is to know both sides of the equation, is to know the work of art. The reader may enter, with Marcel, the rooms of the past – the "vast structures of recollection" – and read therein those "subjective signs," the furniture which the artist has placed there. So, too, may the reader enter that public Gothic cathedral of *A la recherche* and find, in its innumerable carvings, the artist's private vision, multiple individual worlds. When Marcel suggests that all real knowledge, indeed all true perception of the Platonic essences of things, involves extension (projection) and penetration[18] – from self "imprinted" onto furniture and walls, back into self, symbolic forms and sense impressions – he also makes certain that the reader will be able to penetrate minds, especially the mind of the artist, by imaging those minds in terms of spatial extension, as architectural form.

29

The imperfect, worn image in stone
registers and preserves the vision
of the Gothic craftsman. Ruskin gives
to Proust an appreciation of such
"rude" and expressive carvings.
Proust writes, "It is the very form
of that syntax, stripped of all
covering, made honorable and lovely
by his keen yet ever sensitive chisel,
that moves us." Here "syntax"
suggests that Proust is speaking not
of architectural carving
but of literary architecture.

THREE

Language and Architecture

> Cathedrals are an original expression
> of French genius.
>
> MARCEL PROUST

*

> As for ices (for I hope that you won't
> order me one that isn't cast in one
> of those old-fashioned moulds which have
> every architectural shape imaginable),
> whenever I take one, temples, churches,
> obelisks, rocks, it is like an illus-
> trated geography-book which I look at
> first of all and then convert its
> raspberry or vanilla monuments
> into coolness in my throat. . . . I set my
> lips to work to destroy, pillar after
> pillar, those Venetian churches of por-
> phyry that is made with strawberries,
> and send what I spare of them crashing
> down upon the worshippers. Yes, all
> those monuments will pass from their
> stony state into my inside which throbs
> already with their melting coolness.
>
> MARCEL PROUST
> (Spoken by ALBERTINE)

PROUST PUTS INTO the mouth of Albertine literary language abused. Coming in the course of Marcel's apprenticeship to art, the naive narrator feels only unease at Albertine's speech, but his response, if insufficient, is nonetheless an instructive beginning. Albertine's request is "too well expressed" for conversation. She fills her speech with "images so 'written,' which seemed to me reserved for another, more sacred use, of which I was still ignorant" (II, 468). What confuses Marcel is his own complicity in Albertine's new eloquence: he is flattered to think that he is exerting an influence upon her, and given his own lack of literary accomplishment, he overlooks her extravagances in the hope that these image flourishes prove her love.

To the Proust who wrote a series of *Figaro* essays on behalf of threatened French churches ("In Memory of a Massacre of Churches"), and who assiduously and lovingly translated John Ruskin's *Bible of Amiens* and *Sesame and Lilies*,[19] Albertine's violations are more serious than Marcel, at once her jailer and her captive, can perceive. Albertine slays two arts in the name of eloquence: literature and an art no less sacred – architecture. And, as a final act of cunning, Proust has Albertine come to grief on the very trope that he and Marcel as artist solicit for exactly opposite purposes: architecture as metaphor for great literary art. Rather than an ice which melts, architecture, as an art of stone and marble, preserves and endures. It is an apt metaphor for one who admires literary style of old; in "Days of Reading," Proust's reverence replaces Albertine's rapacity:

> Something of the pleasure that one finds in sauntering through a town like Beaune, which has kept intact its fifteenth century Hospital, with its well, its wash-house, its vaulted and panelled rooms with their painted beams, its high gabled roof pierced with dormer windows below a fretted covering of hammered lead (all of them things that a vanished epoch has . . . left behind it; things that belonged to it alone . . .) one can

still feel ... in wandering through a Racine tragedy or a volume of Saint-Simon. For they contain all the lovely forms of a vanished manner of speech, such as preserves the memory of customs or of fashions in feeling that exist no longer, persistent traces of a past which nothing now resembles, but whose colour the obliterating passage of time can still revive.[20]

If Proust jests by sliding bad style–strawberry ices– into Albertine's mouth (for, to Marcel's delight, did she not "hold him there ... whenever she spoke his name"?), he also casts Albertine as a kind of gluttonous iconoclast–a destroyer of churches.

Proust is able to imply much in this incident of light humor. In the character of Albertine, Proust indicts a subjectivity which only internalizes as Albertine ingests, unable to offer forth subjective experience in the unselfish service of communication and art. Whereas Albertine levels a Venice of ice, Marcel releases or springs from the flavor of his tea and madeleine the whole of Combray. It appears that the artist must recognize as necessary but limited these internalizations, either Albertine's subjective sensation or Marcel's involuntary memory.[21] The artist must then labor to penetrate the subjective impression much as he must learn to see behind outward sensuous signs; for all experience, even the memory re-creation of Combray, must release the reason it produces joy or sadness before it can be converted into art. Only then can the artist express as metaphor–that "indescribable bond of an alliance of words"–the results of his internal excavations, metaphors as delicate as those carved images preserved in Gothic cathedrals (II, 1015). The conversion into art thus has two steps: from matter or feeling is extracted *dematerialized* or spiritualized "essences"; essences are then "imprisoned" in metaphors.[22] Albertine, at best, accomplishes only the first, literally decomposing a solid; but even then, hers is Proust's joke, a labor of jaws and digestive juices. In Albertine's world of ices, Proust condemns the misreading of art (architecture) as sensuous "signs" or "hieroglyphics" and the subsequent misuse of those sensuous signs in which there is no effort at real penetration.[23] The indictment is not only of an end-stopped subjectivism; it is also of the concomitant expressive–stylistic and literary–inadequacies. Albertine's inadequate vision and understanding, her denial of the two-fold, internal and external, nature of art and experience, likewise courts misused images which confuse external with internal and capture the essence of neither. Proust, however, finds that architecture performs a dual function, and it is partly for this reason that he selects it as the art analogue of literature. The cathedral's carved images may preserve the artist's private vision; but the building itself is not primarily referential, a vision of something else, as is the art of painting. Therefore, although Proust accepts painting as an analogue for literary style (which he defines as "subjective vision"), painting is insufficient for literary art as a whole. Proust distinguishes and praises literature as an art form capable of discovering and constituting truths, not only those of internal or private perception, but also those non-referential truths which actually "constitute the real essence of life" and are thereby universal, public, and accessible.[24] The images of architecture–a church, a room–may give to their particular literary worlds ideas of a complex, existential reality, which is relevant to the reader's experience of these worlds in several ways.

MARCEL PROUST

Comprehensively, the architectural images can seem virtually equivalent to a novel in its formal aspect—as a constructed entity, as a determinate, articulated object of the mind; an object which, even though purely ideal, seems independent of individual, subjective apprehension. The images of architecture can, at the same time, suggest the opposite idea of existential reality, which is no less complex and no less important to the experience of a literary world—that is to say, an idea of interiority, radically subjective, utterly peculiar to individuals; either the interiority of characters in a novel or the visionary authorial presence itself; Proust and, as we shall see, Henry James are among its denominations. Analogous to literary art, architecture can embrace and subsume these experiential and aesthetic possibilities, juggling each without ever demanding from readers or artists belief in one and repudiation of another. That architecture is out there, in the physical world, occupying and seizing space, flatters the expansiveness of minds and art worlds so small in their literal space extensity but so immense and space hungry in their capacity to conceive and invent.

The architectural analogue Proust finds so serviceable to literary art preserves, in its relative immunity to destruction, at least two strains of time. In the stones of architecture, which are to Proust "living thoughts," there shows "not only the light of a particular moment as it struck the surface; but the colours of the centuries as well."[25] In this statement, culled from the principles of Ruskin, Proust has distinguished the artist's carved image (particular light) from architecture's material (the centuries' colors). For Proust, the image and the material

LITERARY ARCHITECTURE

have separate life histories in which there exists only a one-way contingency and identification: the artist's image cannot exist without its material embodiment, whereas the material has a history predating its emergence as architectural form. And Proust, like Ruskin before him, cautions the artist not to "mutilate" the stone itself, for, as Proust translates Ruskin,

> there is history in them [the stones] . . . and in all their veins and bones and flame-like stainings . . . they write various legends, never untrue, of the former political state of the mountain kingdom to which they belonged, of its infirmities and fortitudes, convulsions and consolidations, from the beginning of time.[26]

Proust had discovered from Ruskin and then proclaimed for himself in his architectural essays and prefaces to the Ruskin translations, that cathedrals, with their two-fold geological and aesthetic lessons, are "books to be read," "written in a solemn language whose every character is a work of art."[27] In his literary essays, as in *A la recherche*, Proust simply takes Ruskin's coupling of architecture and literature and reverses the analogical relationship: books are built cathedrals, still to be read. But it is to Proust's advantage to preserve, in this exchange, the dual nature of architectural history or time. In so doing, he is able to present a notion of literature which distinguishes language as thought–particular carved images–from language as material–stones of old.

> A Racine tragedy, a volume of the Memoirs of Saint-Simon are gracious things the like of which we have not with us now. The language in which they have been carved by great artists, with a freedom that brings out its soft gleam, and sets its native force a-leaping, moves us like the spectacle of certain marbles

now used no longer, but which once the artist worked in. Doubtless, in some of these old edifices the stone has faithfully preserved the craftsman's very thought, but also, thanks to him, the stone itself, of a species unknown today, has been preserved for us, clothed in all the colours which the master could draw from it, could bring to the eye, and set in harmonious order. It is the living syntax of seventeenth century France—and of customs and manners of thought now dead—which we love to find in Racine's lines. It is the very form of that syntax, stripped of all covering, made honourable and lovely by his keen, yet ever sensitive, chisel, that moves us, familiar though we are with its every oddity, its every daring turn, and whose concentrated design we see pass like a swift dart of light, or hang fire in beautiful, broken rhythms, in the gentlest and most tender passages.[28]   [See Plate 29]

With grace and subtlety, in an argument for preserving and revering the "old" literature of Racine and Saint-Simon, Proust has employed in his service a metaphor even older than the seventeenth century. Proust's trope reconverted from Ruskin—syntax as stone—is itself classical in origin. Thus Proust recalls the literary past and, in so doing, revives the rhetorical tradition which bequeathed notions of good literary style to the modern world.[29] Yet in this instance, even preservation is not enough for Proust: architecture, as analogue, in fact defies mutability and death. The image he ordinarily uses to elucidate a literature which records age—the passage of time—and does the office of memory, Proust uses here to suggest time immutable and its new but necessary handmaiden, forgetfulness.

It is these forms of language, wrested from the past, that are offered to our eyes as might some ancient and unruined city. In their presence we feel the same sort of emotion as when we

LITERARY ARCHITECTURE

find ourselves confronted by certain architectural shapes, they, too, outmoded, which we can admire only in such rare and magnificent examples as have been bequeathed to us by the past that fashioned them: city walls, castle keeps and towers, the baptisteries of churches, the little cemetery close to the cloister or beneath the charnel-house at Aitre, which dreams in the hot sun, forgetful, under its butterflies and flowers, of the Funerary Urn and the Lantern of the Dead.[30]

Among the gifts of language made explicit by its architectural analogue are the notions of spatial extension with its variant, also spatial, enclosure. Like Marcel's reconstructed bedrooms of old, these may suggest the qualities or special dimensions of the writer's mind. But more strikingly, language may be hermetically sealed, preserving what is inside. Thus, much as the rooms of Marcel's aunt's house in *A la recherche* function as synaesthetic repositories or depots, sealing in "air saturated with a bouquet of silence," so, too, language may enclose a silence of synaesthetic richness. In *Days of Reading*, Proust writes languorously:

> But it is not only the single phrases that give us the very shape and contour of vanished minds. Between the phrases – I am thinking now of ancient books that, originally, were recited – in the intervals that separate them, as in some inviolate shrine, filling the interstices of stone, there lies for us today a silence as old as all the ages.... I seem to hear the silence of the speaker pausing before beginning to intone the following verses.... That silence fills the pause in the phrase which, though broken to make room for the canticle, still keeps its form. More than once as I read it, it has brought to me the perfume of roses drifting through the open window and spreading through the lofty room where the Assembly sat. Though two thousand years have passed, that perfume has not evaporated.[31]

MARCEL PROUST

Proust is able to preserve and evoke, through his architectural analogue, the vestiges of an oral tradition impossible to record in its precise particularity. As architectural space can be defined by its antithesis, enclosing structure or *not-space*, so by a kind of imaginative reversal afforded by the image of space and walls, Proust presents silence and is able to infer its antithesis, sound. Proust's is a definition by opposition. While in this instance stones, as architectural/linguistic materials, separate or distinguish space, in other situations they unite or connect what is already separate. In his discussions of Racine and Flaubert, Proust reveals his fascination with modes of connection, and in his so doing, these essays of literary criticism suggest paradigms for Proust's own style in *A la recherche*. Proust writes:

> Racine's most famous lines have become celebrated because they can produce this sense of delight by reason of a familiar piece of linguistic daring which stands like a dangerous bridge between two gently-rounded banks. "Je t'aimais inconstant, qu'aurais-je fait fidèle?"[32]

Racine's structural "bridge" finds a kind of parallel in Flaubert:

> But if Flaubert took pleasure in such phrases, it was not, I need scarcely point out, because of their correctness, but because, by setting the root of a flying arch fast in the heart of one statement, and letting its other end touch earth in the middle of another, they guaranteed a narrow and closed continuity of style.[33]   [See Plate 24]

Proust's own "linguistic daring" likewise involves connection, and turns upon the architectural image of enclosure. Marcel, in *A la recherche*, writes, "The writer must strive to imprison forever in a single phrase the two separate terms of the experience" (II, 1009). That single phrase, the metaphor, connects; but in so doing, it preserves the distinctness of each term.[34] The metaphor can do this because it comprises the "essences" of "the two separate terms of the experience," essences which are similar and extractable without threat to the terms themselves.

> Truth will begin only when the writer takes two different objects, establishes their relationship—analogous in the world of art to the sole relationship in the world of science, the law of cause and effect—and encloses them in the necessary rings of a beautiful style, or even when, like life itself, comparing similar qualities in two sensations, he makes their essential nature stand out clearly by joining them in a metaphor, in order to remove them from the contingencies of time, and links them together with the indescribable bond of an alliance of words.
> (II, 1008–1009)

Proust, or rather Marcel as writer, has come full circle. The final declaration of style throws into full relief those stylistic sins which Albertine had formerly committed but which Marcel could only recognize at the end of *A la recherche*. Albertine's earlier metaphors of architectural ices were based on conversion, not upon extraction, of the "essential nature" of two objects or two sensations: "Yes," Albertine had said, "all those monuments will pass from their stony state into my inside which throbs already with their melting coolness" (II, 468). The churches she "crashes down upon the worshippers" are the linguistic churches Marcel has come to cherish. The similarity between architecture and ices is coincidental and arbitrary; it is beautifully metaphoric and does not reveal anything about their "similar qualities" except that both, or all three—architecture, ices, and language—can be destroyed or, to use Proust's term, "massacred," if they are misused and abused. Clearly Proust's sympathies go with "The Churches Saved," his lament with Albertine, with "Death Comes to the Cathedrals."[35]

30
Literary architecture as a gathering device.
The whole town of Combray and all its residents
seemed to gather at the Church.
(Notre-Dame d'Amiens)

FOUR

Memorial Architecture

> We may live without [architecture]
> and worship without her, but
> we cannot remember without her.
>
> JOHN RUSKIN

*

> We have slept too long, we no longer
> exist.... But then from the highest
> heaven the goddess Mnemotechnia bends
> down and holds out to us in the formula
> "the habit of ringing for our cup
> of coffee" the hope of resurrection.
>
> MARCEL PROUST

MARCEL'S TRIBUTE to the goddess Mnemotechnia constitutes Proust's charge against her.[36] In his complex critique of memory, "habit" and the *technics* of voluntary memory are Proust's Janus-faced twins, friends to a practical, functioning life but enemies to an art of imagination and truth. To Proust, it is only in those moments when the controls of habit and memory are in abeyance, when they have not yet adjusted him to the conditions of the world, that "we can have before us ... a truth composed of different realities among which we imagine that we can choose, as among a pack of cards" (II, 464). Dreams, accidents, sudden assaults on the senses—all experiences in which habit and memory have not time to intervene—enable the artist to perceive new truths or to re-create a past freed from the contingencies of time (memory), reconstituted in the present and inseparable from it.

Proust's charge against Mnemotechnia is carefully couched in the language of praise, and for good reason. Because moments of involuntary memory, perception of essences, "are too rare for the work of art to be composed wholly of them" (II, 1015), Marcel expressly will write as he has lived—in Time. And Mnemotechnia is a goddess not only of memory (time past) but of method (technia): she offers a way of remembering and recording the passage of time and is therefore integral to the formal structuring of *A la recherche*, its narrative patternings of association, and the recalling of a different sort of past, one defined as relative to the present. Thus despite Proust's aesthetic hierarchy which relegates to second place memory and time, in deference to a past "*sine materia, sine tempore*," Proust is careful to retain the method or device bequeathed by his goddess—architecture as model. Like its classical predecessor, Proust's architectural device stimulates and structures memory, helping Proust to reconstruct time past as fiction and helping Marcel to reconstruct it as history, sensation, and thought. Proust's book presents places or buildings, people, and art as the elemental images of Marcel's memory system, which distinguishes them architecturally, as cathedral or house (*loci*), statues (*imagines agentes*), and pictures or frescoes (*notae*). Marcel's recreation of Combray is a paradigm of memory's dependency upon the architectural stimulus: no other art form "keeps in dependence on it a whole section of my inmost life as does the memory of those aspects of the steeple of

Combray" (I, 50). But architecture not only initiates and aids recall; it actually provides the image for the memory process itself, that "vast structure of recollection," raised from the "ruins of the past." Marcel observes:

> My memory need only find in it [any church steeple] some dim resemblance to that dear and vanished outline [Combray] and . . . [I can be found] standing still on the spot, before that steeple . . . trying to remember, feeling deep within myself a tract of soil reclaimed from the waters of Lethe slowly drying until the buildings rise on it again. (I, 51)

Reminiscence shares the architectural analogue with Marcel's book-as-art; in this way, reminiscence itself becomes an analogue of literary art.[37] Involuntary memory, being extra-temporal, is the analogue of metaphor and is thus in service to art. Marcel's final image of his book as cathedral, by incorporating memory or reminiscence, suggests how the architectural analogue becomes literary architecture: the book builds a memory system and stocks it while actually recording the building process. The book therefore finally produces and enables Marcel's reminiscence, hence his art. But since the book *is* his art, to produce, in this case, is also to constitute: the book *is* what it produces. Thus the paradox works; and only at the end of *A la recherche* can Marcel begin to write.

One of the first principles of the artificial memory system is that reminiscence, requiring a starting "place," may profitably use the childhood home and thereby gain access to "all those things which were raised in it."[38] Within the overall scheme of *A la recherche*, Marcel's childhood Combray functions as his starting place; but if this memory system is to work, it must presume that ideas or images–the objects of memory–cling in some way to place. When, at the end of *A la recherche*, Marcel puts into operation his system, seeking to recall the women in his life, he proclaims as inseparable memory of person (object) and of place. In the course of his description, Marcel also distinguishes dream-places from memory-places. His brief discourse is worth repeating in its entirety.

> In the case of the women I had come to know, this setting [place] was at least double. Each of them stood out prominently at a different point in my life, rising like a protecting local deity, first, from the midst of one of those dream-world landscapes which, side by side, made a checkerboard of my life and in which I had become fond of imagining her; secondly, seen with the eyes of memory in the setting where I had come to know her, which she recalled to me by fixed association – for even though our life be a roving one, our memory is sedentary and, no matter how ceaselessly we may rush about, our recollections, riveted to the places from which we tear ourselves away, continued to lead their stay-at-home existence there, like the temporary friends a traveller makes in a town and has to abandon when he leaves because it is there that they, who do not go away, will end their journey and their lives, as if he were still there, by the church, before the door, under the trees of the promenade. (II, 1081–1082)

And it is thus that Marcel recalls Gilberte, as a shadow "before a church in the Ile de France" (II, 1082). There exists, it seems, a curious reciprocity between place and memory: place triggers or yields remembering and remembering yields place. Likewise, the memory process, in which recollections of people retain an imaged fixity, functions to throw into relief time's changes. Partly for this reason, at the *coup de théâtre* of the final book, Marcel mistakenly thinks his aged friends are in masquerade costume, so bizarre are the expressions of time passing in comparison with Marcel's remembered images. If any evolution or change of these memory-images is possible, that change reveals a flaw in the memory process: change "is at the mercy of our forgetfulness" (II, 1071).

Since memories lead this "stay-at-home existence," so, too, the evocative power of memory, such as the "spell" of the Guermantes mansion, cannot "be carried over into another setting [as] memories cannot be divided into sections" (II, 985). Within the formal structure of the book, as within individual reminiscences, place thus grows into emblematic stature, fixed and inviolate. Specific buildings stand for and enable recall of entire towns: "Combray at a distance . . . was no more than a church epitomizing the town, representing it, speaking of it and for it to the horizon" (I, 37). The building becomes a kind of gathering device, and Marcel is able to introduce virtually all the people of Combray, with their genealogies, and all the events and thoughts occurring there, through his intricate description of the church.[39] [See Plate 30] Likewise, evocation of a church, as in the instance of Balbec, enables Marcel to give to the town "its place in the order of the centuries," its historical and aesthetic classification which, without the church's "stored consciousness of the romanesque epoch," the town and people would have lacked (I, 294). Here again, however, Proust plays with reciprocal evocations: for just as church recalls town, so town brings to mind church. Furthermore, into this system of recall, Proust introduces another triggering device for memory: words as place names. Like the classical art of memory which formed images for words and placed those images as paintings or art-objects inside architectural structures, that from the images words might be recalled, so Marcel

157

LITERARY ARCHITECTURE

connects images and words as tools not only for recollection, but also for explanation or definition. This architecturally based memory device, with its classical ancestry, is striking; Proust presents it with ease, enriches it by a modern, even mundane, setting:

> Words present to us little pictures of things, lucid and normal, like the pictures that are hung on the walls of schoolrooms to give children an illustration of what is meant by a carpenter's bench, a bird, an ant hill. . . . But names present to us—of persons and towns which they accustom us to regard as individual, as unique, like persons—a confused picture, which draws from the names, the brightness or darkness of their sound, the colour in which it is uniformly painted, like one of those posters, entirely blue or entirely red, in which, on account of the limitations imposed by the process used in their reproduction, . . . are blue or red not only the sky and the sea, but the ships and the church and the people in the streets.[40]
>
> (I, 296)

From his discourse "Place Names: the Name," Marcel proceeds to "Place Names: the Place," in which "certain names of towns, Vézelay or Chartres, Bourges or Beauvais, serve to indicate, by abbreviation, the principal church of the town" (I, 500). The causal memory sequence itself—name to image, name to church to town—makes it possible for Marcel to form emblems or equations in which that causality ceases to be necessary as the linking device between name, church, and town. The colon in "Place Names: the Name" and "Place Names: the Place," signifies the new equivalence between name and place which Marcel carefully describes:

> The partial acceptation [of town name as church], in which we are so accustomed to take the word, comes at length—if the names in question are those of places that we do not yet

158

know—to fashion for us a mould of the name as a solid whole, which from that time onwards, whenever we wish to convey the idea of the town—of that town which we have never seen—will impose on it, as on a cast, the same carved outlines, in the same style of art, will make of the town a sort of vast cathedral. (I, 500)

In his explanation of the emblem and of its construction, the narrator has subtly transposed memory devices into imaginative or fantasy devices. His painstaking qualifications which interrupt his descriptions—"if the names in question are those of places that we do not yet know" and "of that town which we have never seen"— make room not only for the operation of imagination as fantasy but for the more important operation of imagination as fiction. Syntax itself, that connective tissue of style, is the space-place for artistic freedom, that is, *context*. The built combination of words calls attention either to individual words as they need to be noticed or to the shape of the creator's mind which constructs out of the words of others a new, not habitual, way of perceiving the world (i.e., objects of old). The passage suggests then, not only how Marcel comes to imagine Venice and Saint Mark's before he goes there, but also how Proust as writer can construct, emblematically and descriptively, the fictional ("never seen") Combray with its fictional cathedral, Saint-Hilaire. Thus remembering constitutes fiction-making just as much as does fantasy, either of the not yet seen and historically real, or of the never seen. Memory and projection utilize the same memory and architectural devices because they both comprise art. Once again, Proust has defined art while describing process; but even more, he has defined art in such a way that it assumes what is for Proust its proper relationship to the "real," or "historical." Proust's counterpoint between the rhythms of the historical and the fictional, the real and the ideal, between Saint Mark's and Saint-Hilaire, Venice and Combray, is so loaded that the historical real is always less than its fictional analogue; for the latter enables and presents "truths" of creative perception, whereas the other can only be "described," with unavoidable distortion. Like all great visionaries, Proust must un-build the world and our conception of it in order to make room to show us how to see not the *is* but the *might be*, not that we walk in an imaginary world but that we remake our real world by a creative seeing of it. This is to abandon habit and convention (past) for the immediate and moving (unstatic). Syntax, as the linguistic space-place for arrangement of the new edifice built from old stone-words, is like *imagines*: imaginary churches are but the structured rearrangements of real churches, built from them, too; the benefit of these churches, like that offered by syntactical daring, is that they throw into relief what is. They change how we see, which is as close as we can get to changing what we see. This is an act of conserving rather than of replacing: the old monument remains, but comes to sit inside a larger whole, our newly constructed way of seeing, perceiving, conceiving. Within his inherited tradition, Proust's delicate critique of memory and her devices also constitutes his critique of contemporary realistic fiction with all its mimetic and imaginative inadequacies.

The literature that is satisfied merely to "describe things," to furnish a miserable listing of their lines and surfaces, is, notwithstanding its pretensions to realism, the farthest removed from reality, the one that most impoverishes and saddens us, even though it speak of nought but glory and greatness, for it sharply cuts off all communication of our present self with the past, the essence of which the objects preserve, and with the future, in which they stimulate us to enjoy the past again. (II, 1009)

So Marcel preserves the parallel between literature and memory. Realistic literature is like inadequate memory pictures; the one "lists lines and surfaces" while the other furnishes "façades" which seem to Marcel "only illustrations and not impressions" (II, 1069). While the analogues for poor literature and deficient memory devices are both architectural, they constitute only parts of architecture; what is noticeably absent from them is depth or spatial extension, that plastic, three-dimensionality necessary to an art which "penetrates" to truths.[41] But even more glaringly, a literature of realism "sharply cuts off all communication of our present self with the past" (II, 1009). The past and an art of truths are allies, sharing a whole architectural analogue, one preserving that three-dimensionality which distinguishes it from two-dimensional or surface arts such as painting. For all these reasons, the section titles Proust had rejected—"Porch," "Windows-in-the-Apse"—give way, in these sections at least, to titles no less architectural in substance ("Place-Names: the Name," "Place-Names: the Place") but formalistically and structurally far richer. These titles suggest those organizing architectural memory devices which Proust selects, the fictional process he believes in and uses, and the structure or order of evocations, either as memory or as fantasy, which he follows. By this memory system, the reader learns to supply the unstated half of any equation: for Combray he may read or recall Saint-Hilaire, for Saint-Hilaire, Com-

LITERARY ARCHITECTURE

bray. Thus the reader translates not only from one art to another, but from emblem to elaboration or substance, from general to particular, and back again. Above all, the reader translates from "many churches [to] one church," from many perspectives to the cathedral of many perspectives, *A la recherche* (II, 1114).

Within *A la recherche*, the architectural memory devices, when not elucidated as such, often pose as interart or art associations; therefore the emotional impetus a device may give to Marcel's—and the reader's—memory is masked by the richness of texture which the analogue gives to the text. When, for instance, the young Marcel first sees Françoise, she is compared to a statue:

> No sooner had we arrived in my aunt's dark hall than we saw in the gloom, beneath the frills of a snowy cap as stiff and fragile as if it had been made of spun sugar, the concentric waves of a smile of anticipatory gratitude. It was Françoise, motionless and erect, framed in the small doorway of the corridor like the statue of a saint in its niche. (I, 40) [Plate 31]

Françoise is no ordinary statue—statue as free-standing sculpture—but one of a particular sort: like those statues in the classical memory tradition, she is made vivid by her frame and by a striking or unusual feature, her spun-sugar cap. Still more important, she figures as a saint-statue in a cathedral, statues so carved and placed by medieval architects as to strike the worshippers forcibly as a symbol, that they recall a particular virtue or vice. While Proust knew, and discussed in his essays on Ruskin, that conscious tradition of Gothic craftsmanship,[42] in *A la recherche* he translates the tradition into an art simile which appears not once but many times,[43] thereby creating a continuity of imagery and the possibility of ordered

31
The Prince of Darkness
and Foolish Virgins:
West Portal, Strasbourg Cathedral.
This will recall for us
Proust's statues in niches
as narrative and memory devices.

recall. The playing-card king in the stained glass of Combray, Gilbert-the-Bad, the Abbots of Combray, the arms and crests of the Guermantes—all occur and recur as images, but function as memory devices to preserve and create order. These characters are surrounded not only by frames but by space, their syntax or context being what distinguishes them. Feeling flies across space; from a window the thrust can be made. Proust may in fact present us with the memory device as context or setting, but if so, it may slip, as simile or allusion, into the text itself. In Venice, for instance, the same "statue in a niche" imagery that distinguished Françoise not only serves to place Marcel's Mamma in a vivid and therefore memorable setting; but the image-ingredients of that setting are also transposed and made to seem part of his mother in the description of her smile.

> As soon as I called to her [Mamma] from the gondola, she sent out to me . . . a love which stopped only where there was no longer any material substance to support it on the surface of her impassioned gaze which . . . she tried to thrust forward to the advanced post of her lips, in a smile which seemed to be kissing me, in the framework and beneath the canopy of the more discreet smile of the arched window illuminated by the midday sun. (II, 822)

For these reasons, Marcel continues, "the window has assumed in my memory the precious quality of things that have had . . . their part in that hour that struck, the same for us and the same for them" (II,823). The window, whether recalled or seen as "a cast in a museum" says " 'I remember your mother so well' " (II,822–823). The window is at once place and space, access; and its shape mimes the shape of his mother. Recall thus remains rooted to contexts which illuminate as much as their contents, but which may exist for Marcel, as for the reader, in "antipodal regions of my past memories" (II, 1070). Reconstruction of a memory whole–a whole retaining its fragmentary nature but not dissolving into disunity–depends upon recall of image and context. Somewhat like the art lover who "is shown a panel of an altar screen" and by remembering "in what church, museum, and private collections the other panels are dispersed," can "reconstruct in his mind the predella and the entire altar," the writer Marcel and his ideal reader can each reconstruct out of the many volumes and scenes stored in his memory the whole of *A la recherche*. But it is a whole which, like the Gothic cathedral, preserves its past and the beauty and individuality of its parts.

IV
THE ARCHITECTURE OF FICTION: HENRY JAMES

A great building is the greatest conceivable work of art because it represents difficulties annulled, resources combined, labour, courage, and patience.

Henry James

*

The best kind of criticism is that which springs from the liveliest experience. There are hundreds of labels and tickets, in all this matter, that have been pasted on from the outside and appear to exist for the convenience of the passer-by; but the critic who lives *in* the house, ranging through its innumerable chambers, knows nothing about the bills on the front. He only knows that the more he is able to record, and that the more he is saturated, poor fellow, the more he can give out. His life, at this rate, is heroic, for it is immensely vicarious.

Henry James

32
The shop of the mind.
I give to this photograph, the frontispiece
to *The Golden Bowl* I (New York Edition, 1909),
the name Henry James gave to it; in fact,
it is titled "The Curiosity Shop."

ONE

The Prefaces: James's Architecture of the Past

> There is the story of one's hero, and then, thanks to the intimate connexion of things, the story of one's story.
>
> HENRY JAMES

TOWARDS THE END of his life, in honor of the commemorative New York Edition of *The Novels and Tales* (1907–1909), Henry James took occasion to confer upon his fiction what Proust, in the final pages of *A la recherche du temps perdu*, had called retrospective illumination.[1] In the form of eighteen jungle-dense prefaces, James's own *temps retrouvé* "encages and provides for" his past life of art, a recollection of the successive geneses, structures, successes, and shortcomings of his literary achievements. But James and Proust share more than a belief that literary form—its structure and unity—is "to be appreciated after the fact." In these prefaces, James narrates his own story, becoming a Marcel-like artist hero of sorts, making it possible for a reader to move from preface to novel or tale as if from one kind of art to another rather than simply from criticism to craft. In this sense, James's collected fiction includes its own tale of tales; as James recalls, then re-creates former states of mind—the special shapes of consciousness from which his fiction issues

LITERARY ARCHITECTURE

—the prefaces become a sort of paradoxical frame that seems to enclose and enter the picture at once.

Because these prefaces are among the most intricate rhetorical flourishes of the aged James, they often seem—to mix my metaphors for the moment—like the serpentine tail of James's fiction reentering that mouth of origin, as if James devours his own creations in endless tangles of self-reflection. The prefaces are, no doubt, convoluted; but they are less self-consuming than generative; and if we return to the inorganic metaphor which James himself selects—the house—I think that we can discover and describe a careful order and construction not only within the prefaces themselves but also in their relationship to James's fiction. Indeed, we can imagine the finely wrought prefaces as the house that James built to house his "houses of fiction"; and what might seem to be an infinite regress of houses within houses, like those forever shrinking houses in Edward Albee's *Tiny Alice*, is in fact finite, ordered according to a complicated spatial and temporal scheme. The prefaces represent the outermost house enclosing the remembered houses in which James wrote his fictions; James then images these fictions as houses which enclose still smaller ones, either those real or imaginary structures which locate and set action or those house-similes which represent the minds and psychological conditions of characters. While even this description defies simple visualization—and James, as if in an *Alice in Wonderland* world, complicates matters still more by tucking outdoor scenes inside—the description recurs, sometimes varied but always richly suggestive and illuminating, throughout James's work.

With our readings of Pater, Hopkins, and Proust in mind, we may go directly to James's architectural analogues and give them attention of a practical sort, a close, critical reading. We will notice immediately the time required to undo James's space-time constructions: James, like Hopkins, collapses normal syntactical distance such that our analysis requires making linear what in James occurs as the depth dimension of space. James does, however, direct us; and, like Marcel, he asks that we see through language as if it were transparent, not follow narrative roads. What occurs in James does so in the space between or behind words; even his signifying, his referring, are spatial activities.

In one preface after another, like a wakeful Marcel rereading his own story in the flickering light of his magic lantern, James conjures up the former houses of his muse: room after room appears, visions of Florence at the Piazza Santa Maria Novella, of New York's East 25th Street, of Boston, of Paris in the Rue de Luxembourg, of Riva degli Schiavoni, of London's Kensington, of Bad-Homburg in the Taunus hills, and many other places in Europe and America. Each scene, in each preface, is transformed according to a pattern of associative recall in which there are at least three and very often four time periods, what we may call frames: James begins by remembering (time frame 1) his rereading of one of his works; that rereading (2) stimulates recall, what James terms *revision*, of the place where and time when he wrote (3), which may in turn solicit recall of a still more distant past (4), one which clings with the tenacity of Proust's "stay at home memories" to the place (3) recalled. That place, as a physical and an aesthetic habitat (his "dwelling of the muse") re-creates and represents for James his particular consciousness at the time he wrote the works he rereads. These time frames are "synchronized," as James would say,[2] within the immediate or present preface-time by complex syntactical arrangements and by the power of his images. This synchronization accomplishes an important effect: while these preface passages describe, as content, past associations, the passages themselves are ordered according to the associations and the patterns which they describe. Thus James can rerender in the immediate (time frame 1) the activity or associative process described as occurring in time frames 2, 3, and 4: the associative pattern *recalled* therefore constitutes the associative pattern *recalling*, the prefaces themselves.

However synchronized these preface passages are, James carefully controls his verb tenses so that we can locate his images temporally. In James's preface to *Lady Barbarina and Other Tales*, we find time condensed and imaged as architectural structure. Rereading his tale "The Point of View" after thirty long years, James recovers his muse in "vanished" but nonetheless revisioned houses of consciousness.

> Only the little rounded composition ["The Point of View"] *remained*; which glowed, ever so strangely, like a swinging, playing lantern, with *light that brought out the past*. The past had been most *concretely* that vanished and slightly sordid tenement of the current housing of the muse. I had had "rooms" in it, and I could remember how the rooms, how the whole place, a nest of rickety tables and chairs, lame and disqualified utensils of every sort, and of smiling, shuffling, procrastinating persons of colour, had exhaled for me, to pungency, the domestic spirit of the "old South." I had nursed the unmistakeable scent; I had read history by its aid.... These complacencies of perception *swarmed* for me *again* – while yet *no brick* of the little old temple *of the revelation stood on another*.
>
> (P, 13) (italics mine)

HENRY JAMES

At its simplest, the passage describes what James remembered when he reread "The Point of View": where he had lived–"tenement" or "temple" "rooms" which, as we can discover elsewhere in the preface, were in Washington, D.C.–and of what he had been thinking when he wrote the tale. But even this paraphrase begins to betray some of the passage's complexities: that James uses at least two architectural metaphors (tenement and temple) to describe what we might think of as one place; and that the past he describes requires, even in our rerendering of it, at least two verb tenses. In fact, if we look at the time scheme alone, all four frames which I had described earlier punctuate this brief passage: (1) the present, preface-time; (2) the past ["'The Point of View' reread]; (3) the pluperfect, tenement ["I had had 'rooms' in it"]; (4) the "old South." Such a description forces into focus James's interest in temporal distancing; but his emphasis in this passage is less on time than on his processes of thinking and composing. While these processes occupy and respect their time frames, their more important feature is order: what activity stimulates what other activity. There are (at least) two processes described: to simplify matters,[3] we may think of one as the process recalled (it really exists in time frames 3 and 4) and the process recalling (which really exists in 1 and 2). The process recalled is this: the "slightly sordid tenement" stimulated recall of the "old South," each or both of which stimulated the composing of "The Point of View":

tenement→"old South"→(writing of) "The Point of View"

The preface passage adds to that process recalled a new initiating stimulus, rereading. The passage, that is the present one recalling, proceeds this way: rereading "The

Point of View" stimulates recall of the tenement, which stimulates a remembered stimulation (recall of the "old South"); in turn, that remembered stimulus initiates recall of composing "The Point of View." James then adds and subtracts something new, "the little old temple of the revelation" of which "no brick . . . stood on another":

rereading "The Point of View"→tenement→"old South"→ (writing of) "The Point of View" ± temple

The preface passage contains and subsumes the past process of association (in which architecture had recalled the past and each or both had stimulated literary creation), while the preface passage also re-presents that process in the present, as *description*. The difference between the preface process and the past process is that, in the first, literary art is the stimulus to memory and architecture, whereas in the second, architecture is the stimulus to memory and literary art. Architecture and literature each assume and share votive power: each evokes memory and each other; each—as Ruskin would proudly concur—"conquers forgetfulness."

If we look still further at the architectural images, we see that the "slightly sordid tenement" is time past (actually pluperfect) embodied spatially, that is, made concrete as architecture (which James as quickly dissolves into an architectural ephemeron, the literary "housing of the muse"). The "temple"[4] seems to be the "slightly sordid tenement" converted still once again; it is converted because James realizes, in remembering, the tenement's importance as a stimulus for recall ("old South") and for creating ("The Point of View"). But why does James say "temple of *the* revelation"? Does he have in mind only the particular revelation, the "old

South"? or does *the* alter the sentence flow, setting-off *revelation* so that we stumble over it and look again? James, it would appear, means to alert us to what he is doing in the preface: *revealing* to us not only the past, his consciousness at that time, and his former method of composing, but also his synchronous, or present, method which the preface passage represents. The passage is "the revelation" of James's literary method. James's description (past) and James's revelation (past and present) appear interchangeable if not identical; and we can appreciate still more why James, with perhaps the merest wink at his own rhetorical performance, rebuilds tenement into temple. But curiously, although James does bow or nod before the temple he creates, as if with a magic wand he also banishes it in his act of obeisance ("no brick of the little old temple of the revelation stood on another") all the while teasing us that these complicated memories are "complacencies of perception." In fact, James can emphasize the ambiguous disappearance of these quasi- or non-literary monuments (the "vanished" tenement and the temple of which "no brick . . . stood on another") because he has replaced them with a structure of a different sort: literary description, literary revelation. For James, describing and revealing come to constitute those aspects of literary activity which are most constructional, as if description and revelation are James's literary architecture.

In so brief but so dense a passage, James thus presents his revision of the past and of his own "complacencies of perception," that is, his own consciousness during that past, his own seeing through. The mention of James's consciousness should remind us of his famous pronouncement elsewhere in the prefaces, notably in the "house of fiction" passage from his preface to *The Por-*

trait of a Lady. There, while describing literary art by an architectural analogue, James boldly declares: if someone tells him "what the artist is," James will tell "of what he [the artist] has *been* conscious" (P, 46). As reader, James contends that he can do with the art of others what he does with his own: read backwards from the achievement, the literary/descriptive monument, to the mind of the artist. In his preface to "The Point of View" James performs that service. That his reading constitutes *re*-reading is therefore not manipulative; it is a device by which James tries to teach us how to read. In this he shares good company: like architectural theorists who instructed viewers to read from buildings to the minds of builders, James teaches readers to move from literary architecture – whether tenement, temple, or description, that is, the preface passage itself or "The Point of View" – to the consciousness of the literary architect. Reading becomes point-of-viewing, our placing of self that we might see. James asks that we regard language as *grounded*. The analogy between James's reading process and that process proposed by architectural theorists is far from incidental. James's *Notebooks* and travel literature document his impressive knowledge not only of architectural monuments, but also of architectural theory and theorists, among whom Ruskin is an acknowledged favorite.[5] The prefaces reproduce, in different literary form, James's understanding of the complex responses individuals were supposed to have to physical and literary architecture. As if he mastered to excellence the lessons of Ruskin and Pater, who encouraged viewers and in-dwellers to be susceptible to and transported by the intoxicating atmosphere of buildings and to read history in them, James reports in his preface to "The Point of

View" all these responses: how he had "nursed" the "unmistakeable scent" "exhaled" by the tenement; how he had "read history by its aid"; how his former perceptions had "swarmed again." James appreciates fully the associative, synaesthetic richness of response to architecture, a response which we have also seen so tantalizing to Pater, Hopkins, and Proust.

To move, then, from Proust to James is to take not a forward step but a side step. James's architectural analogue differs from Proust's in its practical application: his borders are smaller, more particular, appropriate to fictions which are individual structures, specific and limited – what we might think of as situational rather than encyclopedic. What we explore with James is altered focus. James does not advance literary architecture but he adjusts its extent so that it measures and constitutes exactly his perception of the world.

33
An English House.
From *The Portrait of a Lady* I
(New York Edition, 1907).
This is James's ideal
English country-house architecture.

TWO

"The House of Fiction"

LESS THAN twenty years separate the first publication of Walter Pater's essay "Style" from the appearance of Henry James's intricately mannered (what Pater might have called euphuistic[6] in its most positive sense) prefaces to *The Novels and Tales*. What had been a gentle but impressive plea in Pater's essay, for care in matters of literary style and structure—Pater's overture to literary architecture—comes to assume declarative power in the words of the man whose voluminous literary output, whose fiction and theory likewise honor and proclaim in simile and metaphor alike the value of architecture for literary art. In his preface to *The Portrait of a Lady*, Henry James builds fiction into a house of vast proportions but crafts it in detail, with care. The passage, although familiar, is worth quoting in full:

> The house of fiction has in short not one window, but a *million*—a number of possible windows not to be reckoned, rather; every one of which has been *pierced*, or is still pierceable, in its *vast front*, by the *need* of the *individual vision* and by the *pressure* of the individual *will*. These apertures, of *dissimilar shape and size, hang so, all together, over the human scene* that we might have expected of them a greater sameness of report than we find. *They are but windows at best, mere holes in a dead wall, disconnected, perched aloft; they are not hinged doors opening straight upon life*. But they have this mark of their own that *at* each of them stands a figure with a pair of eyes, or at least with a field-glass, which forms, again and again, for observation, a

unique instrument, insuring to the person making use of it an impression distinct from every other. He and his neighbors are watching the same show, but one seeing more where the other sees less, one seeing black where the other sees white, one seeing big where the other sees small, one seeing coarse where the other sees fine. And so on, and so on; there is fortunately no saying on what, for the particular pair of eyes, the window may *not* [*sic*] open; "fortunately" by reason, precisely, of this incalculability of range. *The spreading field, the human scene, is the "choice of subject"; the pierced aperture, either broad or balconied or slit-like and low-browed, is the "literary form"*; but they are, singly or together, as nothing without the posted presence of the watcher—without, in other words, the *consciousness of the artist*. Tell me what the artist is, and I will tell you of what he has *been* conscious [*sic*]. Thereby I shall express to you at once his boundless freedom and his "moral" reference.

(P, 46–47) (italics mine unless indicated otherwise)

The house James raises curiously suggests no building we have ever seen; and if we were to see it, it would be "ugly" by even Victorian standards.[7] Whereas Victorian architects of the eclectic school did claim to rationalize into an aesthetic whole architectural styles which, like James's many-styled windows, clashed and jarred, few would admit with pride to having "pierced" their building façades with a million "apertures" of which only the best were called windows, the others being "mere holes." But matters of style and taste aside, if we simply try to visualize, in all its dimensions, James's house of fiction, all we can conjure up is a fantastical façade with no structure behind it, much like those smaller and peculiarly desolate building-fronts which line the make-believe streets of old movie lots. If the façade is impossible as any real structure, is it nonetheless useful as a metaphor? And what, we might ask, is James's point in constructing it at all? Most façades hide or mask, and perhaps James's does, as well; but what is it hiding and from what? On one side is "the spreading field, the human scene," on the other the "watcher-artists" (may we say simply "life" and "artists"?); and the façade might mask or hide one from the other. But we still would be hard pressed to explain James's transparencies, the holes and windows which do not hide the "human scene" from the watcher-artists but enable them to watch. The façade, it seems, divides rather than masks, as if it were a barrier, more a Berlin wall than a fantasy movie-front. James declares: "it is a dead wall"; and no matter how he might try to beguile us into distraction by describing all the openings, apertures, holes, and windows, the dead wall bars direct intercourse between the voyeuristic watcher-artists and the human scene they observe. Even the windows are emphatically "disconnected, perched aloft"; they do not open "straight upon life." The façade-wall emphasizes how profoundly disengaged the artist is from participatory experience, from the human scene itself. Like the house, the watcher-artist is strangely disembodied, reduced from a "figure" rather abstract to begin with, to a "pair of eyes," much as the house is reduced to a house-face distinguishable only by its windows. Moreover, just as James carefully makes the windows more distanced than windows need be (disconnected, perched aloft), so he elaborates (as the scene they reveal) not a visual world most of us see, but an artificial, field-glass and camera world in which colors are drained into black or white, a world textured coarse or fine as if on grained photographic paper, and imaged in sizes which no normal eye-optics could produce, only the mechanical lenses of cameras and field-glasses.

LITERARY ARCHITECTURE

In detailing the "house of fiction," James provides us with important analogies and metaphors which help us to read his architecture, the house-settings and house-mind similes which spring up throughout the prefaces and throughout the particular novel-houses of his fiction. In a single sentence from this passage, James teaches us about the complexities of his craft:

> The spreading field, the human scene, is the "choice of subject"; the pierced aperture, either broad or balconied or slit-like and low-browed, is the "literary form"; but they are, singly or together, as nothing without the posted presence of the watcher—without, in other words, the consciousness of the artist.

"The spreading field, the human scene, is the 'choice of subject.'" James seems as clear, as simple and explicit in this definition as James can be. But even here, clarity is only a surface shimmer, and we can discover underneath it something of James's fiction-making process itself. In the briefest shift from "field" to "scene" James has moved from the natural to the composed, from the unlimited (open ground) to the limited (territory); only composed can that "field" be suitable for fiction, can it be the "subject" of fiction. We may describe the subject, then, as the "human" composed, no longer actively growing or spreading, but fixed, selected, chosen, closed. James accomplishes in less than a dozen words the transformation process which is his trademark, his chief concern as artist: he has transformed "life [which is] all inclusion and confusion [into] art [which is] all discrimination and selection" (P, 120). With the same deceptive facility, James defines literary form. It is "the pierced aperture, either broad or balconied or slit-like and low-browed." Already he has entered the realm of metaphor, explaining all those apertures he had been detailing earlier in the passage. Literary form is a forced opening in what we know to be a "dead wall." As shape, literary form can be wide and open or narrow and closed; but is the aperture a hole, a window (lifeless), or an eye (alive), or all three, what James describes elsewhere as "open-eyed windows"? In other words, in his definition of literary form has James combined window, eye, and the implied watcher-artist? It seems that he has. And already we are learning to read "windows" as "eyes," as points of view, as literary form. To James, then, "form" seems to be a *shape* or "frame"–it limits and encloses the subject, surrounds the scene, determines the scope–and a *position*, a distance or angle, a vantage point, what we more often think of as literary or narrative technique. By "broad" James can suggest that a frame is wide, expansive, of epic scope; and appropriately it may be "balconied," that is, it may view or render from above, lofty and elevated, heightening the scene-subject which the frame encloses. If the form is "narrow," James may be suggesting that the frame is small and particular, that the subject may be expressed in "low" form as comedy can be low, and that the author may stand "close" to his subject. So, too, James's window-as-eye-as-form may represent a way to distinguish the length of a novel from the brevity of a short story. Because James's concept of literary form suggests both shape and position–scope and authorial distance–it can include great varieties of fiction within it, the art of Homer or Proust, certainly that of James himself and even that of Joyce. The artist may be "far" from a "narrow" or limited subject, may "frame" it "broadly," and "magnify" it large; or he may be "close" to a "broad" subject and render it "fine," in detail.

LITERARY ARCHITECTURE

A third of the sentence yet remains: "they [the apertures? or the choice of subject and the literary form?] are, singly or together, as nothing without the posted presence of the watcher–without, in other words, the consciousness of the artist." James has finally declared who his watcher is and, in so doing, has rarefied him still further into "consciousness," the particular consciousness of the artist. That consciousness not only determines but fathers into being, crafts into form, literary art. James, in this passage, has read his literary architecture while he has built it: he has moved from the house of fiction–from house to windows to wall to individual to scene to literary subject to literary form–to the consciousness of the artist. His prefaces, by his own example, teach us how to read the particular images which fill his fiction. If we reverse the order, we can see how James views and accomplishes literary creation: he moves from consciousness to literary form to literary subject to scene to individual to wall to windows to house. The reader distills images into an understanding of mind; the artist issues forth from consciousness images, builds (out) from mind into literary art. We come to understand, reading this passage in which the house of fiction seems a great democratizer of sorts, that to James the act of seeing (as distinct from the act of participating) constitutes creating, fiction-making, processes which are unavoidably interpretative and subjective and which James generously celebrates. Is there for James a world but for our seeing of it?

THREE

Windows of Indirection: James's Narrative Techniques

> I have but to reread ten lines
> [of *The American*] to recall
> my daily effort not to waste time
> in hanging over the window-bar
> for a sight of the cavalry
> the hard music of whose hoofs so
> directly and thrillingly appealed.
> . . . I have ever, in general,
> found it difficult to write
> of places under too immediate
> an impression—the impression
> that prevents standing off and
> always allows neither space
> nor time for perspective.
>
> HENRY JAMES

JAMES'S RECOLLECTION of his struggle "not to waste time in hanging over the window-bar" while he writes *The American* is teasing and curious. If we think of James's house of fiction "watcher-artists," content to look through their windows at the "human scene," we wonder at his finding his own window view too close and too distracting, the view so thrilling and appealing that it is difficult for him not to waste time, let alone to write. James's description—of life's temptations and his efforts to assert self-control—seems to be a playful pretense of sorts; for the importance of the passage turns less on the felt tension between "life" and "work" than on James's revelation of the conditions or requirements for his art: he needs "space and perspective," even greater distance from his subject than the window affords.

James's own needs find expression in the techniques of his art. The literary methods embodied in his house of fiction metaphor mirror his own, but with one exception: James as artist does not sit at a window, rendering a scene. He watches his subject "through the successive windows of other people's interest" (P, 306). James calls his process—watching through other watchers—indirection;[8] and in defining it, he gives to the house of fiction new meaning. The metaphors which proliferate throughout the prefaces had pre-existed as images in his fiction and were born of those images. James describes, in the preface to *The Wings of the Dove*, how he presents Milly Theale.

I note how, again and again, I go but a little way with the direct—that is with the straight exhibition of Milly; *it resorts for relief, this process, whenever it can, to some kinder, some merciful indirection*: all as if to approach her circuitously, deal with her at second hand, as an unspotted princess is ever dealt with; the pressure all around her kept easy for her, the sounds, the movements regulated, the forms and ambiguities made charming. All of which proceeds, obviously, from [James's] *tenderness of imagination* about her, which *reduces him to watching her*, as it were, *through the successive windows of other people's interest in her*. So, if we talk of princesses, do the balconies opposite the palace gates, do the coigns of vantage and respect enjoyed for a fee, rake from afar the mystic figure in the gilded coach as it comes forth in the great place. *But my use of windows and balconies is doubtless at best an extravagance* by itself, and as to what there may be to note, of this and other *super-subtleties*, other *arch-refinements*, of tact and taste, of design and instinct, in *The Wings of the Dove*, I become conscious of overstepping my space without having brought the full quantity to light.

(P, 306) (italics mine)

James confirms our reading of the "windows and balconies" of his house of fiction: they are windows of revelation; and they tell us as much about James's literary form, his techniques as a writer of fiction, as they do about the subjects they frame, in this instance about Milly herself. Every time we read architectural descriptions in James–whether houses, rooms, windows, or balconies; whether Milly's Venetian palace, Ralph Touchett's Gardencourt, or Spencer Brydon's vacant New York house–we are asked to read about fictions as well. Literary fictions are as houses are and houses are like the forms of fiction.

James speaks of his use of windows and balconies as "merciful indirection," a literary technique issuing from his "kindness" and "tenderness" towards Milly Theale (who is, incidentally, modelled after William Dean Howells's "Minny Temple"!).[9] Why is James so kind to his dying princess? Is *The Wings of the Dove* like Ravel's *"Pavane pour une infante défunte"*? James's show of concern might win our respect; but what it conceals is James's pride in his own careful narrative achievement. James's kindness covers for him, freeing him to distinguish what he suggests we might otherwise overlook: his "supersubtleties," his "arch-refinements," those architectural devices in the service of narrative technique. Even in his puns, James offers pointers to his audience; once again, he tells us what to notice and how to read.

What James describes here as a "chosen" narrative

technique appears elsewhere to be unavoidable, to proceed not from James's kindness toward the fragile life he tries to render but from his fear of a participatory life. Once again, it is useful if we recall the "dead wall" of James's house of fiction; for just as it protects, so it makes impossible direct access from the world of watcher-artists to the "human scene." In his preface to *The Spoils of Poynton*, James declares that because the spoils—his "center of interest"—are "inanimate things," they "bar" him from presenting them directly. In other words, they do not have a life of their own but must be given life by being presented through a life. For this reason James states that he must create a watcher, Fleda Vetch,[10] who can express the "felt beauty" of the "splendid Things." But "things" are not always James's center of interest; in fact, they rarely are. And yet James invariably—even when his center of interest is the human scene—invents at least one watcher through whose "window of interest" James may peer. In the preface to *The Spoils*, James betrays and reveals other reasons for his literary "indirection"; and we come to realize that his retreat from window-views is more complicated—and more rich with implications for his art—than we might have thought. James writes of rereading *The Spoils* and describes his "revision" of his past, where and how he created this tale.

It [*The Spoils*] began to appear in April 1896, and, as is apt blessedly to occur for me throughout this process of revision, the old, the shrunken concomitants muster again as I turn the pages. They lurk between the lines; these serve for them as the barred seraglio-windows behind which, to the outsider in the glare of the Eastern street, forms indistinguishable seem to move and peer; "association" in fine bears upon them with its infinite magic. Peering through the lattice from without inward I recapture a cottage on a cliff-side, to which, at the earliest approach of the summer-time, redoubtable in London through the luxuriance of still other than "natural" forces, I had betaken myself to finish a book in quiet and to begin another in fear. The cottage was, in its kind, perfection; mainly by reason of a small paved terrace which, curving forward from the cliff-edge like the prow of a ship, overhung a view as level, as purple, as full of rich change, as the expanse of the sea. The horizon was in fact a band of sea; a small red-roofed town . . . clustered within the picture off to the right; while above one's head rustled a dense summer shade, that of a trained and arching ash, rising from the middle of the terrace, brushing the parapet with a heavy fringe and covering the place like a vast umbrella. Beneath this umbrella and really under exquisite protection *The Spoils of Poynton* managed more or less symmetrically to grow. (P, 125)

As James rereads *The Spoils*, he "revisions" the past: "the old, the shrunken concomitants muster again as I turn the pages." "Shrunken concomitants" seem to be experience, the perceptions, the feelings, and the circumstances of the writing of *The Spoils of Poynton*. These shrunken concomitants may not exactly be the same as "forms *indistinguishable*." Forms "indistinguishable" means indistinguishable in themselves or from one another or from shrunken concomitants—that is, the original experiences from which these indistinguishable forms derived. Thus the cottage is a shrunken concomitant and it is *in* the seraglio even as it was in fact the place *in which* the seraglio was created.[11]

James has created and elaborated a striking simile: the black lines of the text of *The Spoils of Poynton* are to the memories they evoke what the bars of a whore-house

LITERARY ARCHITECTURE

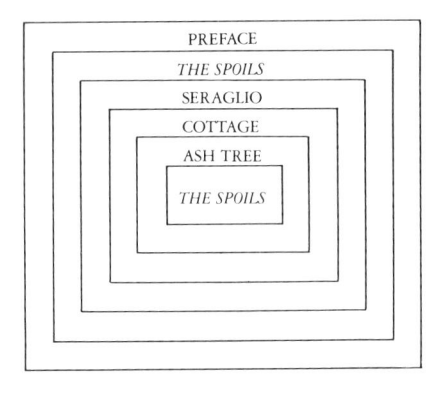

```
┌─────────────────────────────────────────┐
│  PREFACE                                │
│  ┌───────────────────────────────────┐  │
│  │  *THE SPOILS*                     │  │
│  │  ┌─────────────────────────────┐  │  │
│  │  │  SERAGLIO                   │  │  │
│  │  │  ┌───────────────────────┐  │  │  │
│  │  │  │  COTTAGE              │  │  │  │
│  │  │  │  ┌─────────────────┐  │  │  │  │
│  │  │  │  │  ASH TREE       │  │  │  │  │
│  │  │  │  │  ┌───────────┐  │  │  │  │  │
│  │  │  │  │  │*THE SPOILS*│ │  │  │  │  │
│  │  │  │  │  └───────────┘  │  │  │  │  │
│  │  │  │  └─────────────────┘  │  │  │  │
│  │  │  └───────────────────────┘  │  │  │
│  │  └─────────────────────────────┘  │  │
│  └───────────────────────────────────┘  │
└─────────────────────────────────────────┘
```

window are to the indistinguishable forms behind. James seems to be an outsider; and as one, he understandably lacks clarity of vision: he cannot distinguish the forms which "move and peer" behind the barred window. But ironically, James does not acquire the clarity he desires until he has distanced himself still further from direct experience: until "association"—an activity of the mind—bears upon those forms and, like an optic glass, sharpens them into focus. Simultaneously James is freed to look "through the lattice from without inward." We expect an interior view, but what we receive is, to our appreciable surprise, an exterior, a cottage on a cliff-side, with a small paved terrace. James has distanced himself still another time. In fact, the view he finally describes has nothing of the seraglio about it; it is a land-and-sea-scape in open air.

But here, it seems, James's finer optics betray him: they reveal to us James seated in a new sort of interior, not the sexual, experiential one of a seraglio but a cloistral, protected interior of a converted exterior. The paved terrace has a "*trained* and arching ash" tree which "brushes" the "parapet with a heavy fringe and [covers] the place like a vast umbrella." The fiction of *The Spoils* thus grows within an enclosure built from natural, exterior forms. What we have discovered and described is James's paradoxical state of mind in which he desires to look inside, is terrified of looking in, converts the interior into a safer exterior, only to remake that safer exterior into another sort of interior, as if he cannot escape being inside and outside simultaneously. Thus we have that *Alice in Wonderland* world where even outsides are inside and are insides. James's fear of immediate or direct experience is imaged by him in terms of distance–spatial relationships–and by means of architectural similes and metaphors. For James, architecture is as protective and distancing as is time.

The paved terrace alongside the cottage is a fit setting for James's creative expression. It is natural (the ash) and yet architected (the tree is "trained" and "arching"); and the view suggests both a window view and a composed scene. Similarly, James's own art attempts to mediate between nature and architecture, as if James wants to assure us that his art is both alive and controlled. We can thus appreciate James's last description, in the passage above, of *The Spoils*: it "managed more or less symmetrically to grow." "More" and *The Spoils* would have had no life; "less," it would not have been art. In a sense, the entire passage juggles the worlds on either side of James's wall of fiction: art and life, the indirect and the direct, the distanced and the immediate. His passage images the one as the "lines" and "windows" of literary architecture, the other as the "shrunken concomitants," the moving "forms" of experience.

34
Some of the Spoils.
From *The Spoils of Poynton*
(New York Edition, 1908). We might think
of this as the "furniture of thought,"
the "splendid Things" of one
of James's interior views.

FOUR

Furnished Rooms: "Objects" and "Size" in James's Fiction

IN THE MIDST of his parody of James, *The Guerdon*, Max Beerbohm writes of the character Stamfordham that

> he caught himself wondering whether, on this basis, he were even animate, so strong was his sense of being a "bit" of the furniture of the great glossy "study"–of being some oiled and ever so handy object moving smoothly on castors, or revolving, at the touch of a small red royal finger, on a pivot.[12]

Beerbohm's aim is exquisite: unerringly, not only does he mock James's late style, but his eye keenly assesses and then captures James's technique of describing the "subject." In James's work itself, we miss the smile–was there a trace of one?–when, for instance, in the opening pages of *The Wings of the Dove*, James writes of a Kate Croy who waits for her father in his rooms, that "she wasn't chalk-marked for auction" (XIX, 6). While James denies that Kate is auctionable "furniture," the suggestion (even though couched negatively) that Kate is a "bit" of the furniture, an inanimate thing like the Poynton spoils, is difficult to avoid. Throughout his fiction, James himself, or by literary proxy, compares those characters inside his houses of fiction with furnishings: Ralph Touchett compares his reception of Isabel with the receiving of valuable art objects: "Suddenly I receive a Titian, by the post, to hang on my wall, a Greek bas-relief to stick over my chimney piece" (III, 86–87); similarly in Gilbert Osmond's eyes, though she suffers some loss of grandeur,

LITERARY ARCHITECTURE

Isabel is, simply, a "piece of silver." To Densher, Kate is a "whole library of the unknown, the uncut" (XX, 62); and Milly Theale, when sitting in the doctor's office, thinks, "She should be as one of the circle of eminent contemporaries, photographed, engraved, signatured, and in particular framed and glazed, who made up the rest of the decoration, and made up as well so much of the human comfort" (XIX, 237). Maud Manningham is like her own "massive, florid furniture," while Mrs. Lowder has "something in common, even in repose, with a projectile, of great size, loaded and ready for use" (XIX, 169).

Perhaps James is extravagant, his most mannered self, in his use of these analogies; and to the extent that he luxuriates in them, we may appreciate Beerbohm's observations and understand what in James's work tickled (if not goaded) Beerbohm to parody. But it would be unfair to assume that James was not aware of what he was doing when he identifies his characters with objects. When James as artist envisages, he places characters inside his houses, whether the generalized "house of fiction," the particularized house-novel (such as *The Portrait of a Lady*) [see Plate 33], the house-as-setting (such as Gardencourt), or the house-as-mind (such as Ralph Touchett's); and characters become like objects (if not ideas about objects) to other characters who perceive them, to themselves at certain moments of self-reflection, or to us as readers while we read them. James establishes a set of parallels in which characters inside these houses of fiction stand to the fiction as furnishings to a house, as ideas to the mind. In this way, architecture and furniture images make it possible for James's fiction to concern itself with descriptions of thought processes. Indeed, since characters enter and leave houses, their activity can parallel the complex movements of thoughts (Freud's "alien guests") which likewise enter and leave our minds or else remain affixed inside, furnishing and decorating our perceptual structures. Perhaps for this reason metaphors for fiction are also the metaphors for our conception of consciousness. When we see that James envisages characters who, in turn, envisage other characters as furnishings, we, too, learn to envisage all characters as furnishings, to see them as idea-objects within a larger house-mind structure. We also recognize that James's capacity to envisage a scene—to write fiction—requires distancing: he must project his ideas outside his own mind-house into other (literary) houses in order to give to his ideas a structural independence all their own. We see these projected ideas as independent fictional characters inside independent literary edifices. And since distance is spatial, we may begin to understand that to someone who, like James, holds a conception of the mind which is tinged with spatiality, with the concepts of inside and outside, it is essential to introduce into or preserve within his definition of fiction some concept of distance, that is, of space. We can freshly appreciate the implications of James's belief that "the deepest quality of a work of art will always be the quality of the mind of the producer."[13]

Perhaps for this reason James asked the young photographer Alvin Langdon Coburn to photograph architectural monuments for the frontispieces of the beautiful New York Edition of *The Novels and Tales*. James calls these photographs the optical symbols of his fiction. Fittingly, James selected "the doctor's door" [Plate 35]—which opens "straight upon life"—for the first volume of *The Wings of the Dove* and a Venetian palace for the second [Plate 36]. When James describes choosing a frontispiece for the first volume of *The Golden Bowl* [Plate 32], he expresses his keen awareness of the mind-house symbolism and so confirms our reading: this particular frontispiece is "a shop of the mind."

> The problem [of finding a small shop] thus was thrilling, for though the small shop was but a shop of the mind, of the author's projected world, in which objects are primarily related to each other, and therefore not "taken from" a particular establishment anywhere, only as an image distilled and intensified, as it were, from a drop of the essence of such establishments in general, our need (since the picture was, as I have said, also completely to speak for itself) prescribed a concrete, independent, vivid instance, the instance that should oblige us by the marvel of an accidental rightness. (P, 334)

Among the wonderful monuments photographed by Coburn is one which is expressly not architecture per se: it is one of Coburn's portraits of James in which James is seated and somber, one hand resting on but not supporting his chin. [Plate 37] While Coburn's image—is this one of James's optical symbols?—is somewhat reminiscent of Rodin's *The Thinker*, we know from other of his photographs that, had he wished the allusion to be direct, he would have had James pose differently. Nonetheless, the picture does present a striking image of a meditative James, and it is striking not only because of James but also because of the care with which Coburn sets off his subject. We receive from Coburn a tremendous sense of mass, not as if Coburn intended that James be compared to a sculpture but as if James's head were sculpture itself. The light comes from above, so striking the becalmed James as to emphasize volume rather than

HENRY JAMES

35
The Doctor's Door.
From *The Wings of the Dove* I
(New York Edition, 1907).
A celebrated entrance:
James's literary openings
are worked and important.

36
The Venetian Palace.
From *The Wings of the Dove* II
(New York Edition, 1907).
The palace has "romance and art and history";
it sets up "a whirlwind of suggestion"
such that there is never "confinement" within
but "the freedom of all the centuries."
There, in the palace,
Milly Theale and
Merton Densher are "blown together,
she and he, as much as she liked,
through space."

the features of the artist. It would seem that Coburn, who greatly admired James and who read him with care, understood that James conceived of consciousness as a great, containing "vessel," a mold, or even more emphatically, as a "square chamber of . . . attention." Ideas, as James remarks when reflecting on those "delicious old houses," may drop *into* the mind; and Coburn, as if to emphasize James's mental and artistic "capacity," chose with much imagination to feature James's great forehead, the chamber or sets of chambers into which ideas dropped and from out of which James projected his

HENRY JAMES

artistic creations. It seems a wonderful gesture of homage to James.

The image, notably, suggests James's own descriptions, in particular those of himself, deep in thought in rooms of every sort, and in general those descriptions of the artists – the "posted presence of the watcher[s]," the "consciousness of the artist[s]" – posed at millions of windows in his house of fiction. What is even more surprising, however, is that our description of the artfully composed James is strikingly similar to James's descriptions of characters throughout his fiction and the prefaces. Susan Shepherd (for one) and Merton Densher (for another) both describe Mrs. Lowder in terms which make us think of James's photo-portrait.

> Susan Shepherd's word for her [Mrs. Lowder], again and again was that she was "large"; yet it was not exactly a case, as to the soul, of echoing chambers: she might have been likened rather to a capacious receptacle, originally perhaps loose, but now drawn as tightly as possible over its accumulated contents – a packed mass, for her American admirer, of curious detail. (XIX, 168)[14]

Merton's description is similar:

> All this within her [Mrs. Lowder] was confusedly present – a cloud of questions out of which Maud Manningham's large seated self loomed, however, as a mass more and more definite, taking in fact for the consultative relation something of the form of an oracle. (XX, 116–117)

That physical dimensions – in these instances largeness – should matter so much is curious. We may recall that James required a "large subject" for his "large building of *The Portrait of a Lady*," the book itself

37
The "square chamber of attention":
Henry James, 1906.

coming to be a "square and spacious house" (P, 48); and in his preface to *The Wings*, he talks of his "successive centers" not as the "indistinguishable forms" behind a seraglio-window (as in the preface to *The Spoils*), but as "solid *blocks* of wrought material, squared to the sharp edge, as to have weight and mass and carrying power; to make for construction, that is to conduce to effect and to provide for beauty." And James continues:

> Such a block, obviously, is the whole preliminary presentation of Kate Croy, which, from the first, I recall, absolutely declined to enact itself save in terms of amplitude. Terms of amplitude, terms of atmosphere, those terms, and those terms only, in which images assert their fulness and roundness, their power to revolve, so that they have sides and backs, parts in the shade as true as parts in the sun—these were plainly to be my conditions, right and left. (P, 296)

Predictably, James describes the constructing of his character Kate Croy in architectural terms, for she must be able to contain geometrical forms and allow them to revolve; and what other art form besides architecture so suggests amplitude, mass, weight, carrying power, as well as construction and structure? James writes:

> The building-up of Kate Croy's consciousness to the capacity for the load little by little to be laid on it was, by way of example, to have been a matter of as many hundred close-packed bricks as there are actually poor dozens. (P, 297)

James makes clear in his descriptions of particular characters and of his more generalized house of fiction —of literary subject matter and literary form—not only that he requires space, time, and perspective for the making of his art, but that these literary-houses share another property of consciousness, what we hear James call variously largeness, extent, amplitude, or enlargement. The leading "human interest" in any story, James remarks, he sees "but in a consciousness (on the part of the moved and moving creature) subject to fine intensification and wide enlargement" (P, 67). The novel must be able to be large itself in order to embrace its large subject matter, the "whole human consciousness,"[15] and on that point, James writes that "the novel can do simply everything. . . . Its plasticity, its elasticity are infinite; there is no colour, no extension it may not take from the nature of its subject or the temper of its craftsman."[16] Appropriately, in his preface to *The Portrait*, James declares "I would build large – in fine embossed vaults and painted arches" (P, 52).

Scale as such not only reflects the importance or value of subject matter or form; it indicates capacity and relationship between subject and object, between author and internal art objects. The novel must be large, "it would have to be ample [in order to] give me really space to turn round" (P, 82). In other words, it must enable James to see and describe an event, a character, or an object from more than one fixed perspective. In fact, the more room James has in his house-novels, the happier he is:

> The more I, by my intelligence, lived in my arrangement and moved about in it, the more I sank into satisfaction.
>
> (P, 110)

James, it seems, is dissatisfied with any art-analogue which does not provide space for movement, partly because he sees life's experience itself as having, of necessity, to organize "some system of observation" which expresses itself as space, distance, and measurement before it can be converted into art.

LITERARY ARCHITECTURE

> We see it [experience] as pausing from time to time to consult its notes, to measure for guidance, as many aspects and distances as possible, as many steps taken and obstacles mastered and fruits gathered and beauties enjoyed. (P, 3)

But why *largeness* in particular? For James, this word means extent–duration in and as time. When he describes a mind as large, he seems to mean a mind capable of *circumspection* (which we normally think of as spatial), not merely of *insight* or *penetration*; significantly for his art, a character who is circumspect can anticipate events multiplied out or extended in time. We have the sense that as James's late fiction comes to require successive "centers" or "reflectors" who see direction and development, who can predict or structure events in time, so, too, does James emphasize for himself largeness. In this way, largeness may suggest not only the extended or linear (temporal) life of novels about minds which foresee actions and ends in the beginnings, which recognize patterns and parts of patterns, but also novels of space in which many characters can see all around something big as well as something small. Thus, when Mrs. Lowder is described as large, James is saying something about her imagining consciousness: that she can anticipate events and foresee their outcome; and, as a consequence of this oracle-like quality, either she feels capable of controlling those events, or else she can actually control them. Such metaphors enable James to distinguish those characters who "play out"–the "fools"–from those who control or witness the playing out. Kate Croy, Mrs. Lowder, and Milly Theale learn to see or simply do see, in this latter way: arriving at a perception is described as having completely "rounded a corner" (XX, 96);[17] a conversational intricacy is described as "an effort to reach a point in space already so remote" (XX, 99); silence is "gross and thick whereas wisdom should taper, however tremulously, to a point" (XX, 107). Milly feels "Mrs. Lowder as a person of whom the mind might in two or three days roughly make the circuit. She would sit there massive at least while one attempted it; whereas Miss Croy, the handsome girl, would indulge in incalculable movements that might interfere with one's tour" (XIX, 149-150). Milly's "short life" was "queerly a question of the short run and the consciousness proportionately crowded" (XIX, 159); likewise, Milly takes up "room" in Kate's mind:

> It was almost as if room had been made for her. Kate had appeared to take for granted he [Densher] would know why it had been made; but that was just the point. It was a foreground in which he himself, in which his connexion with Kate, scarce enjoyed a space to turn round. But Miss Theale was perhaps at the present juncture a possibility of the same sort as the softened, if not the squared Aunt Maud. (XX, 14)

This might be James speaking directly of his "successive blocks," each "squared"; for we have the sense that James is talking about literary art, about his mind and consciousness. Kate "comes back" to an earlier point in a conversation with Densher:

> She had come back to another, which was one of her own; her own were so closely connected that Densher's were at best but parenthetic. Still she had a distance to go. "You do then see your way?" (XX, 62)

That the descriptive terms James uses for his characters' minds or consciousness are the same as those he uses for the art of fiction suggests that James's art is about art itself and that art is conscious consciousness. James himself, throughout the prefaces, describes his problems of composition in these terms of size and extent, just as his critical interpretations of Balzac, Dickens, George Eliot, are filled with architectural images. Occasionally, for example, he finds he has insufficient room because his fiction is "space hungry," has "space cunning" which must be "kept down" (P, 278). Of the *nouvelle*, he remarks, "Among forms, moreover, we had had, on the dimensional ground—for length and breadth—our ideal, the beautiful and blest *nouvelle*" (P, 220). When James falls into trouble with balance in his fiction, he must use "dodges," or "dissimulate," especially when, as with *The Wings*, he condemned "a luckless theme to complete its revolution, burdened with the accumulation of its difficulties, the difficulties that grow with a theme's development, in quarters so cramped." He must "dress . . . objects in an *air* as of the dimensions they can't possibly have"; in shorter literary forms, then, he has no choice but to "produce the illusion of mass without the illusion of extent" (P, 302).

While we have said that James uses spatial adjectives to describe and qualify his characters' mind-houses as well as fiction's house, as if themes were sculpture and furniture within formal chambers, we have yet to note that these terms also figure in his fictional descriptions of houses. When they do, James intends them to retain rich allusiveness. For instance, the house at Lancaster Gate accumulates mind and literary analogues such that we think James speaks of his house of fiction. As is true throughout *The Wings of the Dove*, the house is large:[18]

> The great historic house had, for Milly, beyond terrace and garden . . . a tone as of old gold kept "down" by the quality of the air. . . . Much, by her measure, for the previous hour,

appeared, in connexion with this revelation of it, to have happened to her—a quantity expressed in an assault of reminders that this largeness of style was the sign of *appointed* felicity.

> The largeness of style was the great containing vessel, while everything else . . . became but this or that element of the infusion. (XIX, 208)

It does not seem sufficient, then, to see James's architectural structures only as social symbols (as do some of James's critics),[19] or as psychological indices (as do other critics): these structures refer, more importantly, to James's theory and practice of fiction-making.

What happens in fiction that is about itself to descriptions of actual monuments such as St. Mark's, Lancaster Gate, or the Vatican? For James these serve less as extensions into history (or into a real world) than as extensions into another sort of interior, the reader's mind as it experiences historical or real time/space. We see James, for instance, describe in his nonfiction a real house only to find that he places, through speculation and ironic suppositions, fictional characters into these real structures.

> Miss Burney's and Miss Austen's heroines might perfectly well have had their first love-affair there [in Ludlow]; a journey to Ludlow would certainly have been a great event to Fanny Price or Emma Woodhouse, or even to those more exalted young ladies, Evelina and Cecilia. It is a place on which a provincial aristocracy has left so sensible a stamp as to enable you to measure both the grand manners and the small ways.[20]

James mixes worlds to some purpose. By introducing the fictional into the real he may well be suggesting that our responses to the real are but "fictions," that we in our thought associations are the makers of fiction, that history is fiction, is projection. This holds with his notion that beauty, in architecture—we may therefore presume in literature as well—"proceeds from that which is participatory and relative, not from what we might call abstract principles."[21] In terms of fiction, such extension or enlargement seems necessary to a novel or novella which seeks to re-create in the reader a fiction-making process, a manipulating, controlling, juggling of externals into the more private realms and structures of thought and perspective. It may seem that in James's art Proust's shifting view of the Martinville towers is internalized, not only conceptually as the idea of varied philosophical points of view, but as the process of shifting narrative allegiances. For, as readers, we share first one narrative stance or center of consciousness and then another, and in this juggling we not only experience the changed perspective offered by each center but we in fact enlarge our house of consciousness, so that it shall contain multiple viewpoints. For the process to involve not only imaginary but also real structures confirms in the reader a feeling that changes of perspective, multiple subjective points of view, are not only possible, but are common to all experience whatever. In this way James can be absolved of a charge often levelled at him: that his art is solipsist, that all his fictions are reducible to James's own mind. In this way the reader does not merely learn information he did not know (what one reflector may tell him); he also experiences a new way of knowing, one which requires that he conceptualize many independent but not exclusive vantage points upon, not an object or a character, but a *series* of events and actions.

FIVE

Matters of Construction and Adequacy: Architecture and Painting

WHEN JAMES MOVES from the general to the particular, from the house of fiction to specific novels, he retains his architectural analogue in order to make explicit his attitudes toward construction. James assures his readers that he oversees the largest of his structures without sacrificing careful attention to detail. In his preface to *The Portrait of a Lady*, James reflects upon and admires again the "square and spacious house" he has built, the novel itself:

> It took nothing less than the technical rigour . . . to inspire me with the right confidence for erecting on such a plot of ground the neat and careful and proportioned pile of bricks that arches over it and was thus to form, constructionally speaking, a literary monument. Such is the aspect that to-day *The Portrait* wears for me: a structure reared with an "architectural" competence. . . . On one thing I was determined; that, though I should clearly have to pile brick upon brick for the creation of an interest, I would leave no pretext for saying that anything is out of line, scale or perspective. I would build large—in fine embossed vaults and painted arches, as who should say, and yet never let it appear that the chequered pavement, the ground under the reader's feet, fails to stretch at every point to the base of the walls. (P, 52)[22] [Plate 35]

While James fills his fiction with varieties of architectural styles—the Gothic cathedral simile for Isabel Archer in *The Portrait of a Lady*, the Venetian palaces in *The Wings of the Dove*, and the pagoda of *The Golden Bowl* – he prefers the "square," the "regular," the "well-proportioned" Palladian style as analogue for construction of his fiction. When, however, James characterizes his characters' minds or consciousness, the square, sane Palladian style is scarcely serviceable, and James abandons it for styles as complex as the minds he describes. But curiously, as analogue for construction in fiction, that very "regularity" in overall structure permits James to be "Gothic" and "irregular" in attention to nuances of style and emotion. Of the necessity for careful construction and the consequent freedom to entertain the intricate and "minor," James writes that the novelist and dramatist each

> has verily to *build*, is committed to architecture, to construction at any cost; to driving in deep his vertical supports and laying across and firmly fixing his horizontal, his resting pieces – at the risk of no matter what vibration from the tap of his master-hammer. This makes the active value of his basis immense, enabling him, with his flanks protected, to advance undistractedly, even if not at all carelessly, into the comparative fairy-land of the *mere minor anxiety*. (P, 109) (italics mine)

Like his classical predecessors, James places the greatest emphasis on the laying of a foundation, but his foundation, by a sleight-of-hand, is not a "base" but a "basis": if it is not firm, no amount of ornament or detail will save a literary monument.

> The ground has not been laid for it, and when that is the case one builds all vainly in the air: one patches up one's super-structure, one paints it in the prettiest colours, one hangs fine old tapestry and rare brocade over its window-sills, one flies emblazoned banners from its roof – the building none the less totters and refuses to stand square. (P, 17)

Notable in this passage, in addition to its emphasis on the necessity for careful construction in preparing ground, is that James's selection of the architectural analogue for fiction does not preclude his interest in and use of other art analogues.[23] Tapestry and frescoes adorn the walls of his built structures; and we see in James something of Pater's concern for the mind and soul of style, both of which contribute to great literary architecture. In fact, James – once again like Pater, and also, in this instance, like Proust – only evokes the more exclusive image of writer-as-painter when he wishes to address himself to the issue of subject matter in art. But James never uses painting, only architecture, as an art analogue for mind or consciousness; and it is mind, more than any other quality, that James searches out when he reads and writes. Not only do critics ignore this; they overlook what James feels he must do to painting in order to make the analogy hold: in *The Wings of the Dove*, he has Kate Croy step out of a picture frame and seize space, just as he juxtaposes two Veronese paintings in his palace hall because one vision (one painting) is insufficient. Likewise, when James speaks of the painter's canvas, he must make it "elastic" so that "it will stretch anywhere and it will take in absolutely anything."[24] What is crucial here is that painting for James becomes, in his house of fiction scheme, analogous to the view (on the "human scene") from the house windows. In other words, painting is but one art-aspect of a larger whole; and there is important historical precedent for this relationship between painting and architecture. The literary critic-historian Claudio Guillén notes this:

> In three-dimensional terms – made possible by the laws of perspective – the canvas is an open window on the contents of a

truncated pyramid [Euclid's visual pyramid] and in two-dimensional terms is comparable to the reflection in a mirror.[25]

What seems important for James, then, is that the architectural analogy can gather to it and include other art analogues, even those which eschew depth for an elaboration of surface. In his preface to *Lady Barbarina* James describes one such structure,

> a "great house" forming the SW corner of Piccadilly and with its long and practically featureless side . . . opposite my open-eyed windows . . . the surface always before me. This surface hung there like the most voluminous of curtains. (P, 212)

Elsewhere, when he speaks about surface directly, he supplies notions of space and distance:

> The prime effect of . . . so prepared a surface, is to lead on and on; while the fascination of following resides, by the same token, in the presumability *somewhere* of a convenient, of a visibly-appointed stopping place. (P, 6)

Once again, James's description, in this instance of fiction's "action," expresses itself through architectural images. The analogue, it seems, resists the limitations imposed upon it by James's critics.

To James architecture is not only "the greatest conceivable work of art because it represents difficulties annulled, resources combined, labour, courage, and patience";[26] it is also the greatest conceivable work of art because it never confines—as art or as analogue—the artist. We may almost think that James speaks of himself as artist when he describes what Milly's palace in *The Wings of the Dove* does for her; and perhaps we, no less than Merton Densher, join Milly and James inside his literary monuments:

She wouldn't let him call it keeping quiet, for she insisted that her palace—with all its romance and art and history—had set up round her a whirlwind of suggestion that never dropped for an hour. It wasn't therefore, within such walls, confinement, it was the freedom of all the centuries: in respect to which Densher granted good-humouredly that they were then blown together, she and he, as much as she liked, through space. (XX, 174)

V
THE ANALOGICAL
TRADITION OF
LITERARY ARCHITECTURE

We cannot articulate our feelings
without a language that tradition
and civilization offers to us
for the selection of symbols.

E. H. Gombrich

IN *The Seven Lamps of Architecture* (1849), John Ruskin makes, I think, one of the most eloquent statements on behalf of architecture that we find in nineteenth-century English writing. His tribute has special importance with respect to the concerns of this book. Ruskin not only brings together in one passage themes and theories shared and expressed by the writers we have been discussing; he also does so in such a way as to suggest and I hope affirm the motives that have impelled me, and values I have held by in my critical and appreciative pursuits. Speaking of "The Lamp of Memory," Ruskin writes:

> It is as the centralisation and protectress of this sacred influence, that Architecture is to be regarded by us with the most serious thought. We may live without her and worship without her, but we cannot remember without her. How cold is all history how lifeless all imagery, compared to that which the living nation writes, and the uncorrupted marble bears! how many pages of doubtful record might we not often spare, for a few stones left one upon another! The ambition of the old Babel builders was well directed for this world: there are but two strong conquerors of the forgetfulness of men, Poetry and Architecture; and the latter in some sort includes the former, and is mightier in its reality; it is well to have, not only what men have thought and felt, but what their hands have handled, and their strength wrought, and their eyes beheld, all the days of their life.[1]

Ruskin distinguishes for us, before he reintegrates, the two arts we have been discussing: literature (Poetry) and architecture; he adds, then, that these two arts, independently and interdependently, "conquer forgetfulness," or to restate positively, enable us to remember the past.

LITERARY ARCHITECTURE

Literary Architecture has been about the two arts which Ruskin distinguishes and compares as they find expression in the writings of Walter Pater, Gerard Manley Hopkins, Marcel Proust, and Henry James; it has also been about that special service to memory which literature and architecture, separately and as analogues, perform and which Ruskin celebrates. If we wish to speak of influences, we can scarcely do Ruskin justice enough: not

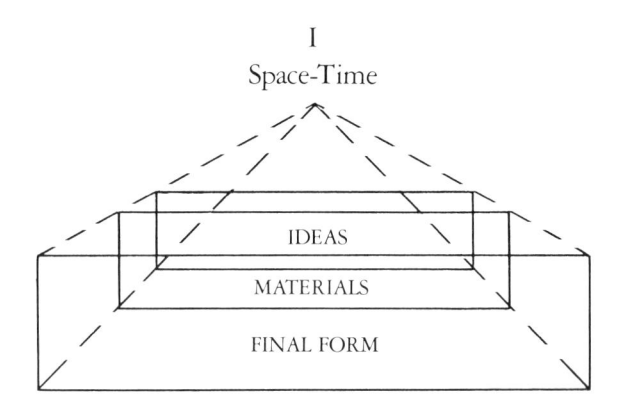

I
Space-Time

only does he announce to the nineteenth and twentieth centuries the importance of architecture, but he enables those writers after him to discover and proclaim for themselves the richness of architecture for their lives and their art.

Architectural places—literary and physical—echo and resonate in the life of our mind. Literature and architecture are separate art forms; and we must qualify their relationships with care, in the same manner Ruskin qualifies them when he says "the latter [Architecture] *in some sort* includes the former [Poetry]" (italics mine). Their separate existence is a consequence of material *form*

THE ANALOGICAL TRADITION

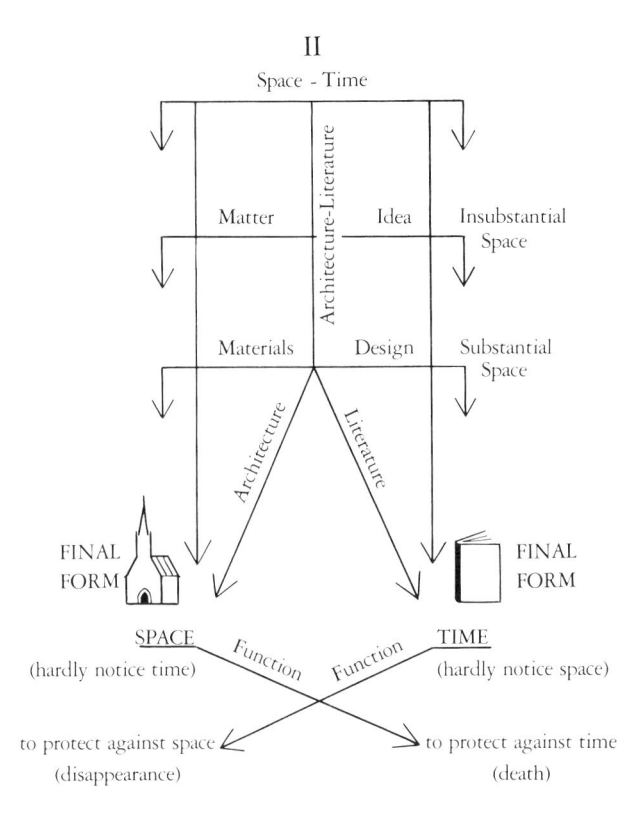

II

Diagram:

Space - Time
↓ ↓ ↓
Matter | Architecture-Literature | Idea | Insubstantial Space
↓ ↓
Materials | Design | Substantial Space
↓
Architecture / Literature
FINAL FORM — FINAL FORM
SPACE (hardly notice time) — Function / Function — TIME (hardly notice space)
to protect against space (disappearance) — to protect against time (death)

and time-life within contexts of separate traditions; and, if we wish to speak on the level of form, we must say that the two arts hold no intrinsic or necessary similarity: the one is an art of stone or concrete, the other of letters and words. This proposition is insufficient, however: it does not raise the cloak of form (express materials) to see basic and elemental underpinnings: both literature and architecture are composed of space, time, matter, energy, this last being a holding-tension, the stress-release bond which constrains matter into form, assigning it place and preventing its explosion into random disconnectedness. Literature and architecture are compositions; they require artist-doers. We persist, of course, in thinking of each art as outward, existing in the solidity it discovers in this final form; but each has an inward motive—

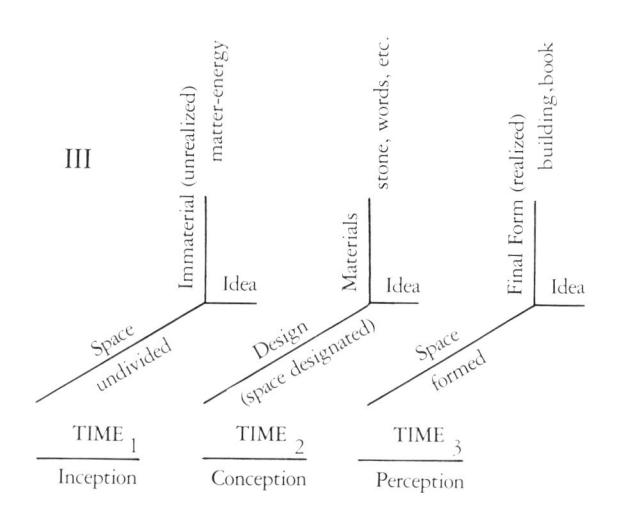

III

Immaterial (unrealized) / matter-energy — Idea
Space undivided
TIME $_1$
Inception

Materials / stone, words, etc. — Idea
Design (space designated)
TIME $_2$
Conception

Final Form (realized) / building, book — Idea
Space formed
TIME $_3$
Perception

Hopkins's and Proust's "essence," James's "germ"—such that outwardness represents conversion from idea—immatter—into matter. This is *embodiment*. I have drawn some diagrams to show the relationships between space-time, idea, matter (material), and form. The first diagram (I) indicates that space-time is common to all three stages of the art activity; in this representation, we may think of space-time as a sea in which artistic creativity occurs, but I think it important to see that sea also as the possibility and power of connection. Diagram II represents where-when architecture and literature di-

IV
Transformation of Materials

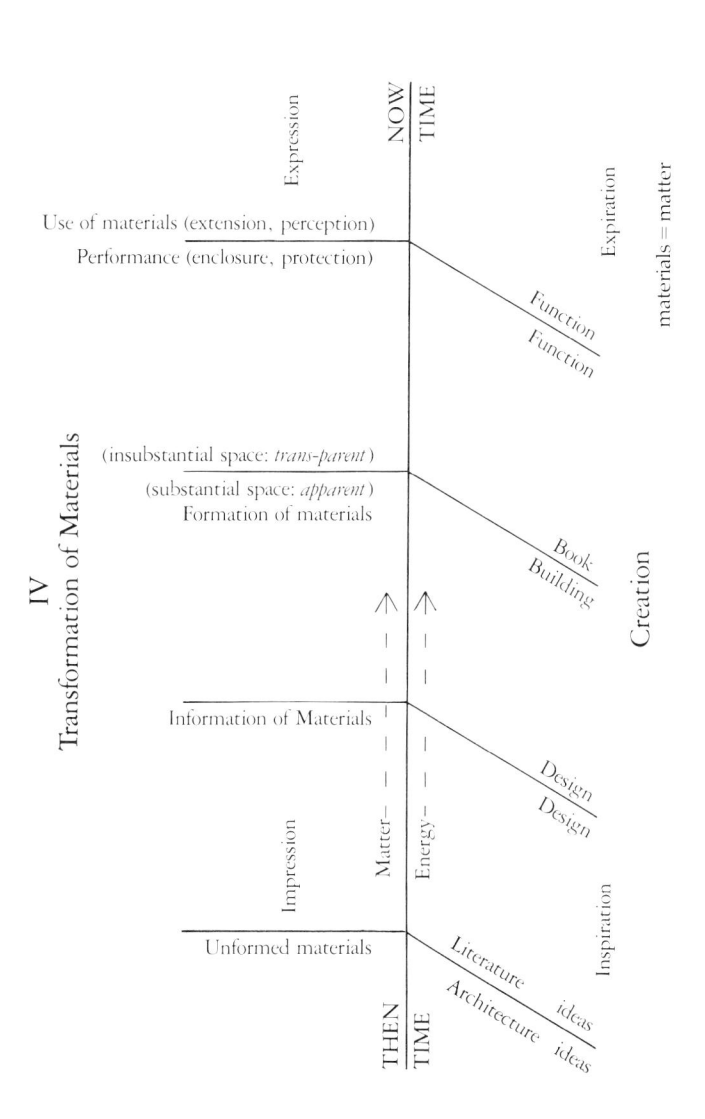

THEN TIME → NOW TIME

Unformed materials — Impression
Matter / Energy
Information of Materials

(insubstantial space: *trans-parent*)
(substantial space: *apparent*)
Formation of materials

Use of materials (extension, perception) — Expression
Performance (enclosure, protection)

Architecture ideas / Literature ideas — Inspiration
Design / Design
Book / Building — Creation
Function / Function — Expiration

materials = matter

verge in form and then again in function. Diagram III shows *idea* as constant, from *inception* to *perception*; IV shows energy-matter as constant throughout the *transform* act; and V shows literary architecture in three space-time intervals. What distinguishes literary from architectural art, then, is not elements (particularity) but the proportion-combination of elements: architecture

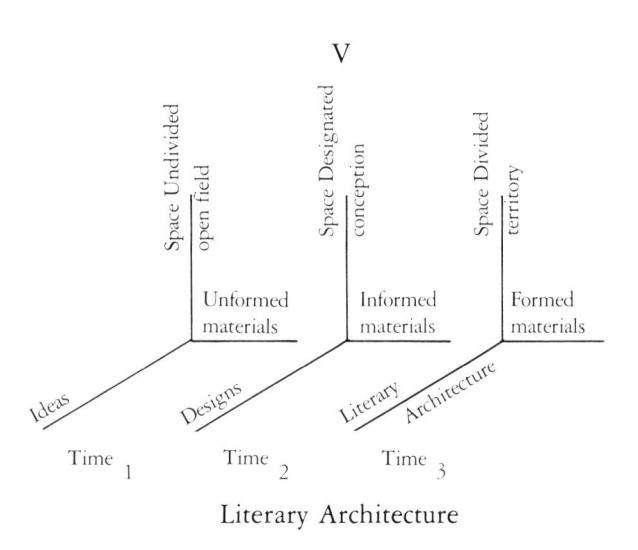

V

Space Undivided — open field
Space Designated — conception
Space Divided — territory

Unformed materials | Informed materials | Formed materials

Ideas — Designs — Literary Architecture

Time₁ Time₂ Time₃

Literary Architecture

celebrates space through enclosure, converting an open field into territory (this is the marking of boundaries); literature celebrates time through expansion, quickening the open field with *imagines* (this is the opening of dream). But even here we must not be deceived by particularity of proportion or emphasis—either space or time—for the distinction is false: we cannot have the one without the other. Despite differences in form, architecture and literature each partake of the other's dominant element. Pater, Hopkins, Proust, and James choose the architectural analogue for literature so that they may emphasize the spaciousness of literary art despite the insubstantiality of that space. They extend literature, but its *where*, unlike architecture's, becomes air unbounded. Space—we may think *void*—is important: it is the area through and the vehicle by which the alive or the quick is realized. As such, it is positive. Space is where time is. In literary art (language), syntax is the most apparent space-place and place-force; in architecture space is the hollow center (Proust's hermetically sealed silence of past or Hopkins's "womb-of-all, home-of-all, hearse-of-all night"). It resonates and records past or potential activity and is necessary for the life of the art. It is also necessary for life: there cannot be movement, life, which we may make analogous to or see as time, without space. The functions of literature and architecture respect the space-time conditions of the arts themselves, of insubstantiality or substantiality: literary art sets in motion (time) our activities of conceiving and perceiving (our transparent dreams or thoughts); architecture moves the other way, representing a conversion from no-thing into something, an activity human, but more importantly natural, in the manner of the universe. It provides space as shelter and space as interior scape or environment. When we think of space in art-life as hollow, this space is death-in-life, the life a field without the center figure, self. Death-in-life is the necessary converse for life, which actually is life-in-death, being-in-field (universe) or being-in-void. (For *being* we may also read architecture, literature, thought.) Solidity or permanence, in this sense, is illusion. Solidity depends, for its illusion, on its time-life. Architecture wears its time slowly (in an analogous system, physics, it undergoes slow configurational change); once we see its time—we go to Rome to see decay and ruin, to Milan to see ghost-admitting frescoes—it assumes a (fertile) trans-parency much like our fugitive thoughts. So, too, once our thoughts (fast configurational change) are embodied in written language, their time-life slows, such that they relinquish their quick transparency-as-thought and seem to endure, as if they were like architecture, substantial.

Substance is, in our senses, our security or refuge from time-death; but architecture as substance is protection of another sort, from uncontrollable (since not self-generated) weather. Weather is kinetic energy, what we should also think of as encounter or experience, while architecture is potential energy. Being-out-of-doors is being without shelter, without either thought structure protection (filters) or physical protection. Being-in-weather requires the nakedness of exposure. Hopkins, of the four writers I discuss, ventures outside the most, into weather—the charged void—and death—the hollow center; Proust follows Hopkins in order of daring but clings for security to a reconstructed past rather than the immediate; Pater, we feel, once risked exposure, but frightened, he too returns to sentimentality, to reconstructed and fortressed enclosures; James, no less fearful than Pater, ventures out into the near-loss of control of his late novels, but, like Pater, returns to safety, wanting to construct against death, not like Hopkins, through or with it. James's novels slow into museums or stiffen into mausoleums, whereas Proust's and Hopkins's quicken to building-as-activity, Hopkins's actually working as breaths of being, making and unmaking. I do not wish to say that Proust and Hopkins are therefore the better;

THE ANALOGICAL TRADITION

but I have thought that they are braver and in some way larger. Their literature spans more, exposes more, and re-creates more of the *extended* world we live in, Pater and James more of the *intended* world we live in. In the end, no matter the scale: each writer is a visionary, each a life-builder.

Pater coins the term *literary architecture*; Hopkins uses architectural terms and concepts to describe and make his poetry; Proust constructs *A la recherche du temps perdu* as a Gothic cathedral; and James writes inside and about a house(-space) of fiction. The architecture of these writers is not just an analogue taken-up but a process for generating a whole range of analogues. It is now an actual creative and a transform-memory process, literary architecture. The close study of literary architecture provides an unanticipated model of the mind in activity, expressing in act, as vital structure, *how* it fuses space-time and recovers buried memories in and for the construction of art. We should not tease ourselves into believing that literary architecture depends upon or presumes a common spirit of the age which marries the two arts, whether we name that spirit a Hegelian *Zeitgeist* or an "*air de famille*."[2] Rather, literary architecture says something about the way Pater, Hopkins, Proust, and James view and work their literary creations. This book has been concerned with architecture as art-model and procedure for literary art and with the implications for creativity and perception architecture provides.[3] What, I have asked, may be accomplished at certain times in history or in certain literary works by architecture when painting, sculpture, and music are available as alternative identities.[4]

Tradition and civilization offer to the nineteenth and

twentieth centuries four sets of parallels or analogues. Architecture figures in each: architecture [and the] human body; architecture [and the] mind; architecture [and] memory; architecture [and] literature. What occurs in the nineteenth century and onwards is a blurring of sorts: these once discrete parallels–used not only by writers but by architects and philosophers–feed into one another so that literature, architecture, and memory share and assume new and complicated meanings as the indistinguishable fusion literary architecture. While two sets of these parallels have been formalized into what we have already called traditions (*ars memoria* and what a few scholars have called *ut architectura poesis*), the other two have been ignored: the relation between architecture and the body and architecture and the mind. Taken altogether, the four represent something in many ways less special but never less important than the formal traditions: the continual search to explain what we mean by metaphor, or, said more simply, *how* we mean. Classical rhetoricians needed to describe structure in periods and could turn to architecture, while architects who needed to describe character and style in architecture could turn to rhetoric. Terms and concepts are borrowed naturally; and the language of comparison becomes a rich *metaphorica* governing all our expression, sometimes in such a way as to lead us to think that all language is metaphorical. I have said that these particular sets of metaphors have something in common–architecture. One possible consequence can be this: when we read, we look for specific effects attained in the use of the architectural analogy for writing and recalling. I hope that my observations have some value in heightening the pleasure we can take in our readings.

ONE

Architecture and the Human Body

THE COMPARISON between architecture and the human body crops up first in the works of Vitruvius, *The Ten Books on Architecture*,[5] written in the time of Augustus. The analogue helps Vitruvius to speak of structure in architecture and to advocate, if not justify, his belief in symmetry. We find a cryptic but paradigmatic use of the analogue in Book I, "The Fundamental Principles of Architecture"; the more elaborate uses of the analogue appear in subsequent books, an example being Book III, "On Symmetry: In Temples and in the Human Body." In the passage from "Fundamental Principles," Vitruvius writes:

> Symmetry is a proper agreement between the members of the work itself, and relation between the different parts and the whole general scheme, in accordance with a certain part selected as standard. Thus in the human body there is a kind of symmetrical harmony between forearm, foot, palm, finger, and other small parts; and so it is with perfect buildings. In the case of temples, symmetry may be calculated from the thickness of a column, from a triglyph, or even from a module; in the ballista, from the hole or from what the Greeks call the $\pi\epsilon\rho i\tau\rho\eta\tau os$; in a ship, from the space between the tholepins ($\delta\iota\acute{a}\pi\eta\gamma\mu a$); and in other things, from various members.[6]

We can document the persistence of the architecture-body analogue in architectural treatises from Vitruvius' time to the present day. Among the seminal reassertions of the analogue is that of Leone Battista Alberti in *Ten*

Books on Architecture (1485):[7] Alberti restates and thereby preserves Vitruvius' analogue; he also expands his predecessor's approach to include mathematics. Alberti states that "an Edifice is a Kind of Body consisting, like all other Bodies, of Design and of Matter";[8] he also breaks from Vitruvian tradition, as we can observe in his title description of Book IX, Chapter VI: "Of the Proportions of Numbers in the Measuring of Areas, and the Rules for some other Proportions drawn neither from natural Bodies, nor from Harmony."[9] What we notice in seventeenth- and eighteenth-century treatises is that terms for parts of buildings are in fact taken from the names of body parts. In *The Builder's Magazine*, 1774, we find, among other terms, *eye, eye-brow, face, elbow, dentells, nose, nude, buttocks,* and *bust,* let alone the more polite terms such as *joint* and *limb.*[10] In the nineteenth century, we find the analogue again: in "The Principles and Practice of Architectural Design," (Essay 7, 1850) from *Detached Essays of the Architectural Publication Society* (London, 1853), the author-architect Wightwick writes:

> A building is a body or a "carcass," lettered over "with beauty of diction, with poetic illustration, and with the charms of rhetoric. . . . What the skin is to the body, the hair to the head, the eye-brows and lashes to the eyes, and the lips to the mouth—such is the marble casing to the walls, the cornice to the façade, the pediment and the architrave to the windows, and the porch to the door."[11]

What is important to notice here is that the analogue has begun to blur, that is, to include a literary analogue as well ("lettered over 'with beauty of diction, with poetic illustration' "). By now this blurring does not surprise us, especially when we discover it in nineteenth-century writings; but it is important to know also that as early as Vitruvius, architectural terms and concepts were borrowed from existing disciplines, specifically from rhetorical treatises;[12] and that in succeeding centuries the borrowing could be made the other way round, from architecture to literature, as is the case with Ben Jonson's *Timber, or Discoveries*, where Jonson applies concepts and terms from Vitruvius and Alberti to the masque, poetry, and drama.[13]

In devotional writing, the analogue seesaws: while architecture may be described by its analogy to body, so, too, is the body described architecturally, most often as church, temple, or house. In English poetry, perhaps a *locus classicus* for such reciprocal uses of the architecture-body analogue is George Herbert's *The Temple*: sometimes the Church is body-like, with veins of human sin, just as at other times the body is house-like, "all symmetrie,/Full of proportions."[14] Herbert's last stanza in "The Church-floore" beautifully bows to one side of the analogue:

> Hither sometimes Sinne steals, and stains
> The marbles neat and curious veins:
> But all is cleansed when the marble weeps.
> Sometimes Death, puffing at the doore,
> Blows all the dust about the floore:
> But while he thinks to spoil the room, he sweeps.
> Blest be the *Architect*, whose art
> Could build so strong in a weak heart.[15]

"Man" bows to the other:

LITERARY ARCHITECTURE

> My God, I heard this day,
> That none doth build a stately habitation,
> But he that means to dwell therein.
> What house more stately hath there been,
> Or can be, then is Man? to whose creation
> All things are in decay.[16]

We need hardly remark that Walter Pater and Gerard Manley Hopkins—Pater's architecture of "old builders," Hopkins's "Harry Ploughman" or "The Wreck of the Deutschland"—must have known this analogue as it was used by Herbert. But it is important to notice once again the words *build* and *dwell*. If we once again take the words back, as Hopkins might have done, to their Indo-European roots, the lines read this way: "That none doth *be* a stately habitation,/But he that means to be seen." The body is the building, that is, the being, of the soul, its temporary place of residence, actually its embodied or seeable form. (*Dwell*, as I have stated earlier, means "to go up as in a cloud," the cloud making the spirit, which rides on the breath, seeable.) *Dwell* also meant "to go astray"; this suggests that our temporary abode—the body, our life on earth—is a departure from that other, correct life, the life of the spirit, which does not know (human) birth and (human) death. We should also be aware that the analogue, while useful for descriptions of structure—proportion (part to whole), symmetry, arrangement—is useful in other ways also: when writers compare architecture with the body, they get the chance to consider architecture "organic," having to do with growth, generation, life-death cycles. We therefore may find that certain writers we might call Romantic use the analogue even when they are intent

THE ANALOGICAL TRADITION

upon dismissing proportion and symmetry as the more bloodless values of a classical sensibility.[17] Perhaps, then, we may begin to see how Pater could remake the analogue into something altogether new, by, as it were, collapsing the parallelism into a point where lines converge: architectural walls are actually composed of "minute dead bodies."[18] In this way, then, the analogue is serviceable for those who wish to speak of structure, as well as for those who seek to use it to describe organic growth, or, simply, human existence.

TWO

Architecture and the Mind

THE IMPORTANT relationship between architecture and mind, whether explicit or submerged, has been noticed and proclaimed throughout the history of Western thought, so much so that it seems commonplace when in fact it is profound. Prior to the eighteenth century, however, the comparison seems to have been used less by architects searching for analogues to architecture than by philosophers and poets who wished to describe mind by an analogue which included notions of place, depth, structure, interior, exterior, light, dark, image, access, barrier. We could chronicle endlessly the occurrence of the analogue: it surfaces in Aristotle (*topos eidon*),[19] while it seems submerged in Ovid and Apuleius ("Palace of the Sun"; "Palace of Psyche");[20] it comes explicit in Augustine and Aquinas, again in Locke and Hegel; the comparison, although carefully qualified, persists through Freud's writings (Roman buildings image mind and memory in *Civilization and Its Discontents*) and is used even now by such writers as Samuel Beckett and Donald Davie, such psychiatrists as W. R. Bion, and such philosophers as Richard Wollheim.[21] We persist, it seems, in feeling that the mind has no extension—to use Descartes' term—and when we seek to describe it, we translate it into metaphors which, of necessity, do have extension. In other words, "mind" without the analogue is shaky, threatening on the one hand to disappear into a puff of abstraction or, on the other, to so reduce itself to essen-

THE ANALOGICAL TRADITION

tials as to be matter no longer, but only energy (a chemical, electrical brain). The comparison of mind with architecture suggests that the mind either has extension or at least has functions or characteristics similar to those things which do have extension. In this way, perhaps, we can appreciate Plato's care in his allegory of the cave: while he does not seek to describe the mind of man as a parthenon or temple, as a finished architectural monument, he more importantly chooses to describe the condition of being (we might read *building*) or mode of existence (we might read *dwelling*) in which the mind functions; and for purposes of description and clarification, he creates the cave metaphor, which, if we wish, we may think of as rudimentarily architectural.[22] Certainly, long after Plato, we can find descriptions—embodiments or extensions in metaphor—of the mind in architectural terms. We might look back in literary history or to the present. The opening of Andrew Marvell's poem "Upon Appleton House, to my Lord Fairfax" may be a *locus classicus* for this occasion: while Marvell establishes an analogous relationship between mind—or sometimes "brain"—and architecture, he also enlarges the analogue to include a literary or poetic significance. The poem begins:

> Within this sober Frame expect
> Work of no Forrain *Architect*;
> That unto Caves the Quarries drew,
> And Forrests did to Pastures hew;
> Who of his great Design in pain
> Did for a Model vault his Brain,
> Whose Columnes should so high be rais'd
> To arch the Brows that on them gaz'd.

LITERARY ARCHITECTURE

"Did for a Model vault his Brain" – the poem extends the complex metaphor beautifully: poet-architect and Fairfax come together in almost every stanza-room.

> V
> And surely when the after Age
> Shall hither come in *Pilgrimage*,
> These sacred Places to adore,
> By *Vere* and *Fairfax* trod before,
> Men will dispute how their Extent
> Within such dwarfish Confines went:
> And some will smile at this, as well
> As Romulus his Bee-like Cell.
>
> VI
> *Humility* alone designs
> Those short but admirable Lines,
> By which, ungirt and unconstrain'd,
> Things greater are in less contain'd.
> Let others vainly strive t'immure
> The *Circle* in the *Quadrature*!
> These *holy Mathematicks* can
> In ev'ry Figure equal Man.[23]

If we jump centuries, we find an equivalent of sorts in Samuel Beckett's *Murphy*. Chapter VI of the novel is devoted to a description of Murphy's mind. This character, the "seedy solipsist" Murphy, holds by a radical Cartesian dualism. The chapter uses the language of abstraction: Murphy's mind has "an actual" and "a virtual," and "three zones, light, half light, dark, each with its speciality." The speciality of the first is "forms with parallel," of the second, "forms without parallel," of the third, "a flux of forms."[24] But Beckett never lets an abstraction "exist" without a concrete, literal parallel or equivalent: thus, although wonderfully delayed until

THE ANALOGICAL TRADITION

Chapter IX, the padded cell for schizoids in Magdalen Mental Mercyseat becomes the extended equivalent, the architectural analogue, to Murphy's mind. Murphy feels that

> the pads surpassed by far all he had ever been able to imagine in the way of indoor bowers of bliss. The three dimensions, slightly concave, were so exquisitely proportioned that the absence of the fourth was scarcely felt. The tender luminous oyster-grey of the pneumatic upholstery, cushioning every square inch of ceiling, walls, floor and door, lent colour to the truth, that one was a prisoner of air. The temperature was such that only total nudity could do it justice. No system of ventilation appeared to dispel the illusion of respirable vacuum. The compartment was windowless, like a monad, except for the shuttered judas in the door, at which a sane eye appeared, or was employed to appear, at frequent and regular intervals throughout the twenty-four hours. Within the narrow limits of domestic architecture he had never been able to imagine a more creditable representation of what he kept on calling, indefatigably, the little world.[25]

The passage, with some subtlety, contains Beckett's critique of solipsism and of all closed or monistic systems: like James, Beckett opens his closed structure to a watcher-intruder, the "sane eye" which appears at the "shuttered judas." Is there a pun on "judas," betrayer of belief systems, outsider, or disbeliever in monotheism? When in his more recent fiction Beckett seems to be imaging being and death, and to be doing so without the biting (but also hopeful) ironic humor of *Murphy*, he still uses architectural metaphors, but composes them of elements (sky, earth, and air) as well as rudimentary structures; and he importantly describes them over and over again as being "issueless."[26] The composing and constructing analogue, mind and architecture, dances in counterpoint to Beckett's de-composing of literary and epistemological conventions.

We can also find the opposite or reverse of the analogue, when architects use it to compare their buildings with mind. This comparison is far more recent than we would suppose: in an essay from July 1839, "On Character and Style in Architecture" from *The Civil Engineer and Architect's Journal*, the architect-writer draws a parallel between matter and mind:

> A style is a method of conveying a character, and is as distinct from that character as the human form, the soul of which it is the external representative; it is the means of explaining to the senses some (insensible) idea; in short is the *matter*, some moral quality being its analogous *mind*.[27]

We also find the analogue used by the architect Wightwick:

> It [The Triumphal Gate] symbolizes MUSEUM. It is a prologue spoken by Retrospection. Like the brain of *Touchstone* [he means Jaques], it is "cramed with observation, the which it vents in mingled forms." It is the "returned traveller," "the picked man of countries...." Having studiously followed the windings of the templed walks to which it leads, you will return, competent to read the significant details of what, now, only *vaguely* addresses your understanding.[28]

Wightwick's belief that buildings symbolize ideas (or even other buildings), and that they may actively address an observer, reveals what is beginning to happen to the relationship between architecture and mind in nineteenth-century architectural theory. Parallelism — Wightwick still uses a simile construction "like" — gives way to what E. H. Gombrich simply calls expression-

THE ANALOGICAL TRADITION

ism:[29] rather than merely parallel, buildings in the nineteenth century come to *express* actively and outwardly, in concrete form, the mind of their builder-architects. Ruskin writes of this expressiveness:

> Exactly in the same manner, we shall find that Gothic architecture has *external forms* and *internal elements*. Its elements are certain *mental tendencies* of the builders, *legibly* expressed in it; as fancifulness, love of variety, love of richness, and such others. Its external forms are pointed arches, vaulted roofs, etc. And unless both the elements and the forms are there, we have no right to call the style Gothic.(italics mine)[30]

Expressionism has two sides to it: not only may buildings express the mind of their builders, but buildings may also impress that expression on an observer's mind. Architects are concerned to make explicit the power of architecture:

> Architecture produces its effect upon the mind quite as much as upon the eye. Its forms are understood by the intellect, not merely painted upon the retina. The pleasures which it excites arise from complicated sources; they spring from the thoughts which we bestow upon the object [after receiving thoughts from it] and not merely from the contemplation of the form.[31]

Ruskin in fact uses the expressiveness of a building as a criterion of its beauty and majesty:

> If we consider how much less the beauty and majesty of a building depend upon its pleasing certain prejudices of the eye, than upon its rousing certain trains of meditation in the mind.[32]

What Ruskin presents should be familiar: we most often speak of it as associationism. Architects, like writers and

LITERARY ARCHITECTURE

philosophers, begin to use their art form as a device to direct specific trains of association. There occurs, thus, a kind of dynamic charge or exchange among builder, building, and observer, of mind expressed to mind impressed.

The literary implications of expressionism and associationism are important. There is the possibility, for viewers, of discovering something about the private vision, even the private life, of the architect-artist from his public monument, whether that monument is an actual edifice or a literary structure. Ruskin had said that "mental tendencies" are "legibly expressed," meaning that an observer may—to use Ruskin's exact term and a term used by other architectural theorists—"read" architecture. One may read backwards from art object to artist, and this is of course what we have seen in this century as psychoanalytic criticism. While in the nineteenth century we find some artists happy about these possibilities, we also find others who feel that such "readings" constitute an invasion of their privacy and an abuse of the artifact. Browning, for instance, is angry that critics read Shakespeare's sonnets, not to mention Browning's own, as the artist's mind-house (like Rossetti's "House of Life" sonnet sequence), which could be entered and understood. When he protests against such an approach, he strikingly chooses to express his objection in poems which themselves exploit the analogue of mind/building/poem. The first three stanzas of "House" (1876) express this clearly.

> Shall I sonnet-sing you about myself?
>   Do I live in a house you would like to see?
> Is it scant of gear, has it store of pelf?
>   "Unlock my heart with a sonnet-key?"

THE ANALOGICAL TRADITION

> Invite the world, as my betters have done?
>   "Take notice: this building remains on view,
> Its suites of reception every one,
>   Its private apartment and bedroom too;
>
> "For a ticket, apply to the Publisher."
>   No: thanking the public, I must decline.
> A peep through my window, if folk prefer;
>   But, please you, no foot over threshold of mine![33]

He ends the poem with the idea that entrance testifies to an "earthquake" or to a weakness of poetic structure. One who wishes to "penetrate" "must dive by the spirit-sense," not force an intrusive visit.

> "Hoity toity! A street to explore,
>   Your house the exception! *With this same key
> Shakespeare unlocked his heart*,' once more!"
>   Did Shakespeare? If so, the less Shakespeare he![34]

Pater and Proust, unlike Browning, wish, it seems, to validate their private worlds and to invite readers inside, much as James, towards the end of his life, attempted to do in the prefaces to his novels. Clearly, architecture offers itself as an analogue to these writers and others who wish to take a stand on the relationship between themselves, their art works, and their viewing public.

THREE

Architecture and Memory

THE *ars memoria* tradition has been documented and analyzed by Frances Yates in her seminal work, *The Art of Memory*;[35] insofar as much of my study has been concerned with vestiges of this tradition, I am indebted to Miss Yates.[36] For our purposes, it is important to recognize that this tradition does not propose an explicitly analogous relationship between architecture and memory: architecture and memory function primarily as *devices*, each in the service of the other. The philosophers and religious thinkers who advanced the *ars memoria* tradition used architecture as a structure or model to facilitate remembering; architects and architectural theorists enjoyed the possibility that architecture, actual edifices, could conquer forgetfulness by embodying the past or by stimulating its recall through architectural style, character, or detail. Quintilian, in his *Institutio oratoria*, describes architecture as memory device:

Places are chosen, and marked with the utmost possible variety, as a spacious house divided into a number of rooms. Everything of note therein is diligently imprinted on the mind, in order that thought may be able to run through all the parts without let or hindrance. The first task is to secure that there shall be no difficulty in running through these, for that memory must be most firmly fixed which helps another memory. Then what has been written down, or thought of, is noted by a sign to remind of it. This sign may be drawn from a whole "thing," as navigation or warfare, or from some "word"; for what is slipping from the memory is recovered by the admonition of a single word. . . . These signs are then arranged as follows. The first notion is placed, as it were, in the forecourt; the second, let us say in the atrium; the remainder are placed in order all round the impluvium, and committed not only to bedrooms and parlours, but even to statues and the like. This done, when it is required to revive the memory, one begins from the first place to run through all, demanding what it is required to remember, all are linked one to another as in a chorus nor can what follows wander from what has gone before to which it is joined, only the preliminary labour of learning being required. . . . We require therefore places, either real or imaginary, and images or simulacra which must be invented.[37]

Quintilian's description of architecture as a memory model is careful and precise; I am not certain whether we shall again encounter it in such clarity. We have already seen that Augustine, in his meditation on memory, demonstrates familiarity with the *ars memoria* tradition; unlike Quintilian, however, Augustine translates the architectural device into metaphor. Memory is the grand "storehouse for countless images" (X, viii, 12) or the "great treasure-house" (X, viii, 14) which holds the permanent collection of the mind's recorded activities; apparently, as Augustine tells us, this storage house for mental events easily adds its own rooms to maintain records of newly acquired mental collectibles, so that in this "inner hiding place" (X, viii, 12) there is a "vast cache" (X, viii, 14) and "vast cloister" (X, viii, 14) which contains a "wonderful system of compartments" (X, ix, 16) and "innumerable caverns and hollows" (X, viii, 26).[38]

As metaphor, architecture remains serviceable to subsequent philosophers who wish to discuss memory but who either do not know or choose not to employ the *ars memoria* techniques. When Locke speaks of memory, he describes structures architectural and tomb-like, where though the brass and marble remain, yet the inscriptions are effaced by time, and the imagery moulders away. The pictures drawn in our minds are laid in fading colours; and if not sometimes refreshed, vanish and disappear.[39]

Freud, too, uses architecture when he seeks to describe conservation, minds which cannot forget experience or sensation. Freud chooses not one building but a city of buildings, Rome, beautifully wearing its history in successive architectural monuments. After describing in some detail the cycles of construction and destruction of specific buildings, Freud asks that we make

the fantastic supposition that Rome were not a human dwelling-place, but a mental entity with just as long and varied a past history: that is, in which nothing once constructed had perished, and all the earlier stages of development had survived alongside the latest.[40]

The spatial analogue offers Freud relief from viewing the mind or memory as temporal and sequential such that he can explain how a remembered experience, even if distant in time, may be experienced as immediate.

Whether we discuss Freud or the *ars memoria* tradition, architecture as analogue, metaphor, or device, we need to ask if the use of the analogue and of the device involves conceiving that memory shares some of the qualities of its analogue.[41] Richard Wollheim, in an essay "The Mind and the Mind's Image of Itself,"[42] presents an architectural image of mind as room or interior space into which thoughts may enter from the outside or in which they may arise, already inside. However much the image is respectful of Freud's, and offered in homage to Wollheim's more immediate teacher, Melanie Klein, Wollheim nonetheless feels that he must

THE ANALOGICAL TRADITION

defend himself; and his defense has much to do with literary architecture. Wollheim writes:

> I foresee two immediate objections. The first would be that I have taken what is no more than a sustained metaphor as though it were, or were intended as, a literal description. We may speak of thoughts entering the mind or breaking in upon the mind or just being in the mind, but when we do so, the phrases that we use do not reflect what we actually believe. They are mere turns of speech. Now whatever sympathy we may have with the general impulse of this argument–which I shall return to later–the argument as it stands is tendentious. For it assumes that we have a clear distinction between what is metaphorical and what is not: which we do not have. As a minimum someone who uses this argument must show that there is an alternative way of describing the facts in question–here it would be, of reporting the relevant mental states–which could make a good claim to be literal description. And I do not see that in the present case this condition can be fulfilled. There is no more reason for holding that the assertion that, say, thoughts are in the mind is a metaphor, than there would be for making the corresponding claim about the assertion that fictional characters are in a novel: a parallel we might remember.[43]

What Wollheim notices here is the language (model) of spatial extension; and he raises the issue of whether our mental experience (act) cannot not be spatial–are not dreams like holograms?–even though the space we experience is not substantial and cannot be recovered on a plane surface. Wollheim also makes explicit another parallel, one we have temporarily neglected but the one this entire book has been about: architecture/memory and literature. That this analogue appears when a philosopher discusses memory and the mind should not sur-

LITERARY ARCHITECTURE

prise us: even Quintilian, preserving and representing Cicero, comments:

> We require therefore places, either real or imaginary, and images or simulacra which must be invented. *Images are as words* by which we note the things we have to learn, so that as Cicero says, *"we use places as wax and images as letters."* It will be as well to quote his actual words:–"One must employ a large number of places which must be well-lighted, clearly set out in order, at moderate intervals apart, and images which are active, which are sharply defined, unusual, and which have the power of speedily encountering and *penetrating the mind."*[44] (italics mine)

Architecture, like literature, may as a device facilitate recall of the past and as an analogue may represent or stand for memory. This leads us, quite naturally, to an idea expressed not by philosophers but by architects: architecture may conquer forgetfulness by embodying the past, by recording the past, or by stimulating recall of the past. It may embody the past by being old; it may record the past by its inscriptions and engravings; it may stimulate recall of the past by its style or character. And as a record, it may be read much as literature is.

We might say, most generally, that revival movements in architecture demonstrate with a kind of explicitness the interest, on the part of architects, in reviving and preserving the past, whether an historical period (Greek Revival),[45] an age of belief (High Gothic),[46] or a past social order (vernacular).[47] Although all architecture in some way influences, morally and aesthetically, its inhabitants, it is not until modern cities–with new buildings, new building materials, industry, mass housing, not to mention slums–threatened to destroy

THE ANALOGICAL TRADITION

the past that we find architects and writers directing more and more attention to this specific attribute of architecture, its "Lamp of Memory." Crucial, however, to the attempt to preserve the past, or newly recreate it, is the possibility that such re-creation can be done, that if one wishes, one may discover what materials were used, how construction was accomplished, in what tasks workers were employed.[48] In this way, the tools for what we commonly call Victorian historicism were available to architects should they choose to have their buildings recall the past. And I think that we can discover what Sir Nikolaus Pevsner calls a clue to Victorian historicism: associationism, that is the power of buildings to *evoke* associations in the mind of the reader/observer/inhabitant. Once architects could assume that their monuments communicated, they were able to direct evocation to historical, memorial, ends. Hence one architect might choose various styles, much as Barry made King Edward's School in Birmingham Gothic in order to evoke the learning of the cloister, while his Edinburgh High School (Hamilton) was Grecian, evoking the wisdom of the *academe*.[49] Barry's clubs, those in the "guise of" Quattrocento palaces, evoke the "highly cultured merchant, say Lorenzo the Magnificent," while the impressive Houses of Parliament had to be either Gothic or Elizabethan in order that they might represent and enable recall of the "venerable English parliamentary past."[50] Some architects, dismayed by modern architecture, wrote that buildings should not try to teach "new things" but should aid one in "recollecting" the past. In *The Civil Engineer and Architect's Journal* (1839), we find such an admonition to architects:

LITERARY ARCHITECTURE

> Texts or inscriptions may be so managed as to become very ornamental and impressive. But the letters should be large and deep, and cut in the hard stone, as a part of the original conception of the building.... The architect should also avoid the most vulgar error, so often committed in printed books, of adding chapter and verse at the end of the line. *Whenever a quotation is addressed to the imagination of the reader we must assume that we are merely bringing to his recollection the words of an author whose works are already known to him. We should not appear to teach something new.*[51]

The writer continues:

> The total want of inscriptions upon our modern buildings is a further proof of the vagueness of modern architecture. It was not thus among the ancients. They built for the people who saw their chronicles upon the marble. The lines were read by the fathers, the children, the grandchildren, and after the lapse of ages, the moss-grown characters add the most powerful charms to the majestic ruin. These means of giving interest to architecture are now always neglected. The Waterloo Bridge, unquestionably the finest in the world, might for anything which appears upon the granite, have been erected by a people ignorant of the art of writing. It does not even bear a date.[52]

Some writers went so far as to supply "mnemotechnic rules" to accompany their architectural treatises.[53] But it is at this point, when it seems so clear that architecture and memory constantly evoke allusion to literature, that we need to turn to our fourth analogue, architecture and literature.

FOUR

Architecture and Literature

OF ALL THE analogues, this one concerns us most. Not only has it been the central subject of this entire study; the architecture-literature analogue also in some way subsumes the other three while preserving an independence and history all its own. The analogue—I sometimes call it *ut architectura poesis*—is prerequisite to literary architecture and is in evidence whenever writers choose to compare their literary art to architecture. The term *literature* in fact is too modern for the analogue as it first appeared; for the comparison was used initially by orators, and its primary function then was not to describe the structure of an entire work of rhetorical art but to describe the composition of periods, the diction, style, and structure of those smaller units. Cicero, in *De oratore*, solicits architecture as one of many analogues for oratory, demonstrating that "the things possessing most utility also have the greatest amount of dignity, and indeed frequently of beauty also":

> In temples and colonnades, the pillars are to support the structure, yet they are as dignified in appearance as they are useful. Yonder pediment of the Capitol and those of the other temples are the product not of beauty but of actual necessity; for it was in calculating how to make the rain-water fall off the two sides of the roof that the dignified design of the gables resulted as a by-product of the needs of the structure—with the consequence that even if one were erecting a citadel in heaven, where no rain could fall, it would be thought certain to be entirely lacking in dignity without a pediment.

The same is the case in regard to all the divisions of speech—virtually unavoidable practical requirements produce charm of style as a result. It was a failure or scantiness of breath that originated periodic structure and pauses between words, but now that this has once been discovered, it is so attractive, that even if a person were endowed with breath that never failed, we should still not wish him to deliver an unbroken flow of words.[54]

Like Cicero, Dionysius of Halicarnassus uses the architectural analogue in his treatise *On Literary Composition* to "illustrate" broadly his general conception of "the science of composition."[55] He solicits the analogue subsequently for more particular purposes, to aid him in describing types of composition. It is applied most extensively to describe what Dionysius calls Austere Composition:

The characteristic feature of austere arrangement is this:—It requires that the words should be like columns firmly planted and placed in strong positions, so that each word should be seen on every side, and that the parts should be appreciable distances from one another, being separated by perceptible intervals. It does not in the least shrink from using frequently harsh sound-clashings which jar on the ear; like blocks of building stone that are laid together unworked, blocks that are not square and smooth, but preserve their natural roughness and irregularity. It is prone for the most part to expansion by means of great, spacious words. It objects to being confined to short syllables, except under occasional stress of necessity.[56]

The passage should bring to mind Pater's, Hopkins's, and Proust's space-word concepts, Hopkins's percussive-word concept, and James's space-literature concept. Both Cicero and Dionysius use the analogue for its structural richness. Quintilian also chooses to describe aspects of rhetoric by analogy to architecture. Of order, Quintilian writes:

> For words are not cut to suit metrical feet, and are therefore transferred from place to place to form the most suitable combinations, just as in the case of unhewn stones their very irregularity is the means of suggesting what other stones they will best fit and what will supply them with the surest resting-place. On the other hand, the happiest effects of language are produced when it is found possible to employ the natural order, apt connexion and appropriate rhythm.[57]

In a similar fashion, Quintilian embarks upon the comparison with architecture after he has been speaking about invention, as if he wishes to make sure that an appeal to emotions and to the inventiveness of a speaker will not be at the expense of order and structure.

> I think that enough has been said on the subject of invention. For I have dealt not merely with the methods by which we may instruct the judge, but also with the means of appealing to his emotions. But just as it is not sufficient for those who are erecting a building merely to collect stone and timber and other building materials, but skilled masons are required to arrange and place them, so in speaking, however abundant the matter may be, it will merely form a confused heap unless arrangement be employed to reduce it to order and to give it connexion and firmness of structure.[58]

Classical rhetorical tradition establishes, to some extent then, the conditions for subsequent use of the architectural analogue, especially when it aids writers in describing matters of composition and structure. We can document the persistence of the analogue through the Renaissance and well into the nineteenth century, discovering it in such temperamentally different writers as David Hume, William Hazlitt, Arthur Schopenhauer;[59] even Ruskin, in his *Elements of English Prosody*, solicits the analogue when he discusses the stanza, which he describes as "the chamber of a house," properly signifying a "piece of a song enclosed or partitioned by itself."[60]

The analogue is also used by writers who wish to describe larger structures, to suggest, perhaps, how separate poems might relate to each other and so constitute a different sort of corpus, or how discrete chapters in a novel work together. "The Temple" is one such example, as is Wordsworth's planned organization of poems: Wordsworth thought of *The Prelude* as "a sort of Portico to *The Recluse*, part of the same building," much as he thought all his "minor Pieces," when "properly arranged," would be equivalent to "little cells, oratories, and with sepulchral recesses, ordinarily included in those edifices."[61] Up to a point it can be said that Pater and Hopkins were more interested in using the architectural analogy to describe smaller units of structure such as sentences or lines (and thus they were closer to classical writers), whereas Proust and James used the analogy to describe entire novel structures, Proust in this way being very like Wordsworth.

The use of the analogue by architects and architectural theorists originates with Vitruvius who, as we have seen, borrowed rhetorical terms and concepts of style to aid him in his treatise on architecture. The analogue remained useful in this fashion as long as levels of literary style, determined by or else generating concepts of genre and decorum, corresponded to the classical orders in architecture. (We might even say that non-Classical architecture, or specifically, that Gothic architecture also

THE ANALOGICAL TRADITION

had a literary analogue in the medieval, Christian Summa, for so Erwin Panofsky maintains in *Gothic Architecture and Scholasticism*.)[62] Even in the nineteenth century, despite the fracturing and collapsing of levels of literary style, and also the shifts in architectural values, we find the analogue still used to describe style and character in architecture:

> As the poet seeks that every phrase and word which he employs be poetical and analogous to the style and character of his poem, so should the architect try to keep every member and portion of his building concordant to its intent.[63]

One architect writes of statues in architecture:

> If we may so express ourselves, he [the architect] should sculpture in a style analogous to blank verse, avoiding the prose of conversation, and the rhyme of French tragedy.[64]

And he elsewhere comments on character in architecture:

> The author too combines narrative with conversation, and the poet song with epic verse. The architect composes a design of Ionic and Corinthian, or of the Doric and Ionic. The true taste of both consists in maintaining one character through the whole, and so combining as to produce harmony without monotony, and so contrasting as to produce variety without confusion.[65]

Even Sir John Summerson in 1963 writes a book entitled *The Classical Language of Architecture* in which his individual chapter titles include "The Grammar of Antiquity" (which might remind us of Raphael Brandon's nineteenth-century work *The Grammar of Ornament*), "Sixteenth Century Linguistics," and "The Rhetoric of the Baroque."[66]

LITERARY ARCHITECTURE

The analogy reaches still further: architects conceive of buildings as books which can be read.

> A public monument is a book opened for the perusal of the multitude; unless it declares its meaning fully, plainly, and sensibly, the main use is lost.[67]

Ruskin, in fact, uses the idea of reading a building to help him demonstrate his preference for the Gothic over the classical in architecture: of symmetrical, correct buildings, he comments:

> The idea of reading a building as we would read Milton or Dante, and getting the same kind of delight out of the stones as out of the stanzas, never enters our mind for a moment. And for good reason;–There is indeed rhythm in the verses, quite as strict as the symmetries or rhythm of the architecture, and a thousand times more beautiful, but there is something else than rhythm. The verses were neither made to order, nor to match, as the capitals were; and we have therefore a kind of pleasure in them other than a sense of propriety. But it requires a strong effort of common sense to shake ourselves quit of all that we have been taught for the last two centuries, and wake to the perception of a truth ... that great art, whether expressing itself in words, colours, or stones, does *not* say the same thing over and over again; that the merit of architectural, as of every other art, consists in its saying new and different things; that to repeat itself is no more a characteristic of genius in marble than it is of genius in print; and that we may, without offending any laws of good taste, require of an architect, as we do of a novelist, that he should be not only correct, but entertaining.[68]

The notion of reading architecture presumes that architecture has a language of sorts. And architects do describe their language; in fact, they believe that they have the equivalent of an alphabet:

Symbolic representations were employed by the ancients, who always understood their work with a thorough propriety of invention and of conception. Symbolic figures form as definite a mode of conveying ideas as the letters of the alphabet: when combined they form a word and impart a notion. But the symbols of the classical age are grounded upon a creed wholly foreign to us, and which has reached us only in disjointed fragments. The alphabet has gone out of use, and the language is a dead language; and in its place we mock the ancients by substituting *allegorical* representations, that is to say, by hewing metaphors in stone, vague, strained, and bombastical, affording no satisfaction to the vulgar.[69]

The analogue is even used towards the turn of the century when English architects were abandoning revival modes for English vernacular architecture: consequently, "design" is distinguished from "building," the one having to do with region and appropriateness of materials, the other with those "universal" qualities common to all buildings.

Architecture, while native to each Country, has a Classic tongue. Design has its dialects, but the Art of Building is a Universal Language.[70]

Ironically, while building might be universal, there is "writing" which only architects read:

Now, each house is but a monument recording an idea, maintained against overwhelming odds; a monument on which is often plainly written the memory of many small defeats. There is other writing too, but only Architects will read it.[71]

And so we seem to find that architecture comes to be more and more esoteric, that the layman, especially in the United States, has lost the art of reading monuments, and that even in Europe, to some the art of reading old buildings has given way to commercial interests in the new. For writers in the nineteenth century, however, the notion that one could read a building perhaps suggested that one could architect a book, but more importantly, that readers could read those architectural monuments which comprise the settings of fiction, nonfiction, or poetry.

We thus have four sets of comparisons in which we may observe architecture to be a common "half." I have tried to suggest throughout this book that Pater, Hopkins, Proust, and James each use architecture as an analogue for body, for mind, for memory, and for literature. And I have named the fusion literary architecture. Of course with none of these writers is architecture the only art analogue they appeal to: music is an important analogue for Pater, Hopkins, and Proust, but less so for James, while painting is very important to Pater, Proust, and James, but less so to Hopkins. And it has been made clear to us that architecture as an analogue can coexist with other art analogues. Hopkins and Proust each translate music into architecture and architecture back into music; and Pater and James decorate their literary monuments—either their carefully architected sentences or their broadly but no less carefully articulated fictions—with the colorations and images of paintings, frescoes, or tapestries.

Once we know that in the nineteenth century there was a mode of perceiving architecture as a kind of communications device which was meant to teach or evoke, we may proceed to read literary architecture in a special way: perhaps readers/viewers are supposed to conjure history as they conjure up the Venetian palaces of James or the Poynton spoils; to understand philosophy as they understand the villas in Pater's *Marius the Epicurean* or Hopkins's "Duns Scotus's Oxford"; or to understand an aesthetic statement as they understand Proust's Gothic cathedral which spans time and space. It must be recognized, moreover, and remembered that architectural analogues were not conscripted by writers into performing services never intended; on the contrary, architects explicitly intended buildings to be symbolic, to stimulate trains of association, to be read; it was assumed that buildings would influence the people living in them; and choice of style—whether Gothic, Palladian, Venetian, Norman, Doric, or whatever—was meant to indicate a political or national preference as well as to suggest something about the nature or state of industry, civilization, moral or religious values. It cannot seem trivial, then, that Pater, Hopkins, and Proust each prefer the Gothic to other styles, while James prefers the Palladian, varying his other architectural styles because of national setting, political sentiment, or the particular psychology of his characters.

We also know that architects themselves were becoming, in the nineteenth century, more and more interested in the function of buildings, the use of materials, as well as in inventing or changing aesthetic values concerning space, light, views. In this way, then, when architecture is selected as a model for literary art, it comes ready with its own expressive qualities given it by architectural theorists or architects themselves; and we might well understand how the description of a country house such as Gardencourt in James's *Portrait of a Lady* is meant to evoke in a reader who knows how to read "real" houses all those things which nineteenth-century readers knew about politics, wealth, city and country, and so on.

I have tried to suggest some other uses of the analogue. If we consider the independent history of philosophy, we know that questions of how and what we know, of subjective perception, of the unconscious, were all of concern to nineteenth and early twentieth-century writers. Since architecture also serves as an image for the mind, it could offer to writers an image to describe private perception (being inside), the unconscious (basements), egos and superegos (attics); it could prove or verify that an outside ("objective"?) perception could correspond to or differ from an interior or private ("subjective"?) perspective; that one could talk about the growth and movement of self-awareness by speaking of walking through the house of one's childhood, or for that matter, about frozen awareness, a sort of temperamental determinism or stasis; and that one could talk about unwanted thoughts or feelings as if they were intruders. Language itself may then represent a translation outward of inner thoughts and feelings, just as literature may be viewed as being not only temporal but spatial as well. In still other ways, if poetry and prose late in the century were thought to be reflecting a loss of control, as if a degenerate Wordsworthian spontaneity were still spawning irresponsible writing, then architecture as analogue could represent an alternative: literary structures could be constructed and superintended just as a "finer edge" could be restored to a dulled language. Likewise, writers could use the analogue to suggest that literature and ideas need not strike root and bloom simultaneously but could be built slowly, with foresight and precision, as literary architecture.

THE ANALOGICAL TRADITION

For Pater and Hopkins, architecture helps them to describe controls which would resuscitate language; for James, it helps him to reveal, retrospectively, his craftsmanship, how he trained and restructured organic, germ growth into constructed fictions; for Proust it suggests that he could build with an old language, as with aged stones, but build so that readers would respect and acknowledge the past and his care in reconstructing it. Architecture is the only art object we actually live in. However, we live in another construction—we do not commonly call it art—also of our own making: consciousness. Literary architecture is a gesture toward that.

NOTES

Introduction

1. See C. Watkins in *The American Heritage Dictionary of the English Language*, ed. W. Morris (Boston, New York, 1969, 1970), p. 1509. The Indo-European word is *bheu*. In this context, I should like to add that I am using the word "building" as the category of which "architecture" is the realized art or the idol. Recently come to my attention is an argument by Heidegger in an essay coincidentally titled "Building Dwelling Thinking" in *Poetry, Language, Thought*, trans. A. Hofstadter (New York, 1971). Heidegger isolates and addresses just these terms and concepts. He glosses *building* this way: "The Old English and High German word for building, *buan*, means to dwell. . . . *bauen, buan, bhu, beo*, are our word *bin* in the versions: *ich bin*, I am, *du bist*, you are, the imperative form *bis*, be. What then does *ich bin* mean? The old word *bauen*, to which the *bin* belongs, answers: *ich bin, du bist* mean: I dwell, you dwell. The way in which you are and I am, the manner in which we humans *are* on the earth, is *Buan*, dwelling" (pp. 146-147). Building as dwelling means "as being on the earth." Later, in the same essay, Heidegger states: "But that thinking itself belongs to dwelling in the same sense as building, although in a different way, may perhaps be attested to by the course of thought here attempted. Building and thinking are, each in its own way, inescapable for dwelling" (pp. 160-161). See, for another contrast to Heidegger, my discussion of *dwelling*, pp. 12, 262.

2. I might also have said "structure as consciousness, perception as conventions, belief as systems." The power of movement, perhaps the movement itself, may dissolve place distinctions, outer and inner. For the moment of noticing the

movement, then, our sense of boundaries disappears. The noticing of correspondence is like a noticing of mirrors: it is actually the activity of re-cognition and itself depends on mirroring, that is, on re-flection. Here, once again, we experience, as our activity of perception, the object of our perception: reflection of this sort is actually a mirroring of mirrors.

The words I use throughout the Introduction are chosen with special attention to their prefixes: I use re-, di-, to denote spatial conditions or quantities in space. Such prefixes function as the place organizers of these words, while the roots or verbs as I am using them function as the time co-ordinates: "recognize," like "reflection," for instance, requires the space of "again in time," a space-time lapse or interval having to have occurred.

3. Walter Pater, "Emerald Uthwart," in *Imaginary Portraits*, ed. E. J. Brzenk (London, 1964), p. 57; and Gerard Manley Hopkins, "Spelt from Sibyl's Leaves," in *The Poems of Gerard Manley Hopkins*, ed. W. H. Gardner and N. H. MacKenzie, 4th ed. (London, 1967), p. 97.

4. Watkins, in *American Heritage Dictionary*, p. 1513. The Indo-European root word for *dwell* is *dheu*.

5. We might say this yet another way, using a word with less apparent ontological significance but more suggestive of art-as-craft or *techne*: *bringing* is like *making*, so we have "the making of being," and "the making of being seeable."

Chapter I

ONE

1. "F," "In Pater's Rooms," *The Speaker*, 26 August 1899, p. 208.

2. Ibid., p. 207.

3. Ibid.

4. Walter Pater, "Style," in *Prose of the Victorian Period*, ed. W. E. Buckler (Cambridge, Massachusetts, 1958), p. 566. "Style" first appeared in *Fortnightly Review* (December 1888)

and subsequently in *Appreciations; With an Essay on Style* (London and New York, 1897).

5. Ibid., p. 570.

6. Ibid., p. 560.

7. Ibid., p. 563.

8. Ibid., p. 561.

9. Ibid., p. 562.

10. Ibid. The comparison or parallel between architecture and the human body finds its architectural origins in the writings of Vitruvius, *The Ten Books on Architecture* (trans. M. H. Morgan, New York, 1960) written for the Imperator Caesar. That the comparison persists well into the eighteenth and nineteenth centuries may be seen by consulting such journals as *The Builder's Magazine* or *The Civil Engineer and Architect's Journal*: among other terms in these journals, we find *eye*, *eye-brow*, *face*, *elbow*, *dentells*, *nose*, *buttocks*, and *bust*, let alone those more polite terms such as *joint* used by Pater. See *The Builder's Magazine* (London, 1774) and *The Civil Engineer and Architect's Journal* II (London, 1839), p. 365. Also see my discussion in Chapter V, section one, pp. 229–233.

11. *Window* is actually a combined form of *wind* (weather, air in motion, formless or unembodied, external energy) and *eye* (the seeing or perceiving edge of mind). See E. Klein, *A Complete Etymological Dictionary of the English Language* (Amsterdam, London, New York, 1966). See also my discussion of James, Chapter IV, section two, especially p. 185.

12. Pater, p. 568.

13. Pater, "Conclusion," in *Prose of the Victorian Period*, ed. W. E. Buckler (Cambridge, Massachusetts, 1958), p. 551. "Conclusion" originally appeared in *Studies in the History of the Renaissance* (London, 1873). The title was changed in the 1912 edition to *The Renaissance: Studies in Art and Poetry*.

14. Pater, "Style," p. 570.

15. "F," p. 208.

16. Ibid.

17. Pater, here, is working within the tradition of other Victorians, especially architects, who used buildings to stimulate associations. For an excellent historical account of the architectural tradition, see the opening chapters of George Hersey, *High Victorian Gothic: A Study in Associationism* (Baltimore, Maryland, 1972). Pater's attitude to architecture is typical, I think, of the general English tendency in the visual arts towards the literary, the associational, the picturesque. This view is still, in the twentieth century, widely accepted. See George Hersey (text cited above); Sir Nikolaus Pevsner, *Some Architectural Writers of the Nineteenth Century* (London, 1972); Lord Kenneth Clark, *The Gothic Revival* (London, 1928).

18. Pater, "Style," p. 562.

19. Walter Pater, "Emerald Uthwart," in *Imaginary Portraits*, ed. E. J. Brzenk (London, 1964), p. 58. "Emerald Uthwart" first appeared in *New Review* (June and July 1892) and was reprinted in *Miscellaneous Studies: A Series of Essays* (London, 1895).

20. Pater, *Imaginary Portraits*, p. 17. For an illuminating discussion of Pater published after I had written my essay, see Richard Wollheim, "Walter Pater as a Critic of the Arts," in *On Art and the Mind* (London, 1973), especially pp. 160, 166, and 169. Professor Wollheim recognizes the importance of the genre Imaginary Portraits; he also discusses Pater's philosophy of aesthetics with attention to Pater's concepts of language and mind.

TWO

21. Pater, "A Prince of Court Painters," *Imaginary Portraits*, pp. 95-96. "A Prince of Court Painters" first appeared in *Macmillan's Magazine* (October 1885) and subsequently in *Imaginary Portraits* (London and New York, 1887).

22. For my knowledge of the *ars memoria* tradition, I am indebted to Frances Yates, *The Art of Memory* (London, 1958), not only for her own excellent writing but also for her bibliography on the memory tradition. For an interesting account of the *ut architectura poesis tradition*, see Alastair Fowler, "Pe-

NOTES TO PAGES 34–38

riodization and Interart Analogies," *New Literary History*, September 1972, especially pp. 501–503, and Per Palme, "*Ut Architectura Poesis*," in *Idea and Form*, ed. N. G. Sandblad, Acta Universitatis Upsaliensis, Figura Nova Series, I (Uppsala, 1959), 95–107.

23. For a discussion of architectural manuals, see Chapter V below.

24. For a discussion of architectural borrowings, see Peter Collins, *Changing Ideals in Modern Architecture* (London, 1965), pp. 173–185.

25. Pater, "Prosper Mérimée," in *Miscellaneous Studies: A Series of Essays*, ed. C. L. Shadwell (London, 1895), p. 18. "Prosper Mérimée" was presented as a lecture at Oxford (November 1890); it was published in *Fortnightly Review* (December 1890) and subsequently reprinted in *Miscellaneous Studies* (London, 1895).

26. John Ruskin, *The Seven Lamps of Architecture*, *Works*, VIII, ed. E. T. Cook and Alexander Wedderburn (London, 1902–1912), 224. All my citations to Ruskin throughout *Literary Architecture* will be to this, the Library Edition, of his works.

27. Ibid.

28. Pater, "Emerald Uthwart," *Imaginary Portraits*, pp. 54–55.

29. Ibid., p. 57.

30. Pater, *Plato and Platonism: A Series of Lectures* (London, 1893), p. 245.

31. Pater's *design* is generally static, the fixed structure of house-mind or the equally fixed architectonic of literary style. Predictably, growth or movement, as the soul of character or of style, occurs within spatial confines of structure or outside. While furniture and decor may change, even the "quasi-decorative" people, only rarely would one alter completed structures. More often, especially in Pater's fiction, an entire site is abandoned when its symbolic or associative import has been fully exploited. This movement has been documented

by numerous Pater critics, especially as it occurs in *Marius the Epicurean*.

32. Pater, "The Child in the House," *Imaginary Portraits*, p. 16. "The Child in the House" first appeared as "Imaginary Portrait, The Child in the House" in *Macmillan's Magazine* (August 1878). Pater's use of "home" as the starting-point for this fictional reminiscence suggests to me a passage by Thomas Aquinas. Aquinas writes, "It is necessary for reminiscence to take some starting-point, whence one begins to proceed to reminisce. For this reason some men may be seen to reminisce from places in which they were children, where something was said or done, or thought, using the place as it were as the starting-point for reminiscence; because access to the place is like a starting-point for all those things raised in it" (Thomas Aquinas, *In Aristotelis libros de sensu et sensato, de memoria et reminiscentia commentarium*, ed., R. M. Spiazzi, Turin and Rome, 1949), p. 107. My translation is that of Frances Yates, *The Art of Memory* (London, 1966), p. 82.

33. Florian's first quality of "intelligence," interestingly, perceived by his mother is the quality of his memory. See p. 19.

34. Pater, "The Child in the House," pp. 16–17.

35. Ibid., p. 17.

36. Ibid., p. 18.

37. Ibid., p. 17.

38. Ibid., p. 19.

39. For this discussion, I am using the most generalizable characteristics of the artificial memory system as conceived by classical rhetors. Again, my indebtedness is to Frances Yates for such a summary.

40. Pater, "Style," p. 562.

41. Ibid.

42. While I do not wish to speculate as to the reasons for Pater's fears, I do think it important to notice that Proust, Hopkins, and James do not quite share Pater's pessimism and morbidity; and perhaps the absence of fear—what we might prefer to call the presence of literary daring—helps or enables

these other writers to achieve creatively what Pater could at best understand and suggest.

43. Pater, "Style," p. 559.

44. Pater, "Notre Dame d'Amiens," in *Miscellaneous Studies* (London, 1924), pp. 124–125.

Chapter II

ONE

1. Gerard Manley Hopkins, *The Letters of Gerard Manley Hopkins to Robert Bridges*, ed. Claude Colleer Abbott (London, 1955), pp. 209–210. Further citations to definitive editions of Hopkins's work will appear in parentheses following the passage quoted. I have used the standard abbreviations:

- CD *The Correspondence of Gerard Manley Hopkins and Richard Watson Dixon*, ed. Claude Colleer Abbott (London, 1955).
- FL *Further Letters of Gerard Manley Hopkins*, ed. Claude Colleer Abbott, 2nd ed. (London, 1956).
- JP *Journals and Papers of Gerard Manley Hopkins*, ed. Humphry House and Graham Storey (London, 1959).
- LB *The Letters of Gerard Manley Hopkins to Robert Bridges*, ed. Claude Colleer Abbott (London, 1955).

All references to Hopkins's poems are drawn from *The Poems of Gerard Manley Hopkins*, ed. W. H. Gardner and N. H. MacKenzie, 4th ed. (London, 1967).

2. John Henry Parker, *A Glossary of Terms used in Grecian, Roman, Italian and Gothic Architecture*, 5th ed., enl. (Oxford, 1850). 1st. ed. J. H. Parker, 1846. The *Glossary* is in three volumes, the first giving the terms in alphabetical order, the second two giving drawings as appropriate examples.

TWO

3. This refers to Figure 1 in JP, reproduced here in Plate 11 (upper left).

4. Hopkins refers to the meaning of *keel* at least three times elsewhere in his journals. This particular reference is preceded by a drawing of a Gothic window (JP Figure 23), reproduced here as Plate 10.

5. See JP Figure 17, reproduced here as Plate 15. See also Plates 13, 14, and 16. Hopkins's drawings, especially on these pages, are remarkably similar to the hair and water studies of Leonardo da Vinci and reflect Hopkins's interest in rhythm, motion, mechanical action, interests Leonardo held as well.

6. The rest of the passage is interesting: "One day early in March when long streamers were rising from over Kemble End one large flake loop-shaped, not a streamer but belonging to the string, moving too slowly to be seen, seemed to cap and fill the zenith with a white shire of cloud. I looked long up at it till the tall height and the beauty of the scaping—regularly curled knots springing if I remember from fine stems, like foliation in wood or stone—had strongly grown on me. It changed beautiful changes, growing more into ribs and one stretch of running into branching like coral. Unless you refresh the mind from time to time you cannot always remember or believe how deep the inscape in things is" (JP, 204–205, 1871). (Plate 19)

THREE

7. Walter Pater, "Style" (*Fortnightly Review*, December 1888), as reprinted in *Prose of the Victorian Period*, ed. W. E. Buckler (Cambridge, Mass., 1958), p. 561.

8. Ibid.

9. Hopkins comments, "It is because where the structure forces us to appreciate each syllable it is natural and in the order of things for us to dwell on all modifications affecting the general result or type which the ear preserves and accordingly with such as are themselves harmonious we are pleased, but in prose where syllables have none or little determinate value to emphasize them is unmeaning" (JP, 85, 1865).

10. Its full title originally read "Rhythm and the other Structural Parts of Oratory and Poetry—Verse–." It was cor-

rected by Hopkins to read "Rhythm and other structural parts of Rhetoric–Verse."

FOUR

11. For this letter I thank Paul Thompson, who came across it in reading Butterfield's correspondence in preparation for *William Butterfield* (London, 1972).

12. Hopkins continually spelled Babbacombe "Babbicombe."

Chapter III

ONE

1. Comte Jean de Gaigneron, from a letter in his possession, translated by and quoted from André Maurois, *The Quest for Proust* (London, 1962), pp. 178–179. Because of the controversy over translation of Proust's title *A la recherche du temps perdu*, I am retaining the French. All references to the text are to the two-volume Random House edition (1934), translated by C. K. Scott-Moncrieff and Frederick A. Blossom. Citations appear in parentheses, indicating first the volume and then the page number.

2. Recall Walter Pater's entire statement: "For the literary architecture, if it is to be rich and expressive, involves not only foresight of the end in the beginning, but also development or growth of design, in the process of execution, with many irregularities, surprises, and afterthoughts; the contingent as well as the necessary being submitted under the unity of the whole. As truly, to the lack of such architectural design . . . informing an entire, perhaps very intricate, composition, which shall be . . . true from first to last to that vision within, may be attributed those weaknesses of conscious or unconscious repetition of word, phrase, motive or member of the whole matter, indicating, as Flaubert was aware, an original structure in thought not organically complete." (W. Pater, "Style," in *Prose of the Victorian Period*, ed. W. E. Buckler, Cambridge, Massachusetts, 1958, p. 562.) That Proust knew Pater's writings is documented in conversation with Proust

and by Proust's explicit citations of Pater in his essays. See Sybil de Souza, *L'Influence de Ruskin sur Proust* (Montpellier, 1932), pp. 43–44; and Marcel Proust, *A Massacre of Churches*, trans. G. Hopkins (London, 1948), p. 76.

3. Gilles Deleuze, *Proust and Signs*, trans. R. Howard (London, 1974), p. 143. I am indebted, throughout this chapter, to Deleuze's excellent analysis of Proust.

4. Cf. Richard Macksey, "Architecture of Time: Dialectics and Structure" (pp. 104–122), and Georges Poulet, "Proust and Human Time" (pp. 150–179), in *Proust: A Collection of Critical Essays*, ed. R. Girard (Englewood Cliffs, N.J., 1962). See especially pages 119–121, and 174–177. For a recent and extensive discussion of Proust and architecture, see J. Theodore Johnson, Jr., "Marcel Proust et l'architecture: considérations sur le problème du roman-cathédrale," in *Bulletin de la Société des Amis de Marcel Proust et des Amis de Combray*, Nos. 25 and 26 (1975, 1976). Johnson's discussion emphasizes the parallels between Proust and Ruskin and between Proust and Mâle.

5. See S. T. Coleridge, *Philosophical Lectures* [1818–1819], hitherto unpublished (London, 1949). The whole is larger than, at times prior to, the parts: "Depend on it, whatever is grand, whatever is truly organic and living, the whole is prior to the parts" (p. 196). *Biographia Literaria*, ed. J. Shawcross (Oxford, 1907), I, 180, 185. See also *Shakespearean Criticism*, I, ed. T. M. Raysor (Cambridge, Mass., 1930), 212–213.

6. Proust, "John Ruskin," in *A Massacre of Churches*, p. 59. Proust's definition of stones as "living thoughts" enables him to search for and discover those thoughts imprinted in architectural materials. But Proust carries Ruskin a step further; not only do the stones retain the thoughts of the craftsman, but they contain those of the architectural historian as well. For this reason, Proust finds Ruskin in the stones of Amiens: "Before I knew whether I should find it there, it was Ruskin's soul I sought, that soul which he carved as deeply into the stones of Amiens as did ever they who made the sculptures, for the words of genius are no less effective than the chisel in giving an immortal form to things" (pp. 54–55). Elsewhere

Proust instructs his reader: "You run no risk of spending an afternoon in the town without being able to find him [Ruskin] in the cathedral" (pp. 18-19).

What is also interesting about Proust's essays on Ruskin is his application of associative and memory devices to a work of criticism. Proust writes, "I have tried to equip the reader with, as it were, an improvised memory, furnishing it with Ruskin's other works—a kind of whispering-gallery in which the words taken from the *Bible of Amiens* may establish themselves in his mind by dint of calling forth related echoes" (p. 24). Not only does Proust use the language of architecture to describe the improvised, critical memory he supplies for the reader; but Proust also describes, in this passage, the kind of memory system he adapts to fiction and structures into *A la recherche*. See section four of this chapter.

7. Ruskin as quoted by Proust, "John Ruskin," p. 54.

8. John Ruskin, "The Nature of the Gothic," *The Stones of Venice*, *Works*, X, 190.

9. Ruskin, p. 212.

10. Ibid., p. 240.

11. Macksey, p. 120.

TWO

12. *Translation* is, interestingly, the term used by Alastair Fowler to describe the function of interart analogies. Fowler writes, "Every interart comparison, even between two visual arts, involves a metaphor ('translation')." See A. Fowler, "Periodization and Interart Analogies," in *New Literary History*, September 1972, p. 499. Proust himself uses the term, giving to it a great importance: "The duty and task of a writer," claims Proust, "are those of a translator" (II, 1009). In this sense, the skills required of the reader are also those of the writer; once again, Proust has asked his audience to participate in the making of the "subjective book" *A la recherche*.

Translation, to look back for a moment, was also the term Pater used when he described literary architecture: "Well! All language involves translation from inward to outward," translation of that private "vision." See "Style," in *Prose of the Victorian Period*, p. 568. In Pater, the idea of translation hinges on the opposition between inside and outside; in Proust, the same assumption holds, but the term is used in such a way that it involves skill and control.

13. E. Klein, *A Complete Etymological Dictionary of the English Language* (Amsterdam, London, New York, 1966). For *form*, see *mer-bh*; for *idea*, see *weid*. That *form* comes from a word meaning "to sparkle, gleam" makes sense: we know – can see – form by the light it gives off; in this way, edge of light – beginning of contrast – determines or signifies the shape of the form we see.

14. The image also suggests Picasso collages, which not only display fragments but use the very materials themselves. I have chosen to name Degas since Proust acknowledges his work and since Proust's affinities, in this matter, are more with the Impressionists and Neo-Impressionists.

15. "Mis-knowing" constitutes misreading structures or rooms. Marcel's family misconstrued, probably deliberately, Swann's face, reading it as "a face vacant and roomy as an untenanted house" in which they put their own knowledge of Swann and memory of him. They planted "in the depths of its unvalued eyes a lingering sense ... of idle hours spent together after our weekly dinners, round the card-table or in the garden, during our companionable country life" (I, 15).

16. There are various relationships mind assumes with respect to room: having fantasies involves stopping-up, sealing windows and doors, closing off rooms; seeking or recalling often involves the "mind straying beyond its borders"; thinking involves clearing an empty space; understanding, penetration through façades. Although one mental act can take more than one image, Proust's images are consistent. Likewise, the image can be more or less expansive: the mind can be an entire "city" of which Combray is only a "quarter" (I, 37).

17. Marcel remarks, "Style is for the writer, as for the painter, a question, not of technique but of vision" (II, 1013). For an excellent discussion of inside/outside in terms of visual

NOTES TO PAGE 139

perception and *A la recherche*, see R. Shattuck, *Proust's Binoculars* (New York, 1964), especially pp. 18-19, 21, 42-47; see also H. Moss, *The Magic Lantern of Marcel Proust* (New York, 1962), Chap. 3, p. 37. Finally, for inside/outside in terms of dialectics, see R. Macksey, "The Architecture of Time: Dialectics and Structure," ed. cit. (n. 4 above), especially pp. 104-110.

18. The concept of penetration—which demands an architectural analogue—is crucial to Proust. The work of the artist, Marcel claims, is "to seek to discern something different underneath material, experience, words" (II, 1013); for "reality," Marcel realizes, is to "be found, not in the outward appearance of the subject, but in the extent to which this impression had penetrated to a depth where that appearance was of little importance" (II, 1003). Of supposed truths which do not involve penetration, Marcel writes, "As for the truths which the intelligence—even that of the finest minds—garners right out in the open, lying before it in broad daylight, their value may be very great, but they have harsher outlines and are all on the surface, with no depth, because no depths had to be penetrated in order to get to them and they have not been re-created" (II, 1015). Memory façades are inadequate precisely because they do not permit penetration. See II, 1069, and II, 1122, regarding the difference between "illustrations" which are insufficient and "impressions" which, because one can "plumb [them] to their depths" are adequate. Also see sections three and four of this chapter, including note 22, for a discussion of penetration in terms of language and memory.

Imprinting—as the converse of being impressed—is as necessary as *penetration*: once Marcel can stamp furniture "with the imprint of a living personality," he can return to it or re-conjure it and retrieve from it that special meaning he put there. (See Marcel in Swann's house, I, 411). So, too, in art: "This book, the most difficult of all to decipher, is also the only one dictated to us by reality, the only one the 'imprinting' of which on our consciousness was done by reality itself. No matter what idea life may have implanted within us, its material representation, the outline of the impression it has made upon us, is always the guarantee of its indispensable truth" (II, 1001).

Thus we see Proust's attraction to material architecture as analogue for the immaterial art of literature which conjures feelings and images much as dreams do, assigning no touchable, seeable place to those feelings and images. The great temple—as head, church, literature—protects and embodies the ephemeral and felt. Likewise, the material object Proust has chosen has within it the space necessary for growth: we cannot move (be quick), pay attention (learn, see, act, react), in space crowded with obstacles; this would be to be *pre-occupied*. (The eye-pupil, puns intended, is accessible, open space.) Our habitations, mental and physical, require empty centers as room for aliveness much as these habitations must look out—for health—upon the open universe.

THREE

19. Proust's translations of Ruskin are *The Bible of Amiens* (*La Bible d'Amiens*, 1904) and *Sesame and Lilies* (*Sesame et les lys*, 1906). Much of the preface to *Sesame and Lilies* is repeated in *Days of Reading*, I (1919), trans. G. Hopkins, in *Marcel Proust: A Selection from His Miscellaneous Writings* (London, 1948), pp. 107–146. See also Proust's discussion of Ruskin: *In Memory of a Massacre of Churches*, in G. Hopkins's *Marcel Proust*, pp. 11–107. Throughout these essays Proust concedes Ruskin's formative influence on Proust's art tastes; he also remarks Ruskin's prose style, even his "retrospective unity" in *Sesame and Lilies* (pp. 170–171). For early critical studies of Ruskin's influence on Proust, see: J. Murray, "Influence of Ruskin on Proust," *Proceedings of the Leeds Philosophical and Literary Society*, 1928–32; and S. de Souza, *L'Influence de Ruskin sur Proust* (Montpellier, 1932). Most discussions of Ruskin and Proust emphasize the stylistic influence rather than Ruskin's art-theoretical impact. Recently there has been a critical turning away from claims of stylistic similarities between Ruskin and Proust in an attempt to show Proust's stylistic innovations. See B. Bucknall, *The Religion of Art in Proust* (Urbana, Ill., 1969), for an intelligent discussion of Proust's departures from Ruskin.

NOTES TO PAGES 143-144

The few instances in which Ruskin is mentioned directly in *A la recherche* are generally ironic in tone, meant to distinguish the dreaming, immature Marcel from an architectural critic or literary artist. See, for instance, *A la recherche*, I, 493: Marcel's grandmother gently teases the tearful Marcel on his way to Balbec, for Marcel is already missing his mother. "Surely this is not the enraptured tourist Ruskin speaks of," Marcel's grandmother remarks. At the end of *A la recherche*, the mature Marcel comments on the importance of his architectural studies, "The study of architecture corrected in me some of the instincts I had formed at Combray" (II, 972). There are many quotations from Ruskin throughout *A la recherche*, mostly from *Modern Painters*, I; while these are set off by quotation marks, they are generally not acknowledged as Ruskin's.

20. *Days of Reading*, I, 142.

21. Albertine's action is destructive, Marcel's constructive. Destruction, however, is not equivalent to the dematerializing I speak of later. Albertine destroys the essence of architecture by making it into ices even before she destroys it by eating. In my description of the writer's task, I have chosen the term *must* to suggest Proust's concept of artistic imperative; "necessity" distinguishes art from the voluntarism of the intellectual or philosophical. See *A la recherche*, II, 1001.

22. Among the many ways in which Marcel restates the writer's task are these: "But recreating through memory impressions which must then be plumbed to their depths, brought into the light and transformed into intellectual equivalents, was this not one of the prerequisites, almost the very essence, of a work of art such as I had conceived it in the library a few moments ago?" (II, 1122). And literary style, for Marcel, "is the revelation—impossible by direct and conscious means—of the qualitative differences in the way the world appears to us, differences which, but for art, would remain the eternal secret of each of us" (II, 1013). See also *A la recherche*, II, 1008–1009, and the end of this chapter section. Coupled with his rejection of subjective or solipsistic perceptions not transformed into something public and accessible is Marcel's criticism of superficial thinking which neither "plumbs depths" nor propounds anything of value: for an "art of

reality," Marcel comments, "more than anything else, I would exclude, therefore, all those remarks that come from the lips rather than the mind, clever remarks such as one makes in conversation" (II, 1014–1015). Facile, conversational images have nothing to do with essences and art.

23. Marcel cites his own, early misreadings: *A la recherche*, II, 1000, 1001, and 1003.

24. Cf. *A la recherche*, II, 1013 passim. "Literature is more than art; it is truth" (II, 1014). Music is, for Proust, "pure essence," and "*sine materia*" (I, 160); as such, it, too, is inadequate as an art analogue of literature because it has no material counterpart to metaphor. Re architecture as a non-referential structure, see Ruskin, "The Nature of the Gothic," *The Stones of Venice*, *Works*, X, 213–214. Ruskin states, "A picture or poem is often little more than a feeble utterance of man's admiration of something out of himself; but architecture approaches more to a creation of his own, born of his necessities, and expressive of his nature. It is also, in some sort, the work of the whole race . . . therefore we may expect that the first two elements of good architecture should be expressive of some great truths commonly belonging to the whole race, and necessary to be understood or felt by them in all their work that they do under the sun." While Proust does not put poetry into the category that Ruskin does, he agrees with Ruskin's definition of architecture's greatness, applying the same qualities to literary art. (What must also be noted is that Ruskin distinguishes between "poems" and "poetry," never disparaging the latter.)

In terms of Proust's objection to certain misuses of subjective impressions, see *A la recherche*, II, 1019. The artist must "transcribe [forgotten words] into a universal language, which at any rate will be permanent and would make of our lost ones, in the truest essence of their natures, an eternal acquisition for all human beings." The passage goes on to develop the image of the artist constructing his "building of the monument" out of "stones" brought to him by each woman he has known. The literary structure is thus universal and accessible; moreover, it is a composite of many particulars, of many stones, from the artist's life and can therefore teach "love of the general" as well as the particular. See also II, 1022.

For the two-fold nature of art and experience, see *A la recherche*, II, 1010. Albertine does not perceive that "every impression has two parts, one of them incorporated in the object and the other prolonged within ourselves." Without analysis of both aspects of an impression, there can be no real communication.

25. See note 6 above. Proust's definition stands in contrast to Pater's "minute dead bodies." See Chapter I above.

26. Ruskin as quoted by Proust, "Days of Pilgrimage," from *In Memory of a Massacre of Churches*, p. 54.

27. Proust, "Days of Pilgrimage," p. 53. See also the remarkable rendering or "reading" of Saint-Hilaire, *A la recherche*, I, 45–51. Not only does Marcel decipher every sign in the church; he also attributes to the church literary qualities. The steeple of Saint-Hilaire "inscribes" its form upon the sky; its "memorial stones" overflow their "margins," or are "reabsorbed into their limits, contracting still further a crabbed Latin inscription, bringing a fresh touch of fantasy into the arrangement of its curtailed characters, closing together two letters of some word of which the rest were disproportionately scattered" (I, 45).

28. Proust, *Days of Reading*, I, 142–143.

29. See, for instance, Dionysius of Halicarnassus, *On Literary Composition*, trans. and ed. W. R. Roberts (London, 1910). Of the arrangement of words, he writes: "It must be remembered that, in the case of all the other arts which employ various materials and produce from them a composite result —arts such as building, carpentry, embroidery and the like—the faculties of composition are second in order of time to those of selection, but are nevertheless of greater importance" (p. 73). Even more striking is Dionysius' discussion of the three processes in the art of composition. His analogue is the house builder: "When a builder has provided himself with the material from which he intends to construct a house—stones, timbers, tiling, and all the rest—he then puts together the

structure from these, studying the following three things: what stone, timber and brick can be united with what other stone, timber and brick; next how each piece of the material that is being so united should be set, and on which of its faces; thirdly, if anything fits badly, how that particular thing can be chipped and trimmed and made to fit exactly. A like course should, I affirm, be followed by those who are to succeed in literary composition. They should first consider in what groupings with other nouns, verbs, or other parts of speech, will be placed appropriately, and how not so well; for surely every possible combination cannot affect the ear in the same way" (p. 105). Regarding "Austere Composition," Dionysius of Halicarnassus assents that each word "should be seen on every side, and . . . the parts should be appreciable distances from one another, being separated by perceptible intervals. It [austere composition] does not in the least shrink from using frequently harsh sound-clashings which jar on the ear; like blocks of building stone that are laid together unworked, blocks that are not square and smooth, but preserve their natural roughness and irregularity. It is prone for the most part to expansion by means of great, spacious words. It objects to being confined to short syllables, except under occasional stress of necessity" (p. 211). In this composition, Dionysius of Halicarnassus cites tapestry as an analogue for interweaving, painting for gradations and shading, music for tone and pitch. See my discussion of the architecture-literature analogue in tradition, in Chapter V, section four, pp. 249-252.

30. Proust, *Days of Reading*, I, 143-144.

31. Ibid., pp. 144-145.

32. Ibid., p. 144.

33. Proust, "About Flaubert's Style," in *Marcel Proust*, trans. G. Hopkins, p. 226.

34. In the sense that it connects or spans, the metaphor is the linguistic counterpart of Time which, as it traverses, is likewise rendered incarnate by the architectural analogue. But in another sense, the metaphor is the antithesis of Time

NOTES TO PAGES 150–155

because it presents essences "freed from the contingencies of Time" (II, 1008–1009).

35. These are two of the four section titles from *In Memory of a Massacre of Churches*.

FOUR

36. It is curious that in all Ruskin's discussions of memory (cf. "The Lamp of Memory" in *The Seven Lamps of Architecture*), he only mentions the artificial art of memory, Proust's Mnemotechnia, once; and this comment occurs in the piece Proust chose to translate, *The Bible of Amiens*. There Ruskin, like Proust, decides not to use Mnemotechnia; but he, too, is careful not to slight her: "Without ignobly trusting the devices of artificial memory—far less slighting the pleasure and power of resolute and thoughtful memory—my younger readers will find it extremely useful to note any coincidences or links of number which may serve to secure in their minds what may be called Dates of Anchorage, round which others, less important, may swing at various cables' lengths" (*Works*, XXXIII, 38). See also note 6 above.

37. There is classical precedent, within the memory tradition itself, for this analogue between reminiscence and literature. Bartolomeo da San Concordio (1262–1347) writes: "Of those things which we wish to remember, we should place in certain places images and similitudes. And Tullius adds that the places are like tablets, or paper, and the images like letters, and placing the images is like writing, and speaking is like reading" (*Ammaestramenti degli antichi*, IX, viii, trans. by F. Yates in *The Art of Memory*, London, 1966, pp. 97–98).

Marcel also reads the classics visually; and his assimilation of Berma's acting to his own image—frescoes on vast walls—suggests the artificial memory system. Marcel thinks, "The old plays, the classics which I knew by heart, presented themselves to me as vast and empty walls, reserved and made ready for my inspection, on which I should be able to appreciate without any restriction the devices by which Berma would cover them, as with frescoes, with the perpetually fresh treasures of her inspiration" (I, 339). See Philostratus the Elder and the Younger, *Imagines*; and Erasmus, *Convivium Religiosum*, trans. W. R. Woodward (Cambridge, England, 1904), in *Desiderius Erasmus, Concerning the Aim and Method of Education*, pp. 226-230.

38. Thomas Aquinas, *In Aristotelis libros de sensu et sensato, de memoria et reminiscentia commentarius*, as trans. by F. Yates in *The Art of Memory*, p. 82. Miss Yates renders the entire passage: "It is necessary for reminiscence to take some starting-point, whence one begins to proceed to reminisce. For this reason, some men may be seen to reminisce from the places in which something was said or done, or thought, using the place as it were as the starting-point for reminiscence; because access to the place is like a starting-point for all those things which were raised in it. Whence Tullius teaches in his Rhetoric that for easy remembering one should imagine a certain order of places upon which images (*phantasmata*) of all those things which we wish to remember are distributed in order." Proust, it is true, uses "place"; but he does not so systematize memory as to impose rigid order upon his images. The modification is important; for order, like habit, is destructive to imagination and art. In this, Proust follows late-nineteenth-century values; even Ruskin remarks that "love of order is not love of art" ("Nature of the Gothic," *Stones of Venice*, *Works*, X, 205). Thus, in Proust's "voluntary memory," order is still not in the service of his narrative technique as much as are surprise, interruption, and so forth.

39. See not only the description of Saint-Hilaire (I, 45-51), but the other important church descriptions throughout, especially the church at Balbec, Saint Mark's, and Saint-André-des-Champs.

40. The complete discourse on names as triggering devices for visual images is strikingly similar to the process described in *The Mind of a Mnemonist*, by R. Luria, a psychologist's account of a man with a remarkable memory. Proust, also renowned for his memory, uses almost precisely the same techniques Luria records. Professor Ernst Gombrich first suggested that I look at Luria's book as evidence of Miss Yates's

memory system in modern times and in natural memories; Proust likewise proves the success of the devices proposed by the classical tradition, but like Luria's mnemonist, he does so without the pretext of a system. Furthermore, Proust does so creatively, in the making of a fiction, whereas Luria's mnemonist, because of his memory, could not understand fiction and certainly could not write it. What I find especially interesting in Proust is that love of words and memory for words involve synaesthetic equivalents: "Bayeux, so lofty in its noble coronet of rusty lace, whose highest point caught the light of the old gold of its second syllable; Vitré, whose acute accent barred its ancient glass with wooden lozenges; Coutances, a Norman Cathedral, which its final consonants, rich and yellowing, crowned with a tower of butter" (I, 297 passim). Luria's mnemonist saw colors, lights, and images as well; but he also heard high pitch frequencies or notes with each word. When one tries to recall a word one recalls all the synaesthetic associations first. It is only in our habitual use of language that we forget to feel, touch, taste, and see words.

41. See note 18 above, on "penetration" to "truths." Proust's criticism of realistic fiction extends to his attitude toward facts, which are neither "truths" nor "essences." Hence, the destruction, during the war, of the church at Combray, is treated as insignificant, for it is insignificant narratively, compared with the power of evoking the church or reconstructing it. Likewise facts, what Swann remembers and what the Curé (who describes Saint-Hilaire) reports, are important to those individuals in some way deficient in aesthetic responses. The Curé prefers, for instance, to "read" Saint-Hilaire as a history of facts, whereas Marcel finds it a repository of legends. The Curé reports that the steeple has "seven and ninety steps"; Marcel sees the steeple as the "Finger of God," a "sign of art, this single indication of human existence" upon the landscape. Likewise, the Curé claims, regarding the windows Marcel so loves and so beautifully describes, "But don't talk to me about the windows. Is it common sense, I ask you, to leave up windows which shut out all the daylight, and even confuse the eyes by throwing patches of

colour, to which I should be hard put to it to give a name, on a floor in which there are not two slabs on the same level? And yet they refuse to renew the floor for me because . . . those are the tombstones of the Abbots of Combray" (I, 79). Stones of different levels are crucial to Marcel, for by tripping over an uneven stone, Marcel has his "break-through" involuntary memory (see II, 990–994). The Curé lends to *A la recherche* a kind of pseudo-historical veracity, giving in fact the etymology of words such that the reader learns of the actual Illiers, the town from which Combray is fashioned (I, 80). Within the whole of *A la recherche*, as the reader is educated by Proust and learns how to read and "create" this and his own book, history, facts, etymologies, all become subordinate to fantasy, analysis, vision, fiction.

42. See Proust's direct comparison between people and statues in "The Churches Saved," *In Memory of a Massacre of Churches*, ed. cit., p. 15. Proust discusses his driver, Agostinelli, who was killed in an auto crash, as a cathedral saint, holding a symbol. "But most of the time, he sat there with his hand upon the wheel – the instrument by which he steered, and like enough for comparison to those instruments of martyred consecration borne by the Apostles who stand against the columns of the Sainte-Chapelle in Paris . . . he held it as he might have done some symbolic object with which convention ordained that he should be associated. In just such a way, do saints in cathedral porches hold, one an anchor, one a wheel, a harp, a scythe, a gridiron, a hunting horn, a paint brush. But if these attributes were, in general, intended to recall the art which each, in life, had excellently practised, they sometimes served as a memorial of the nature of their final torment." Clearly, in Proust's essay, his narrative timing is off, the analogy too long; but nonetheless, Proust makes apparent his knowledge of the architectural tradition.

43. See, for instance, *A la recherche*, I, 68; Proust uses the image of a figure before a Gothic cathedral as a prefiguration of Gilberte; the young Marcel can construct the image only because he has been introduced to the author Bergotte. "But the interruption which a visit from Swann once made, and the

commentary which he then supplied to the course of my reading, which had brought me to the work of an author quite new to me, called Bergotte, had this definite result that for a long time afterwards it was not against a wall gay with spikes of purple blossom, but on a wholly different background, the porch of a Gothic cathedral, that I would see outlined the figure of one of the women of whom I dreamed." Similarly, M. de Charlus is linked with the window of Gilbert-the-Bad (II, 564); but the image functions more to recall past associations, since Marcel does not remark the presage of the window when he first describes it fifteen hundred pages earlier.

Chapter IV

ONE

[All references throughout this chapter are to the New York Edition of *The Novels and Tales of Henry James* (1907–1917).]

1. See the opening section above, " 'The Stored-Consciousness': Marcel Proust," p. 119.

2. Henry James, *The Art of the Novel: Critical Prefaces by Henry James* (London, 1937), p. 216. All further citations from the prefaces will be to this edition and will be placed in parentheses (P) with a page reference following.

3. The entire passage only *presumes* but never states time frame (1). As it stands, the passage is framed, as it were, by the past (time frame 2). The passage opens: "Only the little rounded composition *remained* . . ." and concludes, "these complacencies . . . *swarmed* . . . while yet no brick *stood*." I apologize for my use of technical language in this section of my book, but I have found the terms and numbers necessary in order to make James's methods as clear as possible.

4. It is possible to interpret the "temple" as the composition "The Point of View." This would mean that the "complacencies of perception" swarmed before "The Point of View" had been written, thus inspiring its composition. While I find many aspects of this interpretation compelling, my stronger feeling is that James would not switch images

from "lantern" to "temple"; I also think the verb tenses argue against such an interpretation.

5. Henry James, *The Notebooks of Henry James*, ed. F. O. Matthiessen and Kenneth B. Murdock (New York, 1947), especially pp. 325-335. For James's great respect for Ruskin, see *The Art of Travel*, ed. M. D. Zabel (New York, 1958), p. 1-3.

TWO

6. James, in fact, describes his literary muse as the "gentle Euphemia" (P, 1967). For a discussion of the relationship between Pater and James, see S. P. Sherman, "The Aesthetic Idealism of Henry James," reprinted in *The Question of Henry James*, ed. F. W. Dupee (New York, 1945), pp. 86-106. G. Melchiori also discusses this relationship in his essay "Two Mannerists: James and Hopkins," *The Tight-Rope Walkers* (London, 1950). Melchiori describes Pater as the link between Hopkins and James and shows, with wonderful sensitivity, the stylistic similarities between Hopkins and James. Ironically, however, while Melchiori does mention architecture with respect to his term *mannerist* and James's image in his preface to *The Wings of the Dove* (pp. 21-23), Melchiori never mentions Pater's or Hopkins's interest in architecture (although he does quote "Harry Ploughman"). Instead, Melchiori describes Hopkins's terms as primarily musical. Likewise, when he discusses James's "room" images in *The Wings*, what he stresses is how James "inscaped" rooms, ignoring all the rich implications of the architecture itself.

7. There is much controversy among architectural historians over the Victorian architects' attitudes towards deliberate "ugliness" in architecture. See especially P. Thompson, *William Butterfield* (Cambridge, Mass., 1971), and Sir Nikolaus Pevsner, "Review," *The Art Quarterly*, 35, no. 3 (1972).

THREE

8. At times we may think of James's subject matter as the watchers themselves rather than what they watch. This would make of James a "watcher of watchers." James as much as

declares this the case when he writes of Newman in his preface to *The American*: "If Newman was attaching enough, I must have argued, this tangle would be sensible enough; for the interest of everything is all that it is *his* vision, *his* conception, *his* interpretation: at the window of his wide, quite sufficiently wide, consciousness we are seated, from that admirable position we 'assist' " (P, 37). Now not only does the artist sit before the window, but the subject – and importantly – the *reader* all sit indoors, all get inside those mind-houses not ours and view from there the human scene. In other words, we each share the artist's form of perceiving the world, his particular window-view which he constitutes or constructs in and by language. The "dead wall" is opaque; language punctures the wall with windows onto the world. We might therefore suggest that the subject of James's book is the artist, is artistic inspiration, is language, is perception, and is ourselves, our own perception. For James is explicit, over and over again, that we are no different from the teller of a story: "The teller of a story is primarily, none the less, the listener to it, the reader of it, too; and, having needed thus to make it out, distinctly, on the crabbed page of life, to disengage it from the rude human character and the more or less Gothic text in which it has been packed away, the very essence of his affair has been the *imputing* of intelligence" (P, 63). James complicates the whole matter of watchers watching when he has some of his characters watch others who are imaged in architectural similes. Such is the case with Ralph Touchett who, like his narrator, would image the complex Isabel Archer as a "Gothic cathedral": "The key of a beautiful edifice is thrust into my hand, and I'm told to walk in and admire.... The sentiment of these reflexions was very just; but it was not exactly true that Ralph Touchett had had a key put into his hand. His cousin was a very brilliant girl, who would take, as he said, a good deal of knowing, but she needed the knowing, and his attitude with regard to her, though it was contemplative and critical, was not judicial. He surveyed the edifice from the outside and admired it greatly; he looked in at the windows and received an impression of proportions equally fair. But he felt that he saw it only by glimpses and that he had not yet stood under the roof. The door was fastened, and though he had keys in his pocket he had a conviction that none of them would fit" (II, 87).

Life goes on behind faces, life we never see. The face is in some sense dead if we think of it as the wall-façade through which the energy-spirit must pass. Recall, for instance, Marcel's mother sending her love-spirit out her smile-window: "she sent out to me . . . a love which stopped only where there was no longer any material substance to support it on the *surface* of her impassioned gaze which she tried to thrust forward to the advanced *post* of her lips, in a smile which seemed to be kissing me, in the framework and beneath the canopy of the more discreet smile of the arched window illuminated by the sun" (II, 822). The "apertures," James realizes, are the most apparent zones for the transmission of life-energy, eyes for perception.

9. For a brief mention of this debt to Howells, see F. W. Dupee, *Henry James* (New York, 1956), pp. 220–221.

10. James describes at length his difficulties with technique in *The Spoils*, how to present the spoils themselves since they "are not directly articulate." See P, 123–126, in which he also describes his conception of Fleda Vetch as the way out of his dilemma.

11. For great help with this and other passages in James, I wish to thank Leonard Michaels.

FOUR

12. Max Beerbohm, *The Guerdon* (London, 1925), p. 4. Throughout the entire parody, Beerbohm exaggerates the architectural devices James uses. Not only does the entire action take place within a mysterious palace room in which the "seated personage" waits to greet Stamfordham, but ideas, questions, thoughts in general are expressed in terms of those architectural images so abundant in James's later novels. Beerbohm writes of a hope that "fairly burst from him [Stamfordham] and blossomed, this bud, as the royal eye had poised—had from its slow flight around the mouldings of the florid Hanoverian ceiling, positively swooped—on the fat scarlet book"

(5). Beerbohm refers, likewise, to the "prominent, the virtuous yet so lacklustre family eye of the seated reader" (5) as if he knows that the reader is also seated inside along with characters and authors. Of furnishings, James himself writes of other artists: "All a matter of his own, in a word, for each seer of visions, the particular tone of the medium in which each vision, each clustered group of persons and places and objects, is bathed. Just how, accordingly, does the light of the world, the projected, painted, peopled, poetized, realized world, the furnished and fitted world into which we are beguiled for the holiday excursion ... of the ... voyaging mind–just how does this strike us as different in Fielding and in Richardson." See "The Lesson of Balzac 1905," in *The House of Fiction* (London, 1957), p. 70.

13. Henry James, "The Art of Fiction," in *The House of Fiction*, ed. Leon Edel (London, 1957), p. 44. James must also freeze characters out of life into objects that he might "treat" them rather than interact with them. The conversion is thus another safety device; di-stance may create the space for exchange of energy or it may be seized as territory and used to protect one from feeling the impact of another's presence.

14. While Mrs. Lowder is described as large, her friends Milly and Susan Shepherd are something else: "There was a certain implication that they were spacious because they were empty. Mrs. Lowder, by a different law, was spacious because she was full" (XIX, 168). Likewise, some rooms become too small for certain characters, the implication being that their largeness of mind or imagination violates or wars against the limitations of the world around them. Of Isabel Archer's imagination, James writes, "Her imagination was by habit ridiculously active; when the door was not open it jumped out of the window. She was not accustomed to keep it behind bolts" (II, 42). Lambert Strether has similar problems with confinement. In *The Ambassadors* James writes of Strether after his first reunion with Waymarsh, "On leaving him [Waymarsh] he [Strether] went straight to his own room, but with the prompt effect of feeling the compass of that chamber resented by his condition. There he enjoyed at once the first conse-

quence of their reunion. A place was too small for him after it that had seemed large enough before" (XXI, 28).

15. James, "The Future of the Novel, 1899," in *The House of Fiction*, p. 51.

16. Ibid., p. 53.

17. Death for Milly is "turning her face to the wall"; simple Mrs. Stringham's "little life" was visited by "secret dreams that had fluttered their hour between its narrow walls without, for any great part, so much as mustering courage to look out of its rather dim windows" (XIX, 104). James also uses architectural puns throughout his fiction: "premises," "cold views," "arch of associations," represent just a few.

18. James, in fact, has Milly Theale's Venetian palace "speak" to her of its past: "Palazzo Leporelli held its history still in its great lap, even like a painted idol, a solemn puppet hung about with decorations. Hung about with pictures and relics, the rich Venetian past, the ineffaceable character, was here the presence revered and served: which brings us back to our truth of a moment ago—the fact that, more than ever, this October morning, awkward novice though she might be, Milly moved slowly to and fro as the priestess of the worship. Certainly it came from the sweet taste of solitude, caught again and cherished for the hour; always a need of her nature, moreover, when things spoke to her with penetration. It was mostly in stillness they spoke to her best; amid voices she lost the sense" (XX, 135). Similarly, Milly's Doctor's house "put on for her a look of custom and use, squared itself solidly round her as with promises and certainties" (XIX, 237).

19. See Raymond Gill, *Happy Rural Seat* (New Haven, 1972). Gill's emphasis is on James's country houses as "symbols of community," fusing the "historical and the personal," the "traditional and the visionary" (pp. 14–16, 25). Gill unfortunately neglects to relate James's architectural symbols to his concept of mind and of fictional structure. This oversight deprives Gill's work of the suggestive richness his topic should have yielded him.

20. Henry James, "Abbeys and Castles," in *The Art of Travel*, ed. M. D. Zabel (New York, 1958), pp. 150-151.

NOTES TO PAGE 210

21. James writes that the beauty in architecture is "participatory and relative"; see, for instance, his wonderful descriptions of architectural monuments in his travel literature. Of Wells Cathedral James writes:

"It has often seemed to me in England that the purest enjoyment of architecture was to be had among the ruins of great buildings. In the perfect building one is rarely sure that the impression is simply architectural: it is more or less pictorial and romantic; it depends partly upon association and partly upon various accessories and details which, however they may be wrought into harmony with the architectural idea, are not a part of its essence and spirit. But in so far as beauty of structure is beauty of line and curve, balance and harmony of masses and dimensions, I have seldom relished it as deeply as on the grassy nave of some crumbling church, before lonely columns and empty windows where the wild flowers were a cornice and the sailing clouds a roof. The arts certainly hang together in what they do for us. These hoary relics of Glastonbury reminded me in their broken eloquence of one of the other great ruins of the world – the Last Supper of Leonardo. A beautiful shadow, in each case, is all that remains; but that shadow is the 'soul of the artist' " (*The Art of Travel*, pp. 120-121). And of St. Mark's: "Still, it is almost a spiritual function – or, at the very worst, an amorous one – to feed one's eyes on the moulten colour that drops from the hollow vaults and thickens the air with its richness. It is all so quiet and sad and faded and yet it is all so brilliant and living. The strange figures in the mosaic pictures, bending with the curve of niche and vault, stare down through the glowing dimness; the burnished gold that stands behind them catches the light on its little uneven cubes. St. Mark's owes nothing of its character to the beauty of proportion or perspective; there is nothing grandly balanced or far-arching; there are no long lines nor triumphs of the perpendicular. The church arches indeed, but arches like a dusky cavern. Beauty of surface, of tone, of detail, of things near enough to touch and kneel upon and lean against – it is from this the effect proceeds. In this sort of beauty the place is incredibly rich, and you may go there every day and find afresh some lurking pictorial nook" (Ibid., p. 394).

James's *Notebooks* are also replete with architectural descriptions and details (which, interestingly, suggest those similar descriptions which fill the notebooks and journals of G. M. Hopkins). See especially pp. 325-335. James, however, unlike Hopkins, tends to describe monuments in their settings, including mention of city noise and people.

"Here I come suddenly, this same charming day (Aug. 24) on delightfully placed old St. Dunstan's in the East (the mate of which, St. D. in West, Fleet St., I tried to get into, under the image of Queen Elizabeth an hour ago). I never chanced upon this one before—just out of Eastcheap, on the way to the Tower, and beyond (south) the little St. Margaret Pattens. High 'fine' Gothic tower and spire, and built as it is on the steep hill down to the river the little old disused and voided churchyard is raised on deep southward substructions under the south wall of the church and employed as a small sitting-place for the specimens of the grimy public—*such* infinitely miserable specimens—who are dozing and gnawing bones (2 tramps under the south wall doing *that* in it now). The noise of drays from riverward, the clang of wheels, etc., harsh in the enclosed, built-in space; but the tall (3 or 4) thin trees (a lime and a locust?) make a green shade—and the clock in the tower, or at least the bell, gives out an immense deep note (2o'ck.). Come back of course—get in. All these city churches have their *hours* on notices at doors. Make record of these" (VII, 329).

"*September 21st, 1909*. Just back from Overstrand—beautiful September day. Turned in to St. Bride's Fleet St.—great ample handsome empty 'Palladian' church, mercilessly modernized, brightened, decorated, painted and gilded—but so still in the roaring City—with the *rumeur* outside all softened and faint—so respectable, so bourgeois—such a denial of any cognizance of passions, remorses, compassions, appeals—anything but mildest contritions and most decorous prostrations. But big and square and clear and reverend—in all its simplicity and with no altar to speak—neither book nor bell nor cross nor candle. It is one of Wren's churches and the little baptismal font was saved from the Fire. Immense and massive tower to great height, with superpositions of stages in spire atop—*diminuendo*—like a tower of cards" (VIII, 333).

FIVE

22. Perhaps in part because the Prefaces are so richly metaphorical James's critics have spent considerable time assessing the serviceability and adequacy of James's interart analogies. Surprisingly, however, little attention and virtually no thorough study has been made of James's architectural images, the result being that James's use of architecture has been slighted, dismissed as irrelevant, or else treated for its thematic or historical importance, never its aesthetic significance.

A. Holder-Barrell, for one, in *The Development of Imagery and Its Functional Significance in Henry James's Novels* (Switzerland, 1959), states that architectural images occur in only two novels, *The Portrait of a Lady* and *The Golden Bowl*. Likewise, R. L. Gale in *The Caught Image: Figurative Language in the Fiction of Henry James* (Chapel Hill, 1964), comments that "images drawn from architecture, like those from dancing," are "ornamental rather than vital to the fiction" (p. 145). Gale also claims that in the fiction "James fails completely to group his caryatids, cornices, keystones, and lozenges in any functional manner, all of which is surprising in the light of the fact that in his prefaces he images himself repeatedly as a master-builder of fine houses of fiction" (p. 241). Joseph A. Ward, in *The Search for Form: Studies in the Structure of James's Fiction* (Chapel Hill, 1967), does discuss the importance of James's "structures," but he neglects to speak specifically of the architectural analogues or to relate the prefaces to the internal images of the fiction (see pp. 40–44 and 147–154). R. Gill, whose entire book is devoted to country houses (*Happy Rural Seat* [New Haven, 1972]), and who takes special care to document every house that James built, sadly limits the analogue by never seeing that it refers equally to minds and fictional structures; his intent is so sociological that he makes absolutist remarks about character while ignoring all else that James attempts. L. B. Holland, in *The Expense of Vision: Essays on the Craft of Henry James* (Princeton, 1964), claims that the architectural analogues in the prefaces are "inadequate" to describe the fiction (pp. 4–5), especially the analogue in *The Portrait*. But unlike most critics, Holland does concede that the metaphors are "relevant" to the *Portrait* "if for no other reason than that they place the author *inside* his finished dwelling and call into question his edifice by alluding to its 'dead wall' " (p. 4). Elsewhere Holland feels that James opposes the metaphor of architecture to the action of the novel or story (p. 5). It seems to me that James's theory of the "house of fiction" suggests a structure which incorporates action rather than quarrels with it. James explicitly mentions architecture as able to accommodate time and duration of action in his essay on Balzac ("The Lesson of Balzac, 1905," pp. 82–83), and in his preface to *The Wings of the Dove*; in the latter, James describes the culmination of the dramatic action as taking place in Kate's "consciousness" and—the parallel is important—in Milly's "hired palace," both of which he renders in architectural terms. James writes:

"It is in Kate's consciousness that at the stage in question the drama is brought to a head, and the occasion on which, in the splendid saloon of poor Milly's hired palace, she takes the measure of her friend's festal evening, squares itself to the same synthetic firmness as the compact constructionable block inserted by the scene at Lancaster Gate" (p. 301).

23. See V. Hopkins Winner, *Henry James and the Visual Arts* (Virginia, 1970), especially pp. 177–178. Winner argues that painting and tapestry are "incompatible" with architecture.

24. "The Future of the Novel," in *The House of Fiction*, p. 51.

25. Claudio Guillén, *Literature as System* (Princeton, 1971), p. 289. " 'Chi mira una pittura, vede certa intersegazione d'una piramide': Alberti imagined that Euclid's visual pyramid, the apex of which is the observer's eye, was intersected by a flat plane, transparent as if made of glass ('non altrimenti, che se essa fosse di vetro tralucente'). This flat section became the surface of the painting, which no longer acted as such, but rather as an opening, an open window ('una finestra aperta') on the contents of the visual pyramid. Thus the purpose of painting could be defined as the representation of things seen ('rappresentare cose vedute'), a definition which Alberti the humanist associated with the myth of Narcissus: 'che dirai tu essere dipingere altra cosa che simile abbracciare con arte, quella ivi superficie del fonte?' "

26. Henry James, *Transatlantic Sketches* (Boston, 1875), p. 78.

Chapter V

1. John Ruskin, *The Seven Lamps of Architecture*, *Works*, VIII, 224.

2. For an enlightening discussion of interdisciplinary studies, directions, and methodological pitfalls, see *New Literary History: A Journal of Theory and Interpretation* (September 1972), especially essays by J. Seznec and A. Fowler. For a discussion of historical methodology and Hegel, see E. H. Gombrich, *In Search of Cultural History* (Oxford, 1969), especially pp. 32-50. Gombrich specifically addresses the issue of Hegelian Zeitgeist (much as Seznec addresses *l'air de famille*): "Hegel," Gombrich writes, "saw all periods as movements since they were embodiments of the moving spirit" (p. 35); Gombrich feels that much art history and interdisciplinary history presumes an Hegelian metaphysics, even when metaphysics per se is replaced by a kind of "stylistic formalism" such as that advanced by Heinrich Wölfflin in *Renaissance and Baroque* (1888). Gombrich objects to Hegel's assertion that a nation's "religion, constitution, morality, law, customs, science, art, and technology" are all "concrete manifestations of the national Spirit" (p. 10); such belief Gombrich feels is reductive, a false ordering of events and a violation of any belief in the individual. Gombrich indicts historians and scholars who feel "consciously or unconsciously, that if they let go of the magnet (the 'essence,' 'Spirit,' common 'core') that created the pattern, the atoms of past cultures would again fall back into random dustheaps." The questions I am asking of literature and architecture represent an attempt to avoid any assumption of "magnets"; and Gombrich, both personally and through his scholarship, has guided me in the formulation of many of my questions. For this direction, I am indebted and thankful.

While *New Literary History* looks mainly at interdisciplinary studies in the 1960s and early 1970s, J. Hagstrum in *The Sister Arts* (Chicago, 1958) summarizes interdisciplinary studies to the late 1950s, mentioning as he does so the methodological principles and mistakes of earlier studies. See espe-

NOTES TO PAGES 227-228

cially his introduction. One of the frequent targets of criticism most recently has been M. Praz, *Mnemosyne: The Parallel between Literature and the Visual Arts* (Princeton, 1969), a work which unfortunately does assume a common spirit of the age. Ironically for us, in terms of the concerns of this book, Praz equates memory (his work is a tribute to the Goddess Mnemosyne) with art in a general sense; qualified, "aesthetic memory" (unlike "practical memory") is characterized "by its incapacity to be realized on the level of the senses," so becoming the unifier of the arts and the rationale for Praz's critical view. For an intelligent critical essay on Praz's study (which, incidentally, is mentioned throughout the issue cited of *New Literary History*) see B. Richards, *Essays in Criticism*, 21 (1971), 325.

3. The question regarding the selection of art-models is one which avoids the belief that separate aspects of culture reflect and proceed from one privileged center.

4. For discussions of hypotheses, proofs, observation, and theory, see the works of K. R. Popper, especially *Conjectures and Refutations* (London, 1963) and *The Logic of Scientific Discovery* (New York, 1961). Regarding theories, Popper writes, "Theories are our own inventions, our own ideas; they are not forced upon us, but are our self-made instruments of thought: this has been clearly seen by the idealist. But some of these theories of ours can clash with reality; and when they do, we know that there is a reality; that there is something to remind us of the fact that our ideas may be mistaken. And this is why the realist is right" (*Conjectures and Refutations*, p. 117). Popper, to whom Gombrich acknowledges indebtedness in *Art and Illusion: A Study in the Psychology of Pictorial Representation* (New York, 1961), advances the notion of "critical rationalism" in which one attempts never to "prove positively" (since one always can) a theory but to "test" it by an attempt "to falsify it, or to refute it" (*Conjectures and Refutations*, p. 36). I personally have been attempting not to prove a theory but to document and record the occurrence of a theory, or various theories as stated by others and to discuss what I feel to be the implications of these theories.

NOTES TO PAGES 229-233

ONE

5. Vitruvius, *The Ten Books on Architecture*, trans. M. H. Morgan (New York, 1960).

6. Ibid., p. 14.

7. Leone Battista Alberti, *Ten Books on Architecture*, trans. J. Leoni (London, 1965).

8. Ibid., p. xi.

9. Ibid., p. 197.

10. *The Builder's Magazine* (London, 1774).

11. Wightwick, "The Principles and Practice of Architectural Design" (Essay 7, 1850), from *Detached Essays of the Architectural Publication Society* (London, 1853), p. 37.

12. Examples of Vitruvius' indebtedness to the rhetorical tradition are such terms and applied concepts as "Arrangement (in Greek $\delta\iota\acute{\alpha}\theta\epsilon\sigma\iota\varsigma$)," "Order (in Greek $\tau\acute{\alpha}\xi\iota\varsigma$)," "Eurythmy," and "Propriety." See Book I, chapter 2, "The Fundamental Principles of Architecture," in *The Ten Books on Architecture*, pp. 13-16.

13. For an unusual and interesting discussion of Ben Jonson and Vitruvius and Alberti, see Per Palme, "Ut Architectura Poesis," in *Idea and Form*, ed. N. G. Sandblad, Acta Universitatis Upsaliensis, Figura Nova Series, I (Uppsala, 1959), 95-107.

14. George Herbert, *The Works of George Herbert*, ed. F. E. Hutchinson (Oxford, 1941). See especially "Church-lock and key," "The Church-floore," "The Windows," "Man," and "Sion."

15. Ibid., p. 67.

16. Ibid., p. 90.

17. Ralph Waldo Emerson and Henry David Thoreau both refer to organic architecture and draw analogies between body/architecture and literature. Emerson writes, for example, "Fitness is so separable an accompaniment of beauty that it has been taken for it. The most perfect form to answer an end, is so far beautiful. In the mind of an artist, could we enter there, we

should see the sufficient reason for the last flourish and tendril of his work, just as every tint and spine in the sea-shell pre-exists, in the secreting organs of the fish. We feel, in seeing a noble building, which rhymes well, as we do in hearing a perfect song, that it is spiritually organic, that is, had a necessity in nature, for being" ("Thoughts on Art," *Dial*, January 1841, as reprinted in *The Uncollected Writings by R. W. Emerson*, ed. C. C. Bigelow, New York, 1912, p. 47). Emerson also writes in 1844, that "it is not metres, but a metre-making arrangement that makes a poem,—a thought so passionate and alive that like the spirit of a plant or an animal it has an architecture of its own, and adorns nature with a new thing" (*Works*, III [New York, 1883], 15).

Thoreau's values are similar: "What of architectural beauty I now see, I know has gradually grown from within outward, out of the necessities and character of the indweller, who is the only builder,—out of some unconscious truthfulness, and nobleness, without ever a thought for the appearance; and whatever additional beauty of this kind is destined to be produced will be preceded by a like unconscious beauty of life" (*Writings of Henry David Thoreau*, II [Boston, 1906], 134).

18. Walter Pater, "Emerald Uthwart," in *Imaginary Portraits*, ed. E. J. Brzenk (London, 1964), p. 58.

TWO

19. See Aristotle, *De Anima*, 429a, in which he refers to the "place of ideas" (*topos eidon*) when he is discussing the passive and active aspects of the mind. For a discussion of visualization in Plato and Aristotle, see W. Trimpi, "The Ancient Hypothesis of Fiction: An Essay on the Origins of Literary Theory," in *Traditio*, 27 (September 1971). Trimpi writes, "The whole internal world of the imagination is viewed of necessity as one of arbitrarily imposed delimitations of space, which recalls Plato's *Timaeus* (51–52) and looks forward to the art of memory in which images are assigned to geometrically conceived areas. The process of giving imaginary magnitudes to things we think about is certainly pre-requisite to imagining a sequence of actions in time. In the *Poetics* (chapter 7)

NOTES TO PAGE 234

temporal magnitude is compared to the spatial magnitude of animate creatures; the duration of dramatic action is a function of the memory ('such as can be easily remembered as a whole') as the magnitude of a beautiful creature is a function of vision. Time is to space as memory is to visual image."

20. I am grateful to Professor Gombrich for suggesting that I look at these passages. Ovid's "Palace of the Sun," in its carvings "more beautiful than the material," reconstitutes, in a sense, the history of the world and images the gods along with the signs of the zodiac and representation of the elements. "The palace of the Sun stood high on lofty columns, bright with glittering gold and bronze that shone like fire. Gleaming ivory crowned the gables above; the double folding-doors were radiant with burnished silver. And the workmanship was more beautiful than the material. For upon the doors Mulciber had carved in relief the waters that enfold the central earth, the circle of the lands and the sky that overhangs the lands. The sea holds the dark-hued gods: tuneful Triton, changeful Proteus, and Aegaeon, his strong arms thrown over a pair of huge whales; Doris and her daughters, some of whom are shown swimming through the water, some sitting on a rock drying their green hair, and some riding on fishes. . . . Above these scenes was placed a representation of the shining sky, six signs of the zodiac on the right hand doors, and six signs on the left" (Ovid, *Metamorphoses*, Bk. II, p. 61, trans. F. J. Miller, Cambridge, Mass., 1951). The palace is in a sense an architectural microcosm and suggests the world as enclosed by and made known to the human mind; as such, it becomes a *locus classicus* for subsequent representations, an important instance being Tennyson's "Palace of Art," a structure standing for the mind-house of the soul and enclosing not only representations of the macro-world but also representations of artistic renderings of that world:

> Full of great rooms and small the palace stood,
>   All various, each a perfect whole
> From living Nature, fit for every mood
>   And change of my still soul.
>
> .   .   .   .   .   .

NOTES TO PAGE 234

> Nor these alone; but every legend fair
>   Which the supreme Caucasian mind
> Carved out of Nature for itself was there,
>   Not less than life design'd.

For Tennyson, guilt, in fact political and social guilt, as well as what we think of as subconscious fears, also dwell in the mind-palace and drive the soul out, back to what we may think of as a Romantic "cottage in the vale."

> But in dark corners of her palace stood
>   Uncertain shapes; and unawares
> On white-eyed phantasms weeping tears of blood,
>   And horrible nightmares. . . .
>
> She howl'd aloud, "I am on fire within.
>   There comes no murmur of reply.
> What is it that will take away my sin,
>   And save me lest I die?"
>
> So when four years were wholly finished,
>   She threw her royal robes away.
> "Make me a cottage in the vale," she said,
>   "Where I may mourn and pray."

Tennyson's palace also draws upon Apuleius' "Palace of Psyche," which, like Tennyson's, can only be known and judged by entering it, and which, also like Tennyson's, bears the register of error once moral transgression occurs within it. The richness of Psyche's palace is made manifold but the source is unknown; we recognize that it is too grand and that Psyche's interest in it and curiosity about its builder are in some way deficient. "For the embossings above were of Citron and Ivory, propped and undermined with pillars of gold, the walls covered and seeled with silver, divers sorts of beasts were graven and carved, that seemed to encounter with such as entered in. . . . Every part and angle of the house was so well adorned, that by reason of the pretious stones and inestimable treasure there, it glittered and shone in such sort, that the chambers, porches, and doores gave light as it had been the Sunne. Neither otherwise did the other treasure of the house disagree into so great a majesty, that verily it seemed in every point an heavenly

Palace, fabricate and built for Jupiter himself" ("The Most Pleasant and Delectable Tale of the Marriage of Cupid and Psyche," 1566, trans. W. Adlington, London, 1887).

21. See Augustine, *Confessions*, especially III, iv and X, viii. See also pp. 31-34. See Thomas Aquinas, *In Aristotelis libros de sensu et sensato, de memoria et reminiscentia commentarius,* ed. R. M. Spiazzi (Turin and Rome, 1949), especially pp. 85 ff., and p. 107. (For Aquinas, "places" as well as "images" of the artificial memory figure as the "sensible furniture" of a mind, so making the mind an even larger architectural structure which houses or may house diverse place-structures which are useful for the art of memory.) See John Locke, *An Essay Concerning Human Understanding*, ed. A. C. Fraser (Oxford, 1894), especially I, 32. For Locke, minds contain ideas, much as a room contains furniture; ideas and knowledge are quite literally inside the mind. Likewise, Locke images the "knowledge" of Huygenius and Newton as "lasting monuments," built by these "master-builders" who produce outward their "mighty designs" (I, 14). See G. W. F. Hegel, *The Phenomenology of Mind*, trans. J. B. Baillie (New York, 1967), especially pp. 338-342. Here Hegel, in a chapter entitled "Observation of the Relation of Self-Consciousness to Its Immediate Actuality – Physiognomy and Phrenology," speaks of "inner" and "outer," distinguishing language as an outer expression of the inner; "Language and labour are outer expressions in which the individual no longer retains possession of himself per se, but lets the inner get right outside him, and surrenders it to something else. For that reason we might just as truly say that these outer expressions express the inner too much as that they do so too little: too much – because the inner itself breaks out in them, and there remains no opposition between them and it; they not merely give an *expression* of the inner, they give the inner itself directly and immediately: too little – because in speech and action the inner turns itself into something else, into an other, and thereby puts itself at the mercy of the element of change, which transforms the spoken word and the accomplished act, and makes something else out of them than they are in and for themselves as actions of a particular determinate individual"

(p. 340). Among the many things we may see in this passage is Pater's indebtedness to Hegel for his theory of language. See Chapter I, above, on Walter Pater's "literary architecture."

For a more detailed discussion of Freud's architectural analogues, see section three of this chapter below. Of Donald Davie's poems, I especially think of the closing of "Dublin Georgian":

> The author of the genial comedies
> From which this pair plucked fruit,
> The edible stucco of their shared repute,
> Has made no entrance; and yet there he is,
> A brow that's broader than the marble mantel
> There in the wall
> Which thin heads nod in front of. Broad as well
> Behind the brow, the soul. Broadness of soul—
> What an inelegant and Russian notion!
> It's more than Orrery could cater for.
> His walls distend, the cornice is in motion . . .
> Oliver Goldsmith! Samson heaves the floor.
> (Donald Davie, *Collected Poems,*
> *1950–1970*, London, 1972)

See W. R. Bion, *Learning from Experience* (New York, 1962) and *Second Thoughts* (London, 1957); also see Melanie Klein, *Contributions to Psycho-Analysis, 1921–1945* (London, 1948), especially pp. 140–151 and 303, as well as *Narrative of a Child Analysis* (London and New York, 1961), p. 31. See Richard Wollheim, "The Mind and the Mind's Image of Itself," in *On Art and the Mind* (London, 1973), especially pp. 41–53. Wollheim devotes considerable time to discussing a "spatial" conception of the mind: "For the mind to be conceived of as spatial, it is required, I suggest, either that we should have some specific view about mental states, assigning to them an extended or quasi-extended character; or else that we should have some specific view about the relation in which objects of mental states stand to the mind, assigning to this a positional character. Here we have something like a disjunctive criterion for spatiality" (p. 46). Wollheim proceeds to fulfill the two conditions, and in so doing, he refers not only to Freud's conception of a thought which may forcefully enter the mind, Freud's "alien guest," but he also cites Henry James and William Butler Yeats to augment clinical or psychoanalytical arguments.

22. See Plato, *The Republic*, Book III, trans. P. Shorey (London, 1953) as reprinted in *The Collected Dialogues of Plato*, ed. E. Hamilton and H. Cairns (Princeton, 1961), pp. 747–757. The cave image in fact serves as an analogue for still another architectural image, the prison: "This image [the cave] then, dear Glaucon, we must apply as a whole to all that has been said, likening the region revealed through sight to the habitation of the prison, and the light of the fire in it to the power of the sun. And if you assume that the ascent and the contemplation of the things above is the soul's ascension to the intelligible region, you will not miss my surmise, since that is what you desire to hear" (p. 749).

23. Andrew Marvell, "Upon Appleton House, to my Lord Fairfax," *The Poems and Letters of Andrew Marvell*, I, ed. H. M. Margoliouth (Oxford, 1971). Stanza LXXXI offers still another example of Marvell's play with the poet/architect analogue without the mind analogue:

> Oh what a Pleasure 'tis to hedge
> My Temples here with heavy sedge;
> Abandoning my lazy Side,
> Stretcht as a Band unto the Tide;
> Or to suspend my sliding Foot
> On the Osiers undermined Root,
> And in its Branches tough to hang,
> While at my Lines the Fishes twang!

24. Samuel Beckett, *Murphy* (New York, 1957), pp. 107–113.

25. Ibid., p. 181. See also his comparison between Mercyseat and church architecture in the same chapter.

26. Throughout Beckett's work there is an emphasis on descriptions of place, especially architecture and topography. In 1955, with *The Unnamable*, we find Beckett moving toward a narrative I who comes closer and closer to the personal voice of the author himself, but who nonetheless never arrives. Con-

sistent with the movement is the search still to describe the narrator's "abode": "It would help me," he writes toward the beginning, "since to me I must attribute a beginning, if I could relate it to that of my abode" (p. 296). The narrator moves from this quest for a beginning to a definition of himself in terms of language, and that definition significantly preserves the architectural analogue or reference: "I'm in words, made of words, others' words, what others, the place too, the air, the walls, the floor, the ceiling, all words, the whole world is here with me, I'm the air, the walls, the walled-in one, everything yields, opens, ebbs, flows" (p. 386). His despair does not cease, however: "Help, help, if I could only describe this place, I who am so good at describing places, walls, ceilings, floors, they are my speciality, doors, windows, what haven't I imagined in the way of windows in the course of my career, some opened on the sea, all you could see was sea and sky, if I could put myself in a room, that would be the end of the wordy-gurdy, even doorless, even windowless, nothing but the four surfaces, the six surfaces, if I could shut myself up, it would be a mine, it could be black dark . . . I'd be home, I'd say what it's like, in my home, instead of any old thing, this place, if I could describe this place, portray it, I've tried, I feel no place, no place round me, there's no end to me" (p. 399). The novel ends, "perhaps they have carried me to the threshold of my story, before the door that opens on my story, that would surprise me, if it opens, it will be I, it will be the silence, where I am, I don't know, I'll never know, in the silence you don't know, you must go on, I can't go on, I'll go on" (p. 414). By 1969, it seems that Beckett has arrived at a refuge of sorts, and at silence, although it is still a written silence of words: *Lessness* (London, 1970) opens with the analogue for mind and for the condition of being still architectural. "Ruins true refuge long last towards which so many false time out of mind. All sides endlessness earth sky as one no sound no stir. Grey face two pale blue little body heart beating only upright. Blacked out fallen open four walls over backwards true refuge issueless.

"Scattered ruins same grey as the sand ash grey true refuge. Four square all light sheer white blank planes all gone from

NOTES TO PAGES 238-239

mind. Never was but grey air timeless no sound figment the passing light. No sound no stir ash grey sky mirrored earth mirrored sky. Never but this changelessness dream the passing hour" (pp. 7-8). It seems that the narrator/author has found a place that is no place, has conflated body/place with surrounding place, body perception with mind/place, and has found "no sound," the "silence" so desired in *The Unnamable*. *Lessness* seems to describe "becoming less," the movement toward that final silence, an "almost" death but for words. The final two paragraphs are variations (as is the whole work) on basic word combinations, but they seem to achieve something in addition to the curse of despair. The "novel" closes, "Legs a single block arms fast to sides little body face to endlessness. True refuge long last issueless scattered down four walls over backwards no sound. Blank planes sheer white eye calm long last all gone from mind. He will curse God again as in the blessed days face to the open sky the passing deluge. Face to calm eye touch close all calm all white all gone from mind.

"Little body little block heart beating ash grey only upright. Little body ash grey locked rigid heart beating face to endlessness. Little body little block genitals overrun arse a single block grey crack overrun. Figment dawn dispeller of figments and the other called dusk" (pp. 20-21).

27. *Civil Engineer and Architect's Journal*, II (London, July 1839), 365.

28. Wightwick, "The Principles and Practice of Architectural Design" (Essay 7, 1850), in *Detached Essays of the Architectural Publication Society* (London, 1853), pp. 1-2.

29. The relationship between mind and architecture in architectural theory prior to the mid-eighteenth century was what we might call a product relationship: mind *produces* building, but building does not necessarily reflect or express mind. We can see this clearly in Alberti's treatise; the relationship between mind and architecture is in this sense normative. Alberti writes, "In treating of which [architecture in ten books] we shall observe this Method: We consider that an Edifice is a Kind of Body consisting, like all other Bodies, of

Design and of Matter; the first is produced by the Thought, the other by Nature; so that the one is to be provided by the Application and Contrivance of the Mind, and the other by due Preparation and Choice" ("The Preface," *Ten Books on Architecture*, London, 1965, p. xi).

It is interesting to notice, with regard to Ruskin and his attitude toward expressiveness in architecture, that his lines in his drawings are also expressive in terms of traditional classifications of drawing technique. Ruskin's interest in Gothic architecture, then, is of a piece with his more general artistic disposition and taste.

30. Ruskin, "The Nature of the Gothic," *The Stones of Venice, Works*, X, 183. While this passage demonstrates Ruskin's value system in selecting the Gothic style above all others, it becomes an important criterion for evaluation of other architectural styles in his subsequent writings.

31. *Civil Engineer and Architect's Journal*, II, 251.

32. Ruskin, "The Poetry of Architecture," *Works*, I, 17.

33. Robert Browning, *Poems of Robert Browning*, ed. D. Smalley (Boston, 1956), p. 450.

34. Ibid., p. 451.

THREE

35. Frances A. Yates, *The Art of Memory* (Harmondsworth, Middlesex, 1966).

36. See especially my chapters on Pater and Proust above.

37. Quintilian, *Institutio oratoria* (Loeb edition), trans. H. E. Butler, XI, ii, 17–22. I have slightly modified this translation. See also Cicero, *De oratore* (Loeb edition), trans. E. W. Sutton and H. Rackham, II, lxxxvi, 355–lxxxviii, 360.

38. Augustine, *Confessions*, trans. R. S. Pine-Coffin (Harmondsworth, Middlesex, 1961). See also my chapter on Pater above, especially section two.

39. Locke, *An Essay*, II, 62.

40. Sigmund Freud, *Civilization and Its Discontents*, trans. Joan Riviere (London, 1957), pp. 15–20. Freud uses as his

NOTES TO PAGES 244-246

source book *The Cambridge Ancient History*, vol. VII (1928), "The Founding of Rome" by Hugh Last. Freud's model is ultimately inadequate to his purpose—recording the "idiosyncrasies of mental life." The difficulty Freud encounters with the analogue appears to be due to his own limitation of vision: his imagined city is built of solid and therefore opaque structures. Freud did not see what possibilities the analogy would have were he to figure these edifices as transparent. In fact, had he so extended the analogue, his description of the life of the mind might have been less fixed, more spacious and fluid-fertile. I think it important, however, that we recognize in Freud the search for an analogue and the attempt to use existing traditions to describe what to Freud were new observations of mental phenomena.

41. What Miss Yates does not consider is whether these memory systems presume something about the nature of minds: while she does note, for instance, that in the *Ad Herennium* there exists in the architecture-memory analogue a wonderful sense of space, depth, lighting, of images carved on *loci*, and of places being neither too large nor too small, she never suggests that such a description of an artificial memory device involves a concept of the memory and of the mind which shares the qualities of the architectural analogue. See pp. 17–22 in *The Art of Memory*.

42. R. Wollheim, *On Art and the Mind* (London, 1973), pp. 31–54.

43. Ibid., pp. 35–36.

44. Quintilian, XI, ii, 20–22.

45. For an excellent look at the Greek Revival, see J. Mordaunt Crook, *The Greek Revival* (London, 1972).

46. The seminal work on the Gothic Revival is still Lord Kenneth Clark's *The Gothic Revival* (London, 1928). Of all the most recent publications on this movement, I still find the most stimulating to be G. Hersey, *High Victorian Gothic: A Study in Associationism* (Maryland, 1972), and S. Muthesius, *The High Victorian Movement in Architecture, 1850–1870* (London, 1972).

47. See Sir Robert de Zouche Hall, *A Bibliography on Vernacular Architecture* (London, 1972).

48. The roots of this are in the archeological explorations and writings of Winckelmann in the mid-eighteenth century. I have found the best art historical study of historicism to be R. Rosenblum, *Transformations in Late Eighteenth Century Art* (Princeton, 1967), pp. 34 ff., 50 f., 75 f., 98, 107 ff. William Morris's work in reviving methods for dying fabric, for stained-glass windows, for printing, represents what was newly possible in the late nineteenth century, as does Ruskin's work on architectural building materials (honesty in construction) as in "The Lamp of Truth" in *The Seven Lamps of Architecture*.

49. Sir N. Pevsner, "Review," *Art Quarterly*, 35, no. 3 (1972): 315–318.

50. Ibid., p. 317.

51. *Civil Engineer and Architect's Journal* (July 1839), p. 249.

52. Ibid.

53. Cf. T. Kentish, *A Treatise on a Box of Instruments and the Slide Rule* (London, 1839).

FOUR

54. Cicero, *De oratore* III, xiv, 180–xlvii, 182.

55. Dionysius of Halicarnassus, *On Literary Composition*, trans. W. Rhys Roberts (London, 1910), p. 105. See also n. 29 in my notes to Proust above.

56. Dionysius, *On Literary Composition*, p. 211.

57. Quintilian, *Institutio oratoria* IX, iv, 25–28.

58. "Preface" to Book VII, 1–2.

59. See D. Hume, Essay XX from *Essays, Moral, Political and Literary* (London, 1742): "As the eye, in surveying a GOTHIC building, is distracted by the multiplicity of ornaments, and loses the whole by its minute attention to the parts; so the mind, in perusing a work overstocked with wit, is fatigued and disgusted with the constant endeavour to shine and surprize. This is the case where a writer overabounds in wit, even though

that wit, in itself, should be just and agreeable. But it commonly happens to such writers, that they seek for their favourite ornaments, even where the subject does not afford them; and by that means, have twenty insipid conceits for one thought which is really beautiful" (p. 81).

W. Hazlitt writes, "It is not pomp or pretension, but the adaptation of the expression to the idea that clenches a writer's meaning: – as it is not the size or glossiness of the materials, but their being fitted each to its place, that give strength to the arch: or as the pegs and nails are as necessary to the support of the building as the larger timbers, and more so than the mere shewy, unsubstantial ornaments."

See A. Schopenhauer, *Parerga and Paralipomena*, II, xxiii (1851), 151: "As in architecture an excess of decoration is to be avoided, so in the art of literature a writer must guard against all rhetorical finery, all useless amplification, and all superfluity of expression in general: in a word, he must strive after chastity of style." Schopenhauer also uses the analogue to speak of general construction on a larger scale: "Few write in the way in which an architect builds; who, before he sets to work, sketches out his plan, and thinks it over down to its smallest details. Nay, most people write only as though they were playing dominoes; and as in this game the pieces are arranged half by design, half by chance, so it is with the sequence and connection of their sentences. They only just have an idea of what the general shape of their work will be, and of the aim they set before themselves. Many are ignorant even of this, and write as the coral-insects build; period joins to period, and Lord knows what the author means" (p. 155).

60. Ruskin, "Elements of English Prosody," *Works*, XXXI, 327.

61. William Wordsworth, "Prospectus to *The Recluse*," *Poetical Works*, V, ed. E. de Selincourt (London, 1940–58), 2. See also Wordsworth's letter to Sir J. Beaumont on 3 June 1805 in *Letters, The Early Years*, p. 594. L. Stevenson has written on the subject, "The Unfinished Gothic Church," *University of Toronto Quarterly*, 22 (1963): 170–183.

62. Erwin Panofsky, *Gothic Architecture and Scholasticism* (Cleveland and New York, 1957).

63. *Quarterly Review*, vol. 27, as quoted in *The Civil Engineer and Architect's Journal*, II (July 1839), 249.

64. Ibid., p. 251.

65. Ibid., p. 365.

66. See Sir J. Summerson, *The Classical Language of Architecture* (London, 1963); also P. Collins, "The Linguistic Analogy," in *Changing Ideals in Modern Architecture* (London, 1965).

67. *The Civil Engineer*, July 1839, p. 251.

68. Ruskin, "The Nature of the Gothic," p. 186.

69. *The Civil Engineer*, p. 250.

70. E. Newton, *The Architect*, I (1896), 55.

71. Ibid., p. 54.

INDEX

abode, 12, 301–302
Alberti, Leone Battista, 229–231, 302–303, 303–304
Alice in Wonderland, 172, 193
Apuleius, 234, 298
Aquinas, Thomas, 234, 266, 280, 299
Aristotle, 30, 234, 296–297
Augustine, 31–34, 234, 243

Beckett, Samuel, 3, 133, 234, 236–238, 301–303
Beerbohm, Max, 195–198, 286–287
being, 4–5, 12–13, 225–226, 237, 262
Browning, Robert, 104, 240–241
build, 4, 8, 232, 235, 261
Butterfield, William, 64, 88–94, 269; Plate, 92–93

Cicero, 249–250
Coburn, Alvin Langdon, 197–202; Plates, 169, 180, 194, 199, 201, 203

Davie, Donald, 234, 300
Degas, 137, 272
Deleuze, Gilles, 122
Dionysius of Halicarnassus, 250, 277–278
dwell, 12, 57, 232, 235, 261, 262

Emerson, Ralph Waldo, 295–296

Fowler, Alastair, 264, 271
Freud, Sigmund, 234, 244, 304–305

Gombrich, E. H., 218, 238–239, 280–281, 293
ground, 8–10, 130, 178, 184

Hegel, G. W. F., 234, 293, 299–300
Heidegger, Martin, 261
Herbert, George, 231–232
Hopkins, Gerard Manley, 1–13 *passim*, 27, 33–34, 51–111, 118, 120, 126, 172–173, 179, 218–228 *passim*, 232, 250, 252, 256–259 *passim*, 266–267, 284

James, Henry, 1–13 *passim*, 33–34, 144–145, 167–215, 218–228 *passim*, 241, 250, 252, 256–259 *passim*, 266–267

Leonardo da Vinci, 67, 289
Locke, John, 234, 243–244, 299
Luria, R., 280–281

INDEX

Macksey, Richard, *122-132, 273*
Marvell, Andrew, *235-236, 301*

Ovid, *234, 297*

Palme, Per, *264-265*
Panovsky, Erwin, *253*
Parker, John, *54-55, 267*
Pater, Walter, *1-13 passim, 15-49, 53, 57, 77-78, 92, 126, 172, 179, 181, 213, 218-228 passim, 232-233, 241, 250, 252, 256-259 passim, 269-270, 271-272, 300*
Pevsner, Sir Nikolaus, *247, 284*
Plato, *3, 235, 301*
Poulet, Georges, *122-132, 270*
Proust, Marcel, *1-13 passim, 33-34, 144-145, 167-215, 218-228 passim, 241, 250, 252, 256-259 passim, 266-267*

Quintilian, *242-243, 246, 250-251*

Ravel, Maurice, *189*
Ruskin, John, *11, 34-36, 107, 124-131, 140, 142, 145-148, 153, 162-164, 178, 219-220, 239-240, 252, 254, 270-271, 274-275, 276, 279*

Schopenhauer, Arthur, *252, 307*
Summerson, Sir John, *253, 308*

tend, 227
Tennyson, Alfred Lord, *22, 298*
Thoreau, Henry David, *295-296*

Vitruvius, *229-231, 252-253, 263*

Wightwick, *230-231, 238-239*
window, 21-22, 24, 164-165, 181-186 passim, 187-193, 202, 263, 272, 281-282, 285-286, 292, 302
Wollheim, Richard, *234, 244-245, 264, 300-301*
Wordsworth, William, *252*

Yates, Frances, *242, 264, 280-281, 305*

CREDITS FOR PHOTOGRAPHS

I should like to extend my appreciation to the following institutions for permission to reproduce photographs in their collections:

PLATES 1, 30   From *Merveilles de France* by René Huyghe published by Editions Arthaud–Paris/Grenoble.

PLATES 3, 5, 7–9, 17, 26   Photographs by courtesy of the Courtauld Institute of Art.

PLATES 12, 32–37   International Museum of Photography at George Eastman House.

PLATES 2, 22, 28   Royal Commission on Historical Monuments (England). National Monuments Record. Photographs 22 and 28 by Herbert Felton.

PLATES 10, 11, 13–16   From *The Journals and Papers of Gerard Manley Hopkins* edited by Humphry House and Graham Storey, published by Oxford University Press by arrangement with the Society of Jesus.

PLATES 20, 21, 27   Philadelphia Museum of Art: Purchased with funds given by Dorothy Norman.

PLATE 23   Philadelphia Museum of Art: Purchased: Director's Discretionary Fund.

I should also like to thank the following photographers for permission to reproduce their photographs:

PLATE 31   Dr. Harald Busch, Frankfurt am Main-Griesheim.

PLATE 6   A. F. Kersting, London.

PLATES 4, 17   Jean Roubier, Paris.

PLATE 25   Theodor Seeger, Switzerland.

PLATES 24, 29   Jacques Verroust, Paris.

E. E. F.

Designer:	Wolfgang Lederer
Compositor:	Dharma Press
Printer:	Carey Colorgraphics
Binder:	Roswell Book Binders
Text:	Fototronic Garamond
Display:	Fototronic Garamond
Cloth:	Holliston Crown Linen 13160
Paper:	70 lb Lustro Offset Enamel Dull